WHAT'S NEXT:
The Experts' Guide

WHAT

'S NEXT:

→ The Experts' Guide

◄ Predictions from 50 of America's
Most Compelling People ►

JANE BUCKINGHAM
with TIFFANY WARD

HARPER

An Imprint of HarperCollins*Publishers*
www.harpercollins.com

FIRST EDITION

Designed by Kara Strubel

Library of Congress Cataloging-in-Publication Data
Buckingham, Jane.
    What's next : the experts' guide : predictions from 50 of America's most compelling people / Jane Buckingham.—1st ed.
        p.   cm.
    Includes index.
    ISBN: 978-0-06-088535-9
    1. United States—Civilization—21st century—Forecasting. 2. United States—Social conditions—21st century—Forecasting. 3. National characteristics, American. 4. Twenty-first century—Forecasts. I. Title.
E169.12.B782   2008
973.93—dc22   2007033540

08   09   10   11   12   OV/RRD   10   9   8   7   6   5   4   3   2   1

For Michael, for showing me the best of my past,
and for Marcus, for showing me the best of my future.

For J.Ward, for making our past so much fun
and our future so promising. I only wish I married you sooner.

◀ CONTENTS ▶

by Jane Buckingham

In grammar school, my teacher asked us to draw pictures showing how the year 2000 would look. Like a lot of my classmates, I drew a picture of levitating cars similar to Luke Skywalker's, jet propulsion backpacks, and robotic pets. In the era of *Star Wars* mania, *Jetsons* cartoons, and the original *Star Trek* and *Battlestar Galactica* series, we were certain the future would bring us the space age accoutrements we saw onscreen, and more.

Of course I was wrong. However, some amazing things have happened between now and then, things that even a room full of unbridled third-grade imaginations could not have conceived of: the end of the Cold War, the invention of the artificial heart, the Internet, 9/11, and California's Governor Arnold Schwarzenegger.

Even as adults, we find it impossible to draw an accurate picture of the future. Like the year 2000, a lot of what we think we see going forward will turn out to have been just a mirage. And a lot of things we can't imagine now will be as mind-blowing and life altering as the Internet has been in the last twenty years. After all, no one can truly *predict* the future. Too many things can happen in the world that alter how we think, feel, and behave. Too many mistakes provide unexpected enlightenment, accidental breakthroughs, and serendipitous discoveries.

But despite all of this, we desperately want to *try* to know what the future will bring. We seek out psychics, prophets, and great intellects to try to tell us what the future might hold. When it's good news, we embrace it. When it's less appealing, we ignore it. And while I've built a career in research trying to decipher behavior, I've always shunned the term *trend forecaster*. Frankly, it sounds too much like weather forecaster, and I hope to have a better success rate than that profession does. Nonetheless, there are similarities. Like a weather forecaster I am simply looking at patterns out there and trying my best to judge which way the tides will go, how moods will swing, and where storms will erupt. Human behavior, like the weather, is uncertain. All we can do is give our best guesses, our best thoughts, our aspirations, and our hopes.

What makes the future so compelling is that there seem to be limitless possibilities. We somehow imagine that in the future our greatest hopes will be realized and our worst fears somehow eradicated. The future is something that feels far away and fantastical. We anticipate it endlessly, yet somehow it feels sudden when it arrives. It feels like an airplane journey in which you fall asleep in one location and wake up in another, a place almost entirely different and, presumably, better.

In fact, the future isn't any of these things at all. It is a series of small steps that lead to bigger change. It's all of our fantasies slowly realized or rethought. It's like a child growing up. To a parent who is with them every day, the child seems the same. To a relative who comes only once a year, the child is a whole new creature. While a child might seem a different person—dyeing her hair and getting four piercings at the age of sixteen—if you trace back, chances are you can see the need for self-expression or rebellion throughout the child's life. The change didn't happen in a day; it happened progressively over years.

Often when the future becomes the present, we're disappointed. We wonder why we don't have flying cars or cures for every cancer or robots that cater to our every whim. We forget that we have sent a robot to Mars, with miraculous vaccines, wiped out dozens of diseases that might have killed our children, and invented an Internet that has the capacity to connect anyone to anything at any time.

Bill Gates once said that people overestimate the change that can happen in five years and underestimate the change that can happen in ten. Change does not happen overnight, or over a week or month. It takes years. It takes shifts in people, places, technologies, and cultures. But it can and often does happen faster than we think. We are the architects of the future. We create it every day, in big and small ways, in moments and through decades.

We can't change everything in the present; we can't find all of the cures or will the endings to every war, genocide, or environmental disaster. What we *can* do is listen to those who know their field and have real expertise, those who live in their particular world day in and day out, those who adapt, create, rethink, and reshape their universe throughout their careers. There are those who do it based on research and others who do it based on instinct. But they each effect change and alter the way we experience some part of the world.

Virtually every expert we spoke to in creating this book insisted that they could not predict the future. And we had to reassure them that was not what we were seeking. We simply wanted to know what they expected, what they hoped for, what they feared. We hoped that, in collecting their thoughts, others might be enlightened, educated, and inspired. Change might begin to happen from the thoughts that erupted and the picture they presented. Ripples of information might coalesce into new perspectives, and patterns might be Rorschached from the aggregate of their visions.

Of course selecting the topics was daunting. After all, in predicting the future one has to decide what will and won't be important in the years to come. And yes, we've left out many important topics some would like us to include and covered others some might have left out. There were times when experts were loath to talk about the future of their field because the outlook was so grim, and they didn't want their visions to become self-fulfilling. Many experts were too focused on the chaos of the present to feel confident that they had accurate expectations. We tried to limit our focus to domestic concerns because we felt an international outlook would be impossible to capture in one book. But in our interviews, we found that many of our experts were unable to so limit their thoughts; their specialties were inextricably intertwined with thinkers and professionals internationally, as were their lives . . . and our futures.

We felt some topics, such as religion, were worthy of a book in themselves and thus no expert could offer a comprehensive vision. Instead, we chose to focus on the fastest growing and most politically charged religion—Islam—and interviewed the scholar and author Reza Aslan. Aslan's thoughts about Islam are among the most important in the book. An awareness of the truth of Islam, the importance of education about Islam, and an understanding that the terrorist agenda has no true connection to Islam are particularly timely and important to inspire understanding as a first step toward peace in this time of war.

Despite our decision not to tackle religion exhaustively, the relationship between politics and religion in America seemed to echo through many of our interviews. Whether we were talking about the future of censorship with Joan Bertin, the future of medicine with former Surgeon General Richard H. Carmona, or the future of law with Alan Dershowitz, religious beliefs seemed more consequential than we expected of a country founded on the idea of separation of church and state.

More predictably, the experts we interviewed unanimously agreed that rapidly developing technology will have a huge impact on our lives in the future. It is at the nexus of technology and religion—notably with stem cell research, the abortion debate, and end-of-life legislation and decision-making—that our experts felt some of the most momentous decisions will be made in the next ten years.

It's important to note that in virtually every one of these interviews we looked for someone who could offer a unique perspective rather than an agenda. We were not looking for answers. We did not have a plan or a vision we wanted to promote. We did ask many of our experts for prescriptions, but we don't know whether our experts are right. We do know that their responses were smart, thought provoking, and fair. We could hear how much they cared, how hard they were working in their respective fields to make a better future possible.

Will what they've said come to pass? Will their having said it alter what does happen? Should we take their advice? Frankly, it doesn't matter. What matters is that we are collectively working toward a better safer future. We suspect that in 2016 the predictions here will look like a funhouse mirror of that present—distorted in places, bigger in unexpected ways, and smaller in others. What does seem clear is that even if this book offers what will ultimately be a skewed reflection of the way things might be, we're all responsible for becoming better educated about the way things are so that we can join our experts in clearing a path for the way things could be. We're responsible for deciding for ourselves through learning and experience about how we think our world should be—and taking action.

WHAT'S NEXT:
The Experts' Guide

Shaun Alexander ➤ on Sports

SHAUN ALEXANDER *is the current outstanding running back for the Seattle Seahawks. He is the only player in NFL history to record fifteen or more touchdowns in five consecutive seasons and is one of only two players to record ten or more rushing touchdowns in five consecutive seasons. In 2006, he received two ESPY awards—NFL Player of the Year and Record-Breaking Performance. In 2005, he was named Most Valuable Player of NFL and led the Seahawks to the Super Bowl. Married with three young daughters, he received a marketing degree from the University of Alabama and has significant involvement in charity and foundation work. Because of his perspective, talent, and leadership, we thought Alexander would be a great person to tell us about the future of sports.*

◀ An International Unifier ▶

The power of sports lies in its ability to bring together large groups of people from societies all over the world. Overall, we'll be looking more and more at international stars as heroes and hold athletes from different countries in the same light as homegrown U.S. athletes. Currently, athletes like Ichiro Suzuki and Yao Ming are helping to further bridge this gap and blur the international lines of competition. As we have more global influences, and more commonalities, sports will become a greater unifier. Sports bridge language barriers, age barriers, and cultural barriers, and will continue to do this even more so in the coming years as people look for ways to connect with countries around the world.

We've already seen this with the growth of soccer. And I think that with the hype and popularity surrounding David Beckham and the Galaxy, the trend in soccer will continue to increase greatly in the States, and American teams will continue to improve. I also think the LA sports market will continue to expand and add more professional teams. And it wouldn't surprise me if American football became an Olympic sport as well.

On a more local level, I think that leagues will change in that they will have much stricter guidelines in terms of regulations and punishments on players and officials gambling. We'll want our sports to be more wholesome and clean—just about the game.

◀ **Branding Tomorrow's Athlete** ▶

I also think we'll see a rise in the popularity of professional women's sports, both to watch and to participate in. This is going to see a lot of growth. It's great to see young women really participating in sports at younger ages and to see great role models on a professional level. I think ten years from now, there will be an even stronger clear professional path for women in sports.

As for professional athletes, talent alone will not be enough to make athletes successful on the highest level in sport. Fans will want more. They'll want athletes to dominate their sport but also be well-rounded, well-spoken people. The wild bad-boy athlete model is phasing out, as fans want to relate to their athletes. Athletes will need to be smarter, more educated, and think more like business owners. They'll need to think of themselves as brands. Athletes will better understand the economics and business of the game. The athletes of the future will have to be better behaved, more like role models, and more in charge of their future. Today's fans expect it, and future athletes will know that to be successful, their performance off the playing field will be almost as important as on.

◀ A Changing Sports Experience ▶

It's really important to recognize that the Internet will have a big impact on sports. Athlete and league websites will play an increasing role in the sports fan life. Whether it's game highlights or an athlete talking with fans, people will be able to access sports when they want with the convenience of the Web and mobile devices. We'll have to find ways to keep fans watching in real time. This, I believe, is one of the most important factors in sports now and in the next ten years. It's changing how fans relate to the game and the athletes, and how they experience sports. While it's great that more people have more information and more contact, it would be a shame if fewer people wanted to come out to experience the real thing—especially because technology in stadiums is also increasing and games are becoming greater entertainment spectacles. Going to a game is a family entertainment experience now.

But one of the things I really hope we see in the future is getting our kids more interested in sports. I think it's critical to find cool and innovative ways to keep kids interested and participating in sports. Things like active video games that keep kids moving while they play will continue to grow. If we can find a way to make watching sports an interactive experience, this would lead to an increase in participation. With rising obesity rates and so many other problems out there, we need to make sure that sports are a really important part of our kids' healthy futures.

Reza Aslan ➤ on Islam

REZA ASLAN *is a research associate at the University of Southern California's Center on Public Diplomacy, the Middle East analyst for CBS News, and a professor of creative writing at the University of California, Irvine. Born in Iran, he holds a BA in religion from Santa Clara University, a Master of theological studies from Harvard University, and an MFA in fiction from the University of Iowa; he is currently a doctoral candidate in sociology of religions at the University of California, Santa Barbara. His first book,* No God but God, *has been translated into half a dozen languages and was shortlisted for the* Guardian *of Great Britain First Book Award . We were interested in talking to Aslan, because his book so illuminated the history and reality of Islam. We can't imagine anything more important during a time of war and terrorism than understanding what Islam really is, and how radical terrorists misrepresent it.*

According to some estimates, Muslims are already the largest religious minority in the United States. That is bound to have a profound effect not just on the American religious landscape but on Islam itself. On the one hand, Americans are going to have to stop thinking of Islam as some exotic religion of the "other" and instead recognize Islam as a part of the same biblical tradition with which most Americans are already familiar and comfortable. What that means, in practical terms, is that Americans are going to have to expand their concept of religious pluralism in the United States.

Throughout American history, such an expansion has happened a number of times. It happened with the massive Catholic immigration into the United States in the nineteenth century. At the time, there was a great deal of suspicion about Catholics; they didn't really fit into the American social and religious fabric. Very gradually, however, Catholics were assimilated into American society. The same thing happened with Jews in the twentieth century, particularly in the wake of World War II and the influx of Jewish immigrants into the United States. There was a feeling in America that the Jews represented a kind of fifth column—that they were not a part of American religious or social traditions. Eventually that changed, too, to the point that people now refer to the Judeo-Christian values upon which this country was founded.

I think the same process is taking place with Islam. The idea that Islam is beyond what Americans recognize as standard religious expression is going to have to change. And indeed it is changing. Americans are starting to recognize that Islam is not a religion of the "other." It's the religion of their neighbors and their doctors and their lawyers. It represents a similar, though unique expression of the same Judeo-Christian tradition that this country is supposedly founded upon.

◄ The Impact of Muslim Americans ►

There is no Muslim country in the world in which Muslims have the kind of rights and privileges that they have in the United States. Muslims around the world know that. They envy it. They want to reconcile their faith and their values with the realities of the modern world, and they see American Muslims as having done that fluidly and seamlessly. In many ways, American Islam is the best example, not just of how to reconcile Islam with the modern world, but also of what Islam could be.

I think the United States is bound to have a dramatic effect on the future of Islam. There's an old joke among scholars in my field that, regardless of what religion you are, if you are American, you are more or less Protestant. The American ideal of radical individualism, the belief in the so-called Protestant work ethic, and the idea that religion should not play a role in the public realm, especially in the way we discuss our social, political, and economic issues—all of that is deeply American. The reconciliation of democratic and religious ideals is very important in defining what it means to be American. All of these notions have been completely adopted into the Muslim-American experience.

Muslims in the United States are strongly middle class—some 60 percent own their own homes. They are one of the most literate, well-educated immigrant groups in the entire country. They are thoroughly integrated into American society at almost every level. In other words, American Muslims are the shining example of why the clash-of-civilizations mentality between Islam and the West is so wrongheaded. Muslims are a part of the West. They are very much a part of what makes Western civilization and Western culture what it is. At the same time, Muslim Americans are playing an ever-increasing role since September 11, 2001, in helping to define and export a more moderate, more pluralistic, more rational, and more reform-minded understanding of Islam to the rest of the Muslim world. Some of the greatest scholars and religious leaders of Islam are right here in America. Their works, their opinions, their ideas, their radically innovative interpretations of Islamic law are being read not just by Americans, not just by Westerners, but by Muslims around the world. Regardless of its foreign policy and of the ways in which its national interests have drastically and negatively affected indigenous peoples throughout the world, America is famous for its religious freedoms. No other country gives people of faith greater opportunities to express their faith in the public realm.

◀ **Understanding What Religion Is and Is Not** ▶

We're approaching an age in which nations are increasingly identifying themselves according to religion, in which religion and religious rhetoric are playing far too large a role in U.S foreign policy. Such a situation hasn't occurred for a thousand years or so, and if we are going to avoid the kind of horrific religious wars and conflicts that we saw in the last millennium, then we really need to take strong steps to deflate the almost apocalyptic rhetoric that has skewed U.S. foreign policy.

There's no question that over the last few years, America's foreign policy—particularly the war on terrorism and most particularly the war in Iraq—has done tremendous damage to the image of the United States throughout the world, not just in the Muslim world but even among some of our closest allies. But I think that the greatest mistake the United States has made since September 11 is its refusal to reach out to Muslim Americans. The Bush administration did not do a good job of convincing Muslims that the war on terrorism is not a war against Islam. The extremists, the militant groups, and Jihadists groups like Al Qaeda, they've all done a magnificent job of arguing that Islam itself is under attack by the United States. However, we've done a lousy job of marketing the war on terrorism, because we're not taking advantage of our greatest asset: the six to ten million Muslim Americans who recognize that Jihadism—the transnational movement of violent, Sunni puritanism—is more of a threat to them than it is to the West or to Christians or Jews. In fact, the primary target of these militants and extremists—the group they refer to as the "near enemy"—is other Muslims. The West, the Jews, the Christians—these are secondary targets, or the "far enemy."

Americans are finally starting to understand that there's far more going on in this war than the simplified good vs. evil argument they've been fed thus far. It is unfortunate that it has taken this long, but at least it's starting to get through. This is important, because there is an impression that the war on terrorism is a war of cultures or a war of religions. The rhetoric of our politicians—from the moment the president referred to the war as a crusade—has only made matters worse, because it falls squarely into the trap set by the Jihadists, who want to mobilize support for their cause by presenting the war on terrorism as a war against Islam.

The Jihadists, you must understand, are fighting a cosmic war— one that cannot be won in any real terms. They're not going to defeat the American army. They're not going to destroy Israel. These are hopeless causes, and they know it. It's precisely for that reason that they have framed their goals in these cosmic terms—so that they're not fighting an insurgency or battling an American army; they're fighting a heavenly war between the forces of good (themselves) and the forces of evil (us). What we have done is legitimize their belief through our own religiously charged rhetoric. For instance, when Congressman Tom Tancredo suggests bombing Mecca in response to the next terrorist act, Muslims around the world who do not support Jihadism become convinced that this is indeed a holy or cosmic war. What we need to do is to reframe the entire perception of the war on terrorism; we need to now think of it as a criminal enterprise. Only then can we take away the tools of propaganda that the Jihadists have used so effectively to win over Muslims.

I think it's very important for a Western audience, especially an American audience, to begin educating themselves about Islam as a religion, as a history, as a civilization, so as to recognize its incredible diversity. Islam is unquestionably the most eclectic and diverse religion in the history of the world. Yet in the United States it is seen as monolithic, because the only images of Islam we see are those in the media, which, of course, are images of violence, terrorism, and fear.

More important, we must recognize the connections that people of faith have with one another, regardless of the language they speak, to express that faith. Those similarities bind us together in a way that religious dogma and doctrine do not.

◀ **The Key to Future Islamic Democracy** ▶

There is no conflict between Islam and democracy. Quite the contrary. The community that the Prophet Mohammed created fourteen centuries ago was supremely democratic. The world's first constitution was written by the Prophet Mohammed, who enacted radical egalitarian reforms regarding women's rights and minority rights. Islam and democratic values can be reconciled by going back to that original community as the model for a modern Islamic democracy.

Muslim reformers never tire of saying they don't need to look to America or to the West for the paradigm of an Islamic democracy. They can find that paradigm within Islam itself. Embedded within Islam are the ideals of pluralism and human rights, of popular sovereignty and separation of powers, and even the separation of religious and political powers. All of these notions already exist within Islam. It's just a matter of unearthing them and making them the primary principles for creating a modern, indigenous, Islamic democracy.

When I say "Islamic democracy," I'm not referring to some kind of theocratic democracy. I'm referring to a democratic state dedicated to the necessary elements of a democracy, but founded on an Islamic moral framework. That is not such an unusual idea. It can be found in the Jewish moral framework upon which Israel is founded, the Christian moral framework upon which the United States is founded, the Hindu moral framework of India, the Buddhist moral framework of Bhutan, and so on. The key is to make sure that when there is a conflict between traditional Islamic ideals and modern ideas of a democratic state, it's democracy that trumps religious ideology. That's not a problem, either. After all, Islam has long had a history of assimilation and accommodation wherever it is, no matter the society or nation.

It's true that the concepts of citizenship and national identity are quite new to the Islamic world. Islamic nationalism has its roots in the colonialist experience, when Europeans carved out large sections of the Middle East and North Africa and forced the communities to define themselves in a way that they had never done before: nationalistically. But it's also true that in the fifty or sixty years since the end of colonialism, the notion of citizenship and of a national identity have become widely adopted throughout the Muslim world. These days, most Muslims are quite comfortable with defining themselves as both individual citizens and members of a worldwide Muslim community.

◀ Fear and Understanding ▶

What I would love to see happen in ten years is that Muslim Americans are viewed throughout the world as the shining example of how Islamic values and traditions can be reconciled with democratic ideals. Already, the really innovative work of interpreting Islam, and the hardcore academic analysis of the Koran and of Islamic law are taking place here in the United States. These kinds of ideas will shape the future of what will soon become the world's largest religion. I want these ideas to be adopted by Muslims throughout the world as a means of reforming not just their religion but also their social, political, and economic development. I hope to see American Muslims become the bridge between the United States and the Middle East. It's up to American Muslims to foster a sense of understanding and reconciliation with a region that we have, because of our foreign policy, alienated and forced into a state of mistrust and suspicion.

What I fear will happen is that American Muslims will become so isolated from the rest of the Muslim world that they become irrelevant to the larger issues that define where Islam is going. I think what happens in this sphere will play a major role in whether the U. S. government supports the American Muslim community and tries to hold it up as an example to the rest of the world, or whether it continues to see American Muslims as a fifth column in this country, as a source of suspicion, and even as a source of extremism.

It all depends on whether it is going to be fear that defines the U.S. government's relationship with its Muslim citizens, or whether it is going to be understanding and cooperation.

Joan Bertin ➤ on Censorship

JOAN BERTIN is executive director of the National Coalition Against Censorship. After law school, she spent seven years representing indigent clients as a legal services lawyer and more than a dozen years litigating civil rights and civil liberties cases at the American Civil Liberties Union (ACLU). She has taught at Columbia University and Sarah Lawrence College. Our interview with Joan underscored for us that not only is censorship going on every day in a variety of ways in the United States, but that we are likely to experience even more problems with censorship in the future if we don't become more aware of both our rights and how they're being violated.

The political and legal terrain regarding censorship has shifted significantly in the United States since about 2001. Prior to that time, whenever I gave a talk about censorship, I would say that we had a widespread consensus that political speech of all kinds was entitled to strong First Amendment protections. I would describe the censorship issues we encountered as revolving most frequently around social and cultural issues like sex and religion. An example might be government enforcement of broadcast "decency" standards, or teaching "abstinence only until marriage" rather than comprehensive sex education in public schools.

It would no longer be accurate to say that political speech is not censored in the United States. In the immediate aftermath of the events of 9/11, a White House spokesman chastised a television personality for questioning the president's characterization of the bombers as "cowards." We were all warned to "watch what we say." College professors were disciplined for criticizing the government, and the press and media were cowed into not asking too many hard questions. The government embraced policies of secrecy and control over the flow of and public access to information, and these policies affected not just the public generally and the press, but scientists and researchers of all kinds, as well as the ability of foreign and American scholars to collaborate.

For example, foreign scholars traveling to this country from Arab states and other regions began to encounter unprecedented difficulties, as did American scholars traveling to those countries to participate in scholarly conferences or collaborate with colleagues. Even cultural exchange programs involving dancers and musicians were affected. Restraints were placed on the publication of books containing contributions from scholars from certain countries. All these events combined to create a very different picture of the government's approach to political dissent and the free flow of ideas. Even after six years, we're in a precarious moment, and the future direction is likely contingent on world events in the next ten years.

◀ **How Far Will We Go?** ▶

This kind of reaction is not entirely unfamiliar. The McCarthy era, characterized by anti-Communist witch hunts and blacklists, are in the not-too-distant past. We now know that many of those hounded and persecuted at that time simply held unpopular political views but had engaged in no unlawful or "disloyal" conduct. Throughout the 1960s and into the 1970s, the FBI infiltrated "dissident" political groups, including not only socialist and communist organizations but also anti-war and civil rights groups, under the aegis of its Counter Intelligence Program (COINTELPRO). It's not a stretch to imagine programs of the same sort now, especially given the level of government surveillance over individuals that has become accepted since 9/11 and exemplified by the Patriot Act. Who knows how far this will go or has gone? Given the secrecy surrounding these programs, it's hard to tell.

I am especially concerned that in the next ten years we'll also see a dramatic change in the ability to develop and share scientific information. These concerns are not hypothetical. A large group of highly reputable scientists, including more than fifty Nobel laureates, have issued a public statement charging the current administration with undermining scientific research and debate for political purposes.

The U.S. government has a vast amount of control over the conduct of scientific research. Beyond what it sponsors in its own research facilities through government scientists, the government also influences the direction of research through its many programs, agencies, and support for university and corporate research. Take global warming. If the government alters official reports or suppresses information and expert opinion to support a policy questioning the basis for efforts to address global warning, the documentary record of officially sponsored "science" around global warming will be incomplete and misleading. This is precisely what scientists have charged has happened. Similarly, if because of an official position in favor of sexual abstinence, the government refuses to provide condoms to HIV/AIDs patients or to those at risk of infection, such a policy will impact research to determine if condoms are effective in slowing the transmission of disease. If government scientists may not speak publicly about genetic alteration of food crops without prior approval, the information emerging from the United States, one of the biggest producers of genetically modified foods, will be limited in its quality and value.

In other words, we are sticking our fingers in the faucet of information, sometimes sending it squirting out in funny directions and sometimes stopping it altogether. I'm not suggesting that other administrations haven't tried to manipulate science to provide support for their policies. Some of this is inevitable. But when it gets out of hand—as in official adoption of Lysenkoism under Stalin in the Soviet Union—science and society are in deep trouble. While we are certainly not at that point, there is strong consensus within the scientific and academic communities that the current assault on science threatens our ability to observe, describe, and understand natural phenomena and human behavior and that this undermines our ability to detect, confront, and solve real problems.

But if I had to identify the most threatening contemporary development, it would probably be the tendency to restrict the creation and dissemination of information. Any government that keeps its citizens ignorant deprives them of the most basic means to improve their own situation. There is a reason that totalitarian governments have, throughout history, relied so heavily on information control.

◄ The Erosion of Enlightenment ►

I think we are witnessing the erosion of Enlightenment principles, because our government evidences so little respect for knowledge, empirical data, scientific accuracy, or demonstrable facts. President George W. Bush's most senior advisers have bragged that "we create our own reality." Concern over this trend has definitely affected our approach to protecting First Amendment rights and values.

For example, we're involved in a project to document and analyze government suppression and distortion of scientific research and information. We're bringing together First Amendment advocates and scientists who are concerned about this and framing it as an issue of constitutional dimensions with dramatic importance to the community at large, to try to get a little bit more attention paid to it.

In a different but related trend, we are seeing a rise in what I call "garden variety" censorship incidents at the local level in public schools and libraries. Would-be censors everywhere seem to sense the shift and have become emboldened in their efforts to "purge" schools and libraries of material that they find offensive, immoral, or otherwise unacceptable. When *Beloved* by Toni Morrison, a Pulitzer Prize–winning novel by a Nobel Prize-winning author, becomes a target, you know there's been a sea change in attitudes toward intellectual freedom. Another related development is the rise in book censorship at the *high school* level, often based on objections to profanity. Efforts to protect young children from "inappropriate" material are understandable, if often misguided. However, the notion that high school students, who are on the cusp of adulthood, should be protected from language heard in the street every day is almost ludicrous.

Regardless of what one thinks about the use of profanity in literature and life, it's now firmly ensconced in both. People use it in everyday language for special emphasis, and writers of books, songs, film, and other material do likewise. It expresses specific emotions that other words don't. "Gosh darn" just doesn't have much impact, and sounds stilted and inauthentic. The undeniable impulse behind the effort to remove books that contain profanity is an effort to recreate an idealized society of manners, which perhaps never really existed. Even if it did, it certainly does not exist in the United States today, and we do young people a disservice if their education fails to take account of society as it is.

◀ **Creatures and Creators** ▶

Censors fail to account for the constitutional structure of our government that balances majority rule and individual rights. Under this system, certain fundamental human rights, like the freedom of speech, are protected from the "tyranny of the majority." When people seek to remove a book from the local library, ask the FCC to fine TV stations for any broadcast containing profanity, no matter its context, or prohibit discussion of condoms in sex ed classes, they undermine one of our system's core precepts, specifically that no official, however minor, may dictate what people can say, hear, and think.

Many schools and teachers do what they can to educate young people about democratic and constitutional precepts, but when the culture at large gives these lessons short shrift, it's an uphill battle. Maybe a shift will come about as a result of world geopolitical events.

More people are beginning to wonder what distinguishes us from our "enemies." If our government suppresses speech and dissent, uses propaganda to promote its policies, and spies on its citizens, our right to claim to be a free society is deeply undermined.

There's no quick fix, but we must all pay careful attention to what the government is doing in our name and be more thoughtful about what kind of society we are creating as a result. We need to become engaged and hold elected officials responsible for their acts. We can do this by writing letters to the local newspaper, demanding that the press inform the public with skeptical honest reporting, questioning government officials in public forums, rejecting "infotainment," and protesting when the government's acts violate its compact with the governed. All these things matter. We're both creatures and creators of our culture. That's my prescription for change.

Seamus Blackley ➤ **on Video Games**

SEAMUS BLACKLEY *is now an agent at Creative Artists Agency (CAA), where he works with game clients. A top-selling game designer, he joined Microsoft in 1999 and piloted the creation of the Xbox game platform. While at Microsoft, the former physicist and DreamWorks Interactive executive producer wrote the initial proposal for Xbox, assembled and led the team behind the technical design and philosophy for the platform, and established and nurtured support for Xbox within the worldwide game development community. After Microsoft, Blackley and a group of his Xbox business partners launched Capital Entertainment Group (CEG), a game production company that aimed to produce and finance games in partnership with game developers and publishers. From there, he made the leap to CAA. We're interested in Blackley's thoughts about the future of gaming, because he is truly one of the industry's pioneers, and because these days he's trying to change the industry again. He wants gaming to benefit not only the creators of beloved games, but also to help find them new opportunities to create cool new games for you and me.*

Ten years from now, the game industry is either going to look like the promotional arm of other, older media companies—e.g., an "interactive marketing department" for a movie studio—or it's going to look like the movie industry does currently, with creative people being the real assets and the real capital behind the business. It's an inflection point right now in gaming, in that game publishers (the "studios" of the game industry) are much more averse to and much less experienced at taking creative risk than the people who are running the movie studios. Thus we see game companies licensing a lot of stuff out of the movie studios because the Hollywood creative movie executives have already taken the risk and proven the worth of a property. In these cases, the game companies are following the lead of those executives in order to defer their own risk.

If the system can change, and executives with that kind of vision and creative professionalism arise as the norm rather than exceptions in video games, then the video game business could become a lot more like movies, where bets are taken primarily based on creative people and creative ideas rather than exclusively on audience metrics. And then the gaming industry becomes less of a packaged-goods business and more of an entertainment business.

Marketing and such are important as well—I don't mean to say that those things don't matter. But the fact of the matter is—look at Christmas 2006—the biggest-selling, most exciting titles were entirely licensed properties and sequels. Nobody was starting new and original stuff. This is a bad trend—where do sequels come from when there are no new products?

So we have to figure out how to start new stuff. And if we figure out how to start new stuff, the game industry will be an amazing place. If we don't figure out how to start new ideas and take bets on creative ideas and people, it's not going to be such an amazing place.

◀ **Great Mistakes** ▶

In video games most of the big successes you think of have been almost inadvertent—a team just happened to be ignored long enough to do something great, or there happened to be one or two executives who were willing to take a chance on something at a game publisher that normally wouldn't have been allowed. Or a game publisher was purchased by a larger entity and certain creative teams were forgotten about for a few months, which was enough time for them to do something awesome.

If you look at games—anything from *The Sims* to *Tomb Raider* to *Half-life* to *Halo*—these are all cases where for one reason or another (none of which were really intentional), something great was allowed to happen and creative people were managed properly and allowed to do something really awesome. And the audience responded.

This is the exciting and unique thing about games—much more than any other medium, the audience is obsessed and vocal about the quality of the product, so that building a super-high-quality product turns out to offer a lot more commercial "insurance" than it does in other media. From a business standpoint, the vacuum created because of this lack of "intentional innovation" is amplified as an opportunity because the audience so violently craves anything new and interesting—anything with a high level of quality and love and creative care.

◀ **Creative Intersections** ▶

There is and will be a confluence of people with different backgrounds in the game industry. Just because you walk across the threshold of a video game company doesn't mean that you are no longer an animator or a musician; it just means you do it for games. There are so many creative people on both sides of that threshold with so much to give to each other. One of the exciting things about a creatively driven video-game future is that you'll see this flurry of cross-licensing move toward its logical conclusion where the people who create movie and game franchises work together directly from the start, as creative partners, rather than after the fact, under a license agreement, with one subordinate to the other. We have plenty of examples now of movie directors and some TV people working directly with creative people from the game space—doing games, doing TV shows, and working on movie concepts, all at the same time because it is all fundamentally the same creative process at its most basic level.

Reveta Bowers ➤ on Schools and Education

REVETA BOWERS *would never say so herself, but everyone who comes into contact with her knows she's a legendary teacher and school leader. She was born and educated in Los Angeles, California, where she now runs one of the most respected schools in the country. She left the Los Angeles Unified School District in 1972 to teach at the Center for Early Education, where she is currently the head of school. In addition, Bowers is the former president of the Board of Governors of the Fulfill-ment Fund, an organization that provides mentoring, college counsel-ing, tutoring, and other support programs for students in inner-city Los Angeles public schools. Bowers continues to work with national school systems across the country to improve education. For her role within the school system throughout the years and the profound impact she has had on children and parents across America, we felt Bowers would be an important person to talk to about the future of schools and education.*

Everywhere you turn today, there is another theory about edu-cation—why it works or why it doesn't. Many people feel they have some expertise in education quite simply because they went to school and received an education there. When I ponder the future of education, I am less sure of the exact paths our educational institu-tions will take and more concerned that tomorrow's institutions of learning find ways to be responsive to the changes in the students of the future. There's no question that education will change dramati-cally over the next decade, in large part because our students have changed and will continue to change in dramatic ways. As we face certain social imperatives and tensions, the classrooms and learn-ing institutions of the future must, as they always have, become the stage for many of those issues to be worked on and resolved.

Before we look at the future of education, I think it essential to at least acknowledge that there's no single coherent system of education in our country. The politics of education have landed us in a quagmire that many criticize but few have solutions for. In response to uncertainty about our country's educational future, we've seen the growing fragmentation of a system that has in recent years been largely ineffective in achieving its mission. Thus, the future of education hinges on our ability to take a good, hard look at the realities facing the students we'll be called upon to educate in the future.

◀ The Student of the Future ▶

In looking at the future of education, I would start by asking what our students will require from their teachers and their schools. The differences we see in students today are largely the result of the things to which they have been exposed. The future will only accelerate and accentuate those differences. The proliferation of media and technology has changed the ways in which children think, process information, and acquire knowledge. In fact, experts in brain research tell us now that their very brains are different. These changes in brain function, when combined with the differing ways male and female students process information, has meaningful implications for future curriculum development and integration.

In the immediate future, schools should accommodate the multiple forms of intelligence we've come to appreciate and recognize, as well as the multitasking habits of our students. The age-old delivery system of a factory model of education must disappear completely if we are to succeed. Thus, future school size will matter significantly, for small schools can be more efficient, creative, and responsive. The infusion of technology in classrooms and labs will continue to accelerate even more rapidly as the technology becomes increasingly accessible across socio-economic groups. If this is the generation of "digital natives," the future will bring a generation of "digital innovators" as students adjust to our classrooms and our learning settings. This will place our future teachers in the necessary role of not just introducing the curricula, but also of being skilled facilitators who are able support the integration of that technology in seamless ways. Education in the future will engage students with technology as foundational to their research and learning. Intellectual property rights will become a major consideration for educators and institutions whose very classrooms will function more as interactive research and discovery laboratories supporting a generation of creators, publishers, inventors, and consumers of information.

◀ How Schools Need to Change ▶

Our future schools will need to be skilled at accommodating diversity in all its many forms. There's no question that as our population grows and changes we must continue to see the increased inclusion of students from different backgrounds, cultures, religions, classes, learning styles, languages, and family types in all of our educational institutions. It will be in large part because of this increasing diversity that schools will continue to take on new forms and structures. They'll need to foster creativity, honor diversity, value and promote resilience in learners, tolerate ambiguity, and change and address students' underlying conceptual understanding.

The "one size fits all" philosophy that has driven our schools in the past will no longer be tolerated by a generation of parents and students who have seen emerge the kinds of school "choice" alternatives of the last twenty years. The unfunded national education mandates, if continued, will result in more and more entrepreneurial and creative alternatives to the current school systems. Magnet schools and charters, as well as the further privatization of schools will continue, and parents will become more sophisticated about seeking out alternatives for their children. Independent schools will continue to be well regarded and popular choices for families who can afford and appreciate their often distinct missions. The challenge for independent schools will be to provide the kind of financial and admissions access that also furthers diversity.

In a different path to "school choice," some families will increasingly turn to home-schooling and distance-learning alternatives to systems that have been unable to engage and retain the interest of their children while at the same time supporting the values of their homes. The chasm between public and private education will continue to widen unless we have some coherent national as well as local policies that invite the collaboration of those schools and systems in meaningful ways. Much can be learned from and about other schools and the successful ways they employ in delivering instruction.

◀ Resources for Students ▶

The textbook publishing industry, which has so influenced and dominated the direction of educational philosophy and pedagogy, will find itself hard pressed to keep its market share in a future world when information is readily available and accessible. Our future schools will become virtual resource centers, forcing source materials to become more affordable, relevant, timely, and accurate for changing students and schools. Of course, the coinciding challenge for the future will be to teach students to discern what is factual and supported by history and to engage good research principles and theories.

As we attempt to prepare the future generations for occupations that have yet to be conceptualized, schools will need to focus on developing students who simply can't memorize information, but who are adept at knowing where and how to look for the information and skilled at applying it once they find it. The need to develop critical thinking will become an imperative for "good" and an important, well-articulated foundation of the mission of "excellent" schools. The physical design of learning spaces will change to accommodate the future students' need for collaborative work spaces, technology innovations, alternative forms of assessment, and varied internal and external teaching delivery methods.

The crisis in finding enough well-prepared, highly skilled, and motivated teachers will require schools to look for ways to use technology to share information, access specialized subject matter, and fill the void that will be left in front of classrooms as this generation of baby boomers retires from all levels of education. Education will change because the students, the teachers, the delivery systems, and the global standards will force it to change.

◀ On an International Front ▶

As we benchmark our students' progress against those in other countries, American education will have to consider implementing the longer hours and school years, the more concise source materials, and the national standards adopted by the other countries to which we compare ourselves. As one of the wealthiest nations in the world, we have come to understand that the educational accomplishments of students from many other countries have put our students at a serious disadvantage as we compete in a global marketplace. Schools will have to change that paradigm and prepare our students to compete for places in our excellent post-secondary education system and the global job market.

As our socio-economic spectrum broadens educational choice, it has the potential to create more social segregation in classes and in certain school types. The income gulf will widen; more people will be willing to pay for what they believe is quality education for their children, but even more will need to rely on the promise of the public education system. The demands on schools by consumers across the board will only increase, and our ability to be responsive will largely be based on our willingness to decentralize many of our current systems and to begin to prepare a generation of educators and administrators who have the skills to run smaller and more autonomous entities.

The implications for the institutions that offer teacher preparation and certification are obvious. The old methods and paths to teaching must change to invite a more diverse, better prepared and educated, and nimbler workforce into our classrooms and schools. States will no longer be able to afford the kinds of huge state and local systems that have evolved, particularly in our large urban centers. Education will need to rely less on a system of hierarchical layers of bureaucracy and more on single, effective site-based management structures or small clusters of schools that incorporate strategies for direct purchasing of supplies and materials, institutional budgeting, financial management, and curriculum and programmatic development that is responsive to the needs of the students they serve.

In summation, as we look ahead, schools will require some significant paradigm shifts in instruction, the sustainability and development of our physical facilities, and the ability of our schools to respond to changing students. The future of educational progress will hinge on its success in preparing our children to be facile, resilient, creative, and collaborative thinkers and learners. To quote someone from the past as we challenge the schools of the future, I offer this.

Do not try to satisfy your vanity by teaching a great many things. Awaken people's curiosity. It is enough to open minds; do not overload them. Put just a spark. If there is some good inflammable stuff, it will catch fire.

—ANATOLE FRANCE

Rodney A. Brooks, PhD ➤ on Robotics

RODNEY A. BROOKS *stepped down as director of the MIT Computer Science and Artificial Intelligence Laboratory (CSAIL) on June 30, 2007, and remains the Panasonic Professor of Robotics. He is also cofounder and Chief Technical Officer of iRobot Corp. His research is concerned with engineering intelligent robots to operate in unstructured environments and with understanding human intelligence through building humanoid robots. He has published papers and books in model-based computer vision, path planning, uncertainty analysis, robot assembly, active vision, autonomous robots, micro-robots, microactuators, planetary exploration, representation, artificial life, humanoid robots, and compiler design. Dr. Brooks starred as himself in the Errol Morris movie* Fast, Cheap and Out of Control, *named for one of his scientific papers. At home, his Roomba invention has finally made vacuuming fun. But more important, his work and his corporation have practical aims that will continue to change our lives. Robotics will change medicine, entertainment, and the military in the future, and if Dr. Brooks is right, it may even change our ideas about ourselves and our own evolution.*

When you look at the Hollywood scenarios for the future, what is a good story? A good Hollywood story takes the world as it is today and changes one thing. And the storyline comes from that. But the reality is very different. Everything in the world changes, but it doesn't change instantly; it changes gradually over time—things get integrated. So the stories about robots suddenly running amok are not going to fit into our future reality. The future isn't just going to be the result of one thing changing; many things are going to change.

I am fifty-two. The world is pretty much the same as it was when I was a boy, except that I can communicate with anyone anywhere in the world by pulling something out of my pocket, no matter where I am, and it only costs me a few cents. Well, that's a pretty huge difference, and it changes the way I interact, the way I travel, the way I stay in contact with my kids and my mother. Such technology has changed the way we interact with the world, the way we understand everything—there are lots of exponential processes that are still going on.

For example, if you look in my pocket, there is a $400 iPod. First it was 10 GB, then it was 20 GB, then there was 40 GB, and in the middle of 2006 it was 80 GB for $400. What happens if it keeps doubling? In 2009, your iPod will be able to carry the text of a million books; and by 2013, you'll be able to carry the text of all the documents in the Library of Congress. By 2024, you'll be able to carry every movie ever made, including all of the Bollywood movies.

So what's going to be important then? Video search, not Google search, but video search. How do you retrieve a video? How do you organize it? That's where the next big company is going to be. The Recording Association of America has been completely swamped by the technology that allows people to carry around thousands of songs in their pocket. When songs were on pieces of vinyl, that wasn't possible; most people could only own a few hundred songs.

◀ The Household Robot ▶

There are a lot of dual-income households and a lot of things people don't like doing around the house. So what's going to change over the next ten years? There will be multiple companies working on various products with a niche market—like the Roomba.

A key component for the adoption of any technology is to get the first successes out there. We've seen the first mass-market robot go over two million sales—the Roomba. We've gotten some traction now on some robots at a price low enough that people are willing to pay it. As a result, we'll see more and more robots coming into our homes, and we'll see some remote-presence robots.

What's really driving this is changing demographics, in Europe and Japan, Korea, and more recently in the United States, where there are a lot more older people and fewer people between twenty and sixty-five who are service workers. The older people will want to stay in their homes for more years, and they'll have spent their careers dealing with information technology. They'll be more accepting of information technology and robots, which will make them a little different from the elderly of today.

For example, it's going to get more and more expensive to have someone mow your lawn, so there will be more devices that help you complete tasks that otherwise require the strength that the elderly don't always have. In the shorter term, we will have straightforward stuff—robots that can work outside around your house.

Mowing the lawn should probably be automatic; it can be a wheelbarrow that follows you so it doesn't have to figure out where to go. You say, Follow me, and it follows you and carries the heavy stuff. So I think there's going to be a mixture of levels of autonomy, which is good because some of these things are really hard to do autonomously. This doesn't mean that in twenty years we won't know how to do them, but it's going to require some breakthroughs, some different ways of thinking. Like mowing a straight line—we know how to do it. It's just a matter of cost engineering. Lawn-mowing robots are just a little too expensive right now, but that cost is going to come down.

Right now, our robots are poor at grasping, manipulating objects—the sort of manipulation that a six-year-old child can do. If we could get our robots to do that level of manipulation, the number of applications would be wide open and, given the change in demographics, they'd be very timely.

◀ **Robots That Help Us Walk, Hear, and See** ▶

There are a lot of medical robotic companies doing various things in clinical trials. There's a company doing laparoscopic knee surgery—

there's a surgeon involved, but there's also a robot involved. They're putting in a new knee through a tiny little hole in the knee. Robots are inserted that assemble a new knee inside the person.

We're also starting to see the engineering of synthetic biology here at MIT and at Berkeley. It's going to come together in some interesting ways. I have, in my hand, right at this moment, a book called *Rebuilt* by Michael Chorost. He talks about his cochlear implant, for which there are electronics inside his head, and he shows some of the C-code that is running inside of his head connected to his neurons, and how when the code gets changed, he hears a different reality. There are hundreds of thousands of people with these things in their heads now, and there are clinical trials for retinal implants and implants that bypass the eye directly into the V-1 area. For people who are quadriplegic, there are clinical trials that give them control over a mouse, which means they can click around on the Web by themselves. We are starting to see that integration happening for good clinical reasons.

◀ **Unmanned Military Operations** ▶

Congress has mandated that, by the year 2015, one third of all military missions should be unmanned, and that includes ground vehicles. The U.S. Army has a $150 billion future combat system currently under development. My company, iRobot, has one piece of that program, and so I think you'll see more robots in the military. iRobot has delivered more than 1,000 robots that are used to disarm improvised explosive devices (IEDs). They're used every day in Iraq and Afghanistan. They are tele-operated at the moment—the soldier stands off to the side so that when things blow up, the robot is destroyed, not the soldier.

People have speculated about robots being armed and fighting autonomously. Today it would be impossible to find anyone high ranking in the military who would want autonomous armed robots, but that does not necessarily mean that will be the case forever.

For the foreseeable future, there will be a person in the decision loop. Mankind in the past has decided, for example, that they don't want certain things in war, like biological weapons. So I can imagine a scenario in which people get together and decide they don't want autonomous-targeting capabilities in machines, that there must always be a human being in the loop for military actions.

Dr. Joy Browne ➤ **on Dating**

DR. JOY BROWNE'S *nationally syndicated daily radio show on WOR in New York City is the longest-running program of its kind. A licensed clinical psychologist with a PhD from Northeastern University, Dr. Joy is beloved by her listeners for providing advice that is compassionate, practical, and substantive. With a quick wit and an ability to cut to the heart of the issue, Dr. Joy guides her millions of loyal fans through the trials and travails of their daily lives, always asking them, "What's the question?" Her books include* Dating for Dummies *and* The Nine Fantasies That Will Ruin Your Life. *We were interested in Dr. Joy's expert perspective on dating, because the world of dating seems to have become both easier and more complicated. Easier, because all you have to do to meet potential partners is log on to any of many, many dating sites. Complicated, because the safety net of introductions by friends and family is gone, and it's hard to know if what you're told online is what you'll get.*

I think we're in a transition. Internet dating is really a good example of that, because five years ago when I wrote *Dating for Dummies* people were just beginning to Internet-date. People using Internet dating were considered to be those who couldn't get a date anyplace else. It was the nerds and the techno geeks who were doing this, because they didn't have to worry about sex appeal, they didn't have to worry about grooming. The idea was that someone would fall in love with your heart, whether or not you're funny looking.

So in theory, Internet dating was for lonely, shy introverts who are not particularly attractive. Clearly, technology has exploded that stereotype. We know now that if you post a picture, you're going to get eight times as many responses, regardless of what the picture looks like. So what's the next thing going to be? I think they're going to have opt-cams. I mean that is clear; people already do. So the discovery process of getting to know somebody has really changed extraordinarily.

And we know there are studies that suggest there's a false intimacy—that people sitting in front of a blank computer screen will talk about things they'd never talk about with somebody face-to-face. We know that there is a huge level of lying on the Internet. I also think it is changing marriage. In the past, when people got bored with their spouse, they could only go to a bar at the risk of being spotted either there or coming home later. You can go online without anybody being the wiser.

There's going to be more Internet dating, an impatient kind of speed dating. It's going to get more sophisticated in that you're not only going to be IMing people, but everybody will have a webcam. At some point, we will probably have barcodes issued at birth, so somebody will just scan our barcode when they want to go out with us.

◀ **A Shopping Mentality** ▶

Long-distance relationships will become more prevalent just because it seems tempting to find somebody you like and not pay much attention to the fact that you're not actually going to spend much time with them. The whole social fabric is changing. Kids in their twenties aren't getting married anymore. I mean, they're having babies. They're shacking up. They're with each other, but they're not getting married, which I think is destabilizing for kids, and also for the women, because we know that, economically, women suffer substantially more when relationships come undone. The Internet is creating a shopping mentality. Before, if you ran into this great guy, you would date him for a while and see how things went. And now, even if he's great, there's a tendency to think, Well, maybe there's somebody cuter, I'll just go check my listing.

The dating scene is becoming increasingly fragmented. It used to be that people started looking for a mate, started dating, fell in love, got married, and had kids, and lived happily ever after. And now all parts of that have been broken down. People will date without any real goal. There's a new statistic out that says more than half the people who go to online dating sites never go out with anybody. People certainly fall in love without any notion of institutionalizing or formalizing the relationship. People have children without doing it. What we're seeing is that each of the segments we viewed as part of a larger process is being broken down and extracted and fragmented, and I think that is going to continue to happen.

People are getting more and more isolated. I'm convinced that the Sony Walkman was really the death of civilization as we know it. You can be in a crowd and be completely tuned out, and it's only gotten worse, not better.

◀ **Marriage and Sex** ▶

Does marriage really have a use anymore? I'm one of those romantics who thinks it probably does, because raising a child is the hardest thing any of us ever do. All of us are ill prepared for it, and at least having two people, often of the opposite sex, brings two perspectives. I was reading someplace that a thousand years from now men will be extinct; there's really no value in having them. All you need is sperm. You may not even need that. I mean, if you clone, you don't even need sperm. And so that whole issue about marriage, about dating, about courting, about sex is really being altered and has been for a very long time. But it's really a larger issue: how does technology lead or serve?

One of the trends we are sure of is that kids are having sex earlier. They're having unprotected sex. They're having babies earlier. In this country ten years ago, one of every four births was to a girl under the age of eighteen. There are some indications that this trend may be easing a bit, partially because as more single women opt for motherhood later, the median age has gradually increased. Additionally, women are waiting longer to have children, and it is directly associated with education. We're finding that young, uneducated women are having more children earlier, and education is certainly being impacted by that. In addition, educated, middle-class Americans are having fewer children and having them later.

This destabilizes society, because the people who are least capable of parenting are having more children earlier by themselves. Daddies aren't sticking around, so you have young men with multiple children, none of whom they are living with and supporting. And on the other hand, you have the people that, in theory, are best able to take care of children—in terms of income, in terms of education, in terms of stability—having fewer children much later in life.

◄ A Prescription for Love ►

What can you do? Know yourself. What you really want is an addition to your existing life. I think the best relationships are the ones where you keep that in mind. The relationship is not even the icing on the cake; it's the sprinkles on top of the whipped cream on top of the hot fudge, on top of the ice cream. What we know is, *I want you*: great. *I love you*: why not? *I need you*: bad idea. The more self-reliant you are, the better able you are to run your own life, the better the decisions you will make about a partner, and the less you will need to lie to them—and lie to yourself and get yourself in situations where you're tempted by other people.

So if I was in charge: When little boy babies are born, I'd just put a little sticker on them saying they can't procreate until they pass something like a driver's test. They'd have to prove they're not children. The license would only be good for one person for one sexual time or for six months, so all babies were planned and wanted—no accidents—sex wouldn't be taboo, venereal disease could be controlled to a very large extent, and people would commit to somebody only when they wanted to spend the rest of their lives with them. I wouldn't allow people to have babies until they could stick around to take care of them. This way, you don't confuse love and lust, and you don't confuse sex and anything else, and you hook up with somebody because your life works just beautifully without them—but it certainly is a little more fun with them there. And both of you feel the same way, so you both make much better decisions.

Marcus Buckingham
➤ on Management and Leadership

During his seventeen years with the Gallup Organization, MARCUS BUCKINGHAM helped take the group's research into the world's best managers, leaders, and workplaces. He has written two best-selling books based on his broad experience in management practices and employee retention: First, Break All the Rules and Now, Discover Your Strengths. His most recent book is The One Thing You Need to Know. Buckingham graduated from Cambridge University with a master's degree in social and political science. We were interested in Buckingham's thoughts about management and leadership because it seems that, with all the rapid changes in the world, we need real leadership more than ever.

My specialty is the world of work. In many respects, this world will continue to be governed by its time-honored rules.

To be productive as an individual, you must identify your customer and fulfill that customer's felt need—the customer alone defines and judges your performance. To be productive as a team leader, you must make your team great to work with—this means setting clear expectations for each person, praising excellence whenever you see it, pushing decisions down as close to the action as possible, and helping each person find the right ways to grow and develop. To be productive as an organization builder you must do everything to ensure positive cash flow—in our capitalistic system, no cash means no future.

However, in two important areas, this world is being changed by irresistible forces. Both can damage and deplete the world of work. But each also holds the promise of positive change.

First, we're going global. What is sold in Chicago was assembled in Mexico from parts made in Taiwan from materials mined in Australia. For you, the individual employee, this means not only that you will have to become versed in and accepting of the customs of strangers—what is considered bribery in Chicago is considered good business practice in Taiwan, what is impetuousness over there is called "performance orientation" over here, what is responsible to you is reckless to them. More important, it means that you will have to become far more self-reliant. You work in Sunnyvale, California. Your boss works in Brussels. You open your e-mail in the morning just in time to see her signing off for the night. You have a quick question. Her reply takes a day. Very little face time. No tolerance for ambiguity. No handholding. No frank, face-to-face chats as you hammer things out together. This is the future of work in global, vertically integrated organizations.

Why is this a positive change? Because the largest cohort to enter the workforce since the baby boomers, Generation Y, wants this kind of self-reliance. If you are a Gen Yer, you've been cosseted and protected and praised since your first toddling steps. You were given an award for coming in seventh in the high jump, you had an elaborate ceremony when you graduated . . . from third grade to fourth grade. All this lavish attention has given you a sense of entitlement: "I've been coming to work on time for six weeks straight. Where's my promotion?" But it has also made you a volunteer. You believe you have a unique contribution to make at work, and unlike your immediate elders, the fabled, jaded Generation X, you actually believe that your contribution will make a difference. And so you come into work expecting—demanding, even—that you be given the freedom to carve a role for yourself that fits your unique talents. You don't want someone to look over your shoulder and define in explicit, excruciating detail what you are supposed to do. Don't tell me how to do it, you say. Just tell me what you want to get done, and let me figure out my path of least resistance to that outcome. You want freedom, room to maneuver. You want your boss in Brussels.

The smart employee is the one who figures out how to use this freedom wisely. In the future you must identify specifically what your strengths are, and then, with little guidance from above, seek out the unoccupied niche within your organization where your particular strengths will give you a significant advantage.

The smart organization is the one that doesn't try to fight against this self-important volunteerism, but instead strives to channel it.

The second change is the dramatic increase in transparency. A harmless little fudge on your résumé? It will be discovered, you will be humiliated, and you will be fired. A dismissive remark to another guest in a hotel lobby? Tomorrow it will appear on some blog or other, and either your or your company's name will be publicly besmirched. Your recent medical history? Your secret one-cigar-a-week habit? Soon your organization will have the "right to know."

The death of privacy? Perhaps—though I think that we will quickly become more tolerant, and maybe even more forgiving of other people's imperfections.

What is most unquestionably positive about this transparent world is that it will force our leaders to become more accountable to us. If you're paying for your wife's birthday party out of company coffers, we will find out. If you're extracting oil from the Niger delta by destroying the livelihood of those living on the Niger delta, we will learn about it. If you're a political leader whose lifestyle contradicts everything you stand for, and vote for, we will discover it and hold you to account.

And this transparency will allow information to flow both ways. Not only will we be better able to find out about our leaders' actions, but they will be able to find out about our will. In the future they will be forced to hear and act on what we want. Corporate presidents will have to listen more closely to their many constituencies. Politicians will less and less be the representatives of the people, and more and more their mouthpiece. Companies will have to bend to the will of inquisitive, activist shareholder meetings. States will be run by referenda. Accountable capitalism. Direct democracy. This is the future for leaders. We should look forward to it.

Richard H. Carmona, MD, MPH, FACS
> **on Medicine**

RICHARD H. CARMONA, MD, MPH, FACS, *served as the seventeenth Surgeon General of the United States from 2002 to 2006. A first-generation American, he was born and raised in New York City. In 1967, at the age of seventeen, Richard Carmona dropped out of high school, as did many of the kids in his poor Hispanic neighborhood. Soon after leaving school, he enlisted in the U.S. Army, where he earned his Army General Equivalency Diploma and became a Special Forces medic and weapons specialist. He went on to become a combat-decorated Vietnam veteran. When he returned home, Carmona attended Bronx Community College, and later the University of California, San Francisco (UCSF). He graduated first in his class from UCSF medical school, earning the prestigious gold-headed cane. He also completed a surgical residency at UCSF and a National Institutes of Health-sponsored fellowship in trauma, burns, and critical care. Later in his career, Dr. Carmona earned a master of public health degree from the University of Arizona. Dr. Carmona has served in many positions in the health and medical field, including as a medic, registered nurse, physician's assistant, surgeon, and CEO of a health care system. He has also been a professor, a police officer, and a SWAT team leader.*

In many ways, health care is the perfect intersection of two subjects that seemed to echo throughout most of our interviews: technology and religion. Medical ethics seems more important than ever, and religious concerns impact the development and application of this technology daily. For this reason, Dr. Carmona's thoughts on this intersection and how it relates to stem cell research were of particular interest to us.

If we look out around the country of 300 million citizens, we are largely a health-illiterate society. Science is moving so rapidly that even the scientists have trouble keeping up with information outside their own focused field. So what does that foretell for the average American who may be anything from an accountant to an auto mechanic? Do Americans understand all the science and health messages that can help them make good decisions that will keep them healthy and well? As we move the science along, the public keeps getting further and further away from what these great scientific and technological advances mean for their lives and their families' lives.

We need to get the American public engaged in understanding what's being done and what's important in science. We need to improve our nation's health literacy.

Because, ultimately, no matter what I might have done as surgeon general, in order to achieve improved health and wellness, it's all about behavioral change. It's not about CT scans or MRIs or complex surgical procedures. It really is about all of us understanding that information and making some informed decisions that change our behavior. So we get a little physical activity every day. We eat healthier in appropriate portions. We remove the risk in our lives by wearing a seatbelt or a bicycle helmet, and so on. Doing those simple things will greatly reduce the disease burden in our society as well as the economic burden.

Over the past several decades, the United States has made unprecedented advances in medicine and technology. But it is health literacy—the ability of an individual to access, understand, and use health-related information and services to make appropriate decisions—that is fundamental to our individual and national health. Yet more than ninety million Americans have difficulty understanding basic health information. Language barriers add another layer of complexity. Culturally and linguistically diverse groups typically experience less adequate access to care, lower quality of care, and poorer health status and outcomes.

I grew up a poor Latino street kid in New York City. I was often hungry and was homeless for the first time when I was six years old. I know what it's like to be on the fringes of society, to be someone who people were willing to forget and leave alone.

My parents were good people, but they struggled with serious

substance-abuse problems. My grandmother—my *abuelita*—helped
raise my brothers and sister and me. Although she was poor and
uneducated, she was one of the strongest people I have ever known.
I think today of all the parents and grandparents raising the next generation of Americans and trying to understand enough about health
so that they can raise a healthy family, so that they can be well and
continue to be active in their community.

The reality is that very few people understand today's modern
medical world. Few Americans understand the complexities of navi-
gating an HMO, for instance. Very few people understand nutrition.
Even fewer people understand genetics or genomics, or the fact that,
thanks to the Human Genome Project we now have the blueprint for
the human body. What does that mean to the average person? How
do they grasp that information? How do they utilize it?

There are people who believe the vaccines themselves can cause
diseases like autism. The fact is that there's really no proof of that. It's
all hypothetical. We've had study groups at the National Institutes of
Health, universities have done studies, and vaccines are probably
one of the best and safest ways ever invented to prevent disease.
Just look at the polio vaccine. In the 1950s, we had an epidemic
of polio in our country. You still see people my age or older walking
around in braces, with limps, or with undeveloped limbs because
they contracted polio. Polio has been eradicated in the United States
and most of the world largely because of vaccines. When you look
at the incidence of measles, mumps, rubella, whooping cough, and
all of the other diseases, we're a relatively healthy society because
of vaccines. Now vaccines do have some minor side effects. Generally speaking you may have a sore arm or get a little fever for a day,
but that's it. It's very, very unusual to have a significant complica-
tion from a vaccine, so we've spoken out forcefully on this from my
office—especially as it relates to children, because we need to protect our children from all the childhood diseases that can affect their
growth and development.

That falls under the umbrella of health literacy and improving
health literacy. I think we'll slowly evolve, as our society moves to

understanding that we need to embrace health, wellness, and prevention because we can't afford the alternatives.

People are trying to figure out how to pay for the health care
system and the medical technology advances available now. We
spend 16 percent of our gross domestic product on health care, and
that number increases annually. That's unsustainable over time. I
think we'll see broader programs available, but I don't think we're
ever going to have a single-payer, universal health care system. Our
government and businesses will make appropriate relationships with
providers to ensure that all Americans do have access to a basic set
of health benefits (universal care is much different than universal
payer), but I think that's going to be an evolutionary process. It will
be pushed along by lots of little pieces of legislation, lots of little
activities, lots of little bits and best practices that emerge, and a
society that's becoming more informed and less tolerant of the fact
that the richest nation in the world cannot provide basic services for
its people.

The bad news is that this is going to be an intergenerational
endeavor. It's not going to happen in one generation. It's going to
be a cultural shift that will take place over time. We really have to
become a nation that embraces health and wellness and prevention
as much as we've embraced health care over the past half a century
or so. Most of the disease burden and the economic burden we have
today are preventable. Of our health care expenditures, 75 percent is
on chronic diseases, many of which are preventable. We must move
from being a treatment-oriented society to being a prevention-oriented
society.

◄ **Future Preparedness for Emergency Response** ►

When I was a youngster growing up in New York City back in the
fifties and sixties, we knew that there were threats. The people of
the United States knew there was this thing called the Cold War,

and within the Cold War, we knew that these Russian guys had a bomb, and we had a bomb in World War II. If things got tense, the worst-case scenario was that somebody would drop a nuclear bomb on us. So we had what we called Civil Defense, and in Civil Defense, we had air-raid shelters. We would stockpile food and water in the house, just as we're told to do today. People who had enough money had bomb shelters in their backyards. When they didn't, they had a place to evacuate to, like a school that became a community shelter if something happened.

We all knew that when the siren went off, we were to sit under our desks, go to a protected place in the home, find shelter if we were out in the streets. We would have these drills from time to time, never knowing when the siren went off if it was just a drill or the real thing. Our society understood a potential threat, and we understood what actions we needed to take when an emergency occurred.

We don't have that capacity anymore. People hearing a siren in the street wouldn't even think of civil defense anymore. If you ask the average person what threats face us today, they would be hard-pressed to define weapons of mass destruction, the tools that the terrorists use, what terrorism is, or what the problems are, let alone all the other challenges, such as avian flu. So when you look at these threats—challenges that include terrorism, emerging infections such as SARS, avian flu, smallpox, and monkey pox, as well as earthquakes and hurricanes—how does the average person prepare for them? What do you do? We don't have the Civil Defense mentality anymore.

The American public needs to be engaged to understand the concept of "all-hazards" preparation, to understand that in any given emergency, they may be expected to act in a certain way so they can protect themselves and their families and to assist their neighbors and community when needed. That's going to be different from a single response, because there will be multiple potential responses depending on whether it's avian flu or a hurricane or a terrorist event. But to do that we have to engage the American public through communication, public service announcements, stories on the Internet, in the newspaper, magazines, television, radio, and on and on and on, so that we can start to re-build that capacity and resilience in society.

◀ **Stem Cell Research** ▶

I think the *science* of stem cells is not controversial. The fact of the matter is that stem cells hold for us the promise of a healthier future, and that's not the ideological or theological interpretation. That's simply the science. Stem cells have unlimited potential. The child who is paraplegic, the child who may die of a congenital heart, a senior with Alzheimer's—there is so much potential there for the application of stem cell science. But then as a society we have to step back and say, Okay, what happens? What are the unintended negative consequences if we don't control proliferation? Do we want to have reproductive cloning? Do we want to make or manufacture our fellow humans? Most people say that would not be good. We appreciate how we evolve and have our children.

So how do we use this science for the betterment of society and still take into account that there are many complex issues that aren't about science but are ideological, theological, and sociological—and in a country that prides itself on its diversity, that fights for its democracy to its death? How do we integrate all of that and move forward for the betterment of the American people?

The issue with the stem cells really comes down to a lowest common denominator: how do you define life? If you define life as two cells coming together, then you may have difficulty in allowing any kind of research that involves two reproductive cells, because as soon as those cells unite, you define that as life. Others say, Well, that's not really life. The debate rages on: Is it two cells? Is it four cells? Is it when gestation progresses enough so that you see a heartbeat or the rudiments of a neurological system?

I certainly don't pretend to have the answer. That's the beauty of democracy—that we can have this debate and we can decide for ourselves. That debate needs to continue. My sense of this situation is that we have on the right very religious ideologically driven folks who see stem cell research only as destruction of life. On the left, we have very liberal people who say, I don't really think that's true, and this research is for the good of mankind, so we need to let this research go on unchecked. Yet letting this go unchecked offends a lot of people. How do you balance those conflicting in a democratic society?

I think that we will continue this discussion for some time and that, incrementally over time, more stem cells will be used. The only ban now is on federally funded new stem cell lines. But there are industries that are emerging. California set aside millions of dollars to do its own programs without federal funds. Think about this hypothetical case: If you're the mother, father, or sibling, no matter how you are driven ideologically or theologically, and you have a child or a parent or a friend who's about to die because of a defect, what do you do? If you have a girlfriend or boyfriend who's a paraplegic from a car accident and could be sequestered in a wheelchair for fifty years, but there is the promise of science that can make that person walk again—what do you do?

My sense is that what will ultimately drive stem cell research is the betterment of society and mankind, and I think our culture will then redefine how we see life. Even theologically, it will redefine how we see this gift. For those who are driven religiously, theologically to the right—when all of a sudden a child walks again because of that stem cell, they may redefine this stem cell as God's gift to us. Whereas the scientist on the left says, Look, I told you this twenty years ago—this has nothing to do with theology, it's all science.

What will happen is that mankind will benefit. That's how I see it eventually being resolved. New science will engender economic opportunity, which will engender growth, which will engender better health and wellness and cures. And we will discover and embrace better ways to prevent diseases, saving ourselves a lot of suffering and cost. That's going to be the ultimate driver.

◀ **The Doctor's Prescription** ▶

What would I like to see for us in the future? Educate yourself. Get interested in life. Get literate in science. We're in the digital age. The world of the assembly line—the world of making widgets in a factory—is gone. No matter your profession in the future, you're going to have at least a grasp of science and technology. The computer is going to be your portal to the world. You'll be able to access any scientific information. There will be explanations for the human genome. You'll be able to have your medical records readily available, and you'll be able to update them and virtually take them any place in the world you go. All of this is going to be right at your fingertips every single day, but you have to prepare for it. So get involved, get literate, and understand the benefits of health and wellness and prevention.

In the military, we often speak of the concept of "force projection," which is essentially the global demonstration of our power via the visible presence of planes, ships, and uniformed troops. The concept of superpower is now evolving. He who has the digital or genomic codes necessary can project force virtually, invisibly, and globally without *traditional* force projection as we know it today. In fact, I believe that in the future we will see "health diplomacy" prospectively practiced as a "soft force projection" not only for its health benefit globally but equally important for its tangential ability to extinguish global symmetries of health, wealth, ideology, and theology—which are some of the variables that create global divisiveness and sometimes terrorism.

Think globally, because the present and future threats (manmade or naturally occurring) that our nation will face don't respect geopolitical borders.

The goal is to eradicate, eliminate, and reduce all preventable disease in society and the world, in order to make us a healthier nation and world and thereby reduce the economic impact on society. Many people who are living at the margins of life, as I did—hungry and homeless more times than I can count—still don't have high-quality health care, and if we're not careful, the literate alone will continue to advance and leave large parts of society behind to struggle. We must ride this wave together, so we all enjoy healthier and safer and more secure lives, here in the United States and around the world.

Science and health, if used wisely, can be a powerful currency to express global social responsibility as well as a means to a safer and more secure world.

Chip & Pepper ➤ on Fashion

As twenty-somethings, identical twins CHIP AND PEPPER FOSTER *created a Canadian sportswear label that grew into a multimillion-dollar company. In 2003, they began a fashion renaissance in America by launching a high-end denim line that has become a cult favorite among celebrities and hipsters. Its rapid popularity has expanded to include maternity, kids, knitwear, hats, leather goods, and sportswear. In fall 2005 the twins launched Chip & Pepper University, a knit line incorporating vintage and original logos from thirty-five universities around the nation. In addition, Chip & Pepper launched C7P: A Chip & Pepper Production with JC Penney Corporation, Inc., in 2007. With C7P, a juniors' collection, the twins were inspired to give the same premium look and feel without the premium price to a larger audience. Chip and Pepper's energetic personalities have landed them a gig hosting* The Look for Less *on E! Entertainment and the Style Network, and they also proudly serve as fashion correspondents for* Extra. *We wanted to talk to Chip & Pepper because they have their eyes and energy on the trends and know what will be happening in fashion in the future.*

Fashion changes daily. There are no givens other than what may be hot today will certainly not be hot tomorrow. What we love about this industry is that, since it is trend-driven and trends change quickly, things cannot be planned out a decade in advance. Pop culture and a designer's own vision or preference will to an extent influence nuances in a collection, but a key factor that has and always will drive broad trending in fashion is street style. A good designer will keep their blinders on, to a point, and not be influenced by what those around them are doing, yet they will always respect what style trends emerge naturally and organically.

We also expect that the influence of celebrity will play an increasingly significant role in shaping fashion. This influence has grown from the celebrity-designer relationship, often relegated to a celebrity serving as a muse and/or featured in an advertising campaign, to celebrities ultimately becoming designers in their own right. The power of Hollywood is not going unnoticed in the fashion industry, as designers vie for the coveted opportunity to dress celebrities on not only the red carpet, but also in their increasingly private lives. Having an A-list celebrity photographed in and recognized for favoring your brand can have more influence over consumer buying patterns than some traditional advertising campaigns. As such, celebrity courtship will continue in years to come.

◀ Eco-Friendly Trends ▶

We anticipate that the growing environmental trend will have a major effect on fashion, whether it be eco-friendly materials and processes that we're seeing being implemented for the long-term or nature and animal motifs being incorporated into current design. This will be a very positive change. With people becoming more aware of the declining state of the environment and the rather simple solutions and processes that can be implemented to create a smaller footprint, we will see sweeping changes across many different sectors, fashion included. In addition to fabric treatments and wash processes becoming more "green," the fashion industry will use more eco-friendly options including vegetable dyes and saltwater, wash treatments for garments, and organic fabric, which is no longer just a niche offering but a staple in many clothing lines.

To that end, the environment will have a similar impact on fabric. Recycled fabrics will be prevalent, and we'll see even unique fabric made from recycled goods, such as plastics. Current technology is amazing—it's difficult to fathom that the soft fabric of a shirt was once a plastic produce bag or that the material used in a pair of surf trunks was once a plastic soda bottle!

◄ **Denim in the Future** ►

Denim, and especially premium denim, is a trend that will be here for many years to come. What people forget is that the premium denim industry is still relatively new, existing, as we now know it, for only the past five to seven years. The market is still settling and establishing its permanent role. The average American owns seven pairs of jeans. Premium denim is not going anywhere. Once the dust settles, we will see five to ten big brands in the forefront, such as the case with car companies. The offerings will become truly vertical: dark to light washes, skinny to flare fits, and organic fabric to Japanese denim.

Mass retailers will continue to grow and expand their offerings. The biggest change we'll see in years to come is the increased presence of individual brands within stores by way of self-contained "stores within stores" or popshops. Mass retailers will increase business with specific brands and become known for having a healthy collection available of such brands, and this will become a key method of not only highlighting that but also increasing sales.

◄ **The Fate of Couture** ►

But don't expect couture to go away completely. True couture—haute couture—has been in existence since 1945, and its essence will never change. Couture is the art of garment construction and often involves time-consuming, hand-executed techniques. In current years, the term has loosely been used to describe high-fashion custom-fitted clothing, though in France the term is protected by law, and only a handful of government-approved companies have the legal right to refer to themselves as couture. It is the most revered form of fashion and will remain as such.

When it comes to the future of fashion, the trends we don't want to see can be just as important as the ones we do. Since one of the core components of our growing brand and business is denim, we clearly wouldn't like to see a return to a more formal mode of dress in the workplace. In fact, some years back, the trend of casual Fridays in the workplace significantly affected formal menswear manufacturers and helped boost denim sales, as full suits were replaced by denim and casual shirts. The impact of casual Fridays also paved the way for denim as an acceptable staple for going out. Beyond that, our biggest hope is that shoulder pads do not make a comeback!

Loren Coleman ➤ on Cryptozoology

LOREN COLEMAN *is one of the world's leading cryptozoologists.
Since the Abominable Snowman caught his interest more than four
decades ago, Coleman has traveled the world in pursuit of the mys-
teries of unknown creatures, leading him to research everything from
black panther sightings to reports of Napes (North American apes) in
the American Midwest. He has traveled around the world interviewing witnesses of lake monsters, Bigfoot, giant snakes, mystery fields,
Mothmen, thunderbirds, and other unconfirmed creatures. The author
of thirty books and more than five hundred articles, he has been both
an on- and off-camera consultant to reality-based programs on NBC,
A&E, the History Channel, and the Discovery Channel. We were
curious about what kind of creatures he thought we might find in the
future, and what those discoveries would mean.*

In cryptozoology, there is no magic crystal ball. Cryptozoology,
despite what the general public might think about the people
involved, the scientific search for Bigfoot, Yeti, and Nessie, is
grounded in our pursuit and research of these cryptids (hidden or
unknown creatures), through zoology, anthropology, and other sci-
ences. In 2001, I made a series of predictions based upon trends,
patterns, developments, and the history of cryptozoology. Here are
the relevant ones, the ones that still apply as we enter the second
half of this first decade of the twenty-first century:

➤ Intriguing clues will surface of a new population of coel-
acanths (those prehistoric-looking fish that were thought
to have died out 65 million years ago until they were redis-
covered in 1938), far from their native Africa. Look to the
Caribbean, the Gulf of Mexico, or near Australia for some

startling news in this regard. More findings from Africa will also occur.

➤ Laser-triggered cameras will capture good photographic evidence of the small, unknown anthropoid called the Orang Pendek, in Sumatra. More funding will pour into the study and preservation of that primate.

➤ Postcranial remains (bones other than from the skull) will be found of *Gigantopithecus* (a supposedly extinct nine-foot-tall ape) in Asia, and many theories regarding the relationship of *Gigantopithecus* to the Yeti and Bigfoot will have to be revised.

➤ The search for the Loch Ness monsters will continue to be frustrating, with no earthshaking findings for another ten years. Awareness will increase that several different kinds of phenomena have been lumped under the Nessie label.

➤ Most new animals, those yet to be discovered, are not likely to be ones that we domesticate. Any primate discovered may be more intelligent than we have considered.

➤ South America will be the source of a thrilling new discovery of a large mammal, possibly a feline or an animal that looks like a cat, although it may be a marsupial.

➤ Attention will focus again on searches in Africa. Explorers looking for "living dinosaurs" will find new evidence that the animals they're seeking are actually unknown forest rhinos. Researchers will rediscover the importance of old missionaries' diaries and records, and scholars will reopen inquiries into these "dinosaurs," as well as spotted lions in Kenya and unknown apes throughout tropical Africa.

◀ **The Next Generation** ▶

I am entering a phase of my life that I understand is significant for preparing the next generation of cryptozoologists, those who will follow me. I have done much to popularize cryptozoology, I've made materials easily accessible, and I've laid the groundwork for others who have created even more opportunities and knowledge for the general public. I think it's important now to concentrate on books for children on general cryptozoology, field guides that inform specifically as well as single-topic books on certain under-researched cryptids. Having just turned sixty, I look forward to the forty years of work ahead of me.

New discoveries will enhance our knowledge of the globe's biosystems and enrich our understanding of how humans fit into the overall picture. Technology, from DNA analysis to high-speed laser camera traps, has already begun to change cryptozoology, and I expect this to continue. More classes will be offered, and eventually a department of cryptozoology will be established, probably at a state college.

Kellyanne Conway ➤ on Women

KELLYANNE CONWAY *is President and CEO of the polling company, inc/WomanTrend. Her firm specializes in survey research, focus groups, and strategic counsel for political, corporate, legal, and public affairs clients. She appears regularly on television and has written for the* Wall Street Journal, National Review, *and* Campaigns & Elections. *She was profiled in* George *magazine and named by the* National Journal *one of Washington's most influential conservatives who are forty and younger. We spoke to Conway because we felt the book that she co-authored with Celinda Lake,* What Women Really Want: How American Women Are Quietly Erasing Political, Racial, Class, and Religious Lines to Change the Way We Live *(2005), smartly addressed the real concerns women have today, and how they are changing their lives for themselves and their families.*

◄ Women in the Workforce ➤

The traditional workforce will soon be forced to confront two convergent trends being driven by women: motherhood and entrepreneurship.

First, motherhood tends to be the primary reason that women who are already in the traditional workforce leave it for a temporary period. The "temporary" nature of these departures is rooted in the fact that children eventually mature and go to school, and Mom, either at that time or much sooner, returns to the workforce out of need or desire.

A funny thing has happened recently on the boomerang back to work. Some of these women are simply not going. The percentage of stay-at-home mothers in married-couple families has grown from

20 percent in 1996 to 24 percent in 2006, but the declining number of women in the "traditional" workforce cannot solely be blamed on women opting to provide full-time care for their children. Some of them are tapping their savings and converting hobbies into full-grown businesses, or they're setting up a Web site or an extra phone line and gingerly stepping into self-employment by catering on the weekends or designing Christmas cards for sale. I think entrepreneurship offers many of these women the promise of flexibility and the self-designed work-life harmony that many employers in the traditional workforce preen about in their handbooks—about "family-friendly environments" and sensitivity training—but simply do not provide.

The rapid and widespread attainment of higher formal education for many women and technological advances means that now the workplace is everywhere and includes everyone. Women are also on the forefront of Web-commuting and job sharing, and the demand for flex time is really being driven by women. Twenty years ago women were trying to finesse institutional change in corporate America by demanding on-site day-care centers or government-mandated extended maternity leave. Now they're more quietly trying to forge individual flexibility within the private employer-employee relationship and customize arrangements according to their personal situations.

Second, entrepreneurship among a diverse demographic of women in the United States—not just mothers—is explosive and undeniable. In fact, the rate of growth in the number of women-owned firms has grown at two times the rate of all firms. An eye-popping 10.4 million firms have women that possess at least 50 percent ownership, and 74 percent of those firms are majority-owned by women. Their sales figures are impressive; in 2006, they generated $1.9 trillion in sales. Moreover, women business owners hire more individuals than Fortune 500 companies combined (and lay them off far less frequently), and the increase surpasses the growth of male entrepreneurship almost two to one in some of our key states.

In the research we conducted for our book *What Women Really Want*, 46 percent of the women nationwide surveyed said if their financial situation allowed, they would like to own their own business. That figure is even higher among single women, African American women, and younger women. We're also seeing an increase in women who are fifty or older starting their own businesses. They are such a fascinating demographic group anyway. Fifty years ago, when you turned sixty, you were basically winding down, putting your papers in order, and entering retirement and those "final years"— even if you didn't work outside of the home. Now women turn fifty or sixty and exclaim, "Well, half of my life is ahead of me," so they tend to take on new relationships, new friendships, new opportunities in education and career. They're going on interesting travel adventures. They're turning toward entrepreneurship to allow them to feel more fulfilled and engaged and challenged in their professional lives than they felt when they were concerned primarily with earning a paycheck or securing health coverage and other benefits.

Essentially, entrepreneurship has become the contemporary version of the "American Dream." Years ago when you asked men and particularly women to define the American Dream, it was to give their children an education, to buy their first home, to save money for retirement, to find a meaningful and well-paying job themselves. Then in the late 1990s it became much more intangible: to be happy, to feel fulfilled. Now for many women, many of whom already have their educations and educations for their children, own their own homes, and hold some financial security, owning a business is their updated version of the American Dream. It combines tangible needs (livelihood) with intangible desires (freedom *and* security).

◀ **The New Parenthood, Dad Included** ▶

Statistics show that men, especially Generation X dads, are taking a much more active role in their children's physical and emotional development, their children's preschool education, and the actual care and feeding of the children. In fact, despite the prominence of two-working-parent households, both moms and dads of this generation are spending more time with their children than previous generations.

This is also a by-product of a fair number of Generation X men having been latchkey children. Many of them did not have Mom and Dad at home between those critical hours of three p.m. and six p.m. (after school and before dinner) and were then often charged with the care of younger siblings. Forty percent of Generation Xers (those Americans born between 1965 and 1978) lived in a single-parent household by the age of sixteen. Rather than replicate that in their own children's lives, they're taking a much more active approach to parenting.

In the future, the primary responsibility for the caretaking of children, of course, will continue to rest on women. That's the way it's always been, through nature and nurture. At the same time, we're seeing both men and women struggling to find a way to balance their many commitments and desires so that they can spend more time with the children. One example of this is happening in urban and some suburban areas. Some of these women do have at-home care for the children. Most of it is part time. What we're finding is that the women who have at-home care are using it more judiciously so that *they* can spend more time with their children. Many of these women were complaining for years, saying, "Oh, God, my babysitter is at home with the kids and I'm stuck in traffic going to the grocery store and dry cleaner." It made no sense. So now they send their helpers to run errands while they're at home making mud pies with the kids and teaching them the alphabet.

◀ Explosion of Single Women ▶

The increase in the number of single women in this country is one of the most important demographic evolutions in the last thirty to forty years, and will continue to be, because most of these women are delaying, deferring, or denying marriage by choice.

A number of them are waiting until they have finished their formal educations, gained career footing, and concluded that they are ready. Many of these women delay marriage not because they don't take marriage seriously, but precisely because they do. They've seen the skyrocketing divorce rates. They've been from broken homes themselves and believe that when it comes to marriage, you do it once, you do it right, and you do it forever. Women previously had pursued the four magic Ms—marriage, munchkins, mortgages, and mutual funds—in that order. Now they are obtaining them in different sequences, and omitting those they have decided do not fit with their "lives' to-do lists."

In the 2000 Census, it was reported that 51 percent of all women live without a spouse present in the home. Even though roughly 80 percent of all American women will have been married at some point in their lifetimes, women who are divorced or widowed or the women who have never been married are another fascinating group. They don't think like married people at all. They know they're primarily responsible for their health care, their education, and their retirement security, and many become very career focused. They are up for grabs politically. The Right is trying to engage them based on their status as stakeholders in an ownership society in which they are full-throated participants. The Left relies on them as believers in the safety social net, on which women eventually rely disproportionately more than men. As the years progress, many of these women will also feel unencumbered with obligations at home and financially stable enough to forge their way into entrepreneurship.

Consumer America is on to the explosion of single women, and "No Assembly Required" has been replaced with "No Man Required." They recognize that these women don't wait for "me" to become "we" before purchasing the big-ticket items such as homes, cars, and luxury vacations. In only eleven years, single women managed to capture a greater share of the home-buying market, growing from 14 percent to 22 percent between 1995 and 2006. Meanwhile, single men held steady in their share of the home-buying market at 9 percent during the same time span. These single women have the economic wherewithal and the consumer prowess to be full-fledged buyers in their own right.

Women no longer live according to linear paths and traditional sequences. The multitude of lifestyle choices and opportunities available to women means that women might share a gender and age but have little else in common. For an illustration of how non-monolithic women are today, consider the following life stages of three forty-eight-year-old women living just miles apart. The first may be a blue-collar grandmother; the second an unmarried, college-educated, tireless executive; and the third a mother of a kindergartener pregnant with her second.

◀ Balancing Health Care Needs ▶

Health care will continue to be one of the most persistent issues on the so-called women's agenda. Women tend to be the health gatekeepers for the entire family. The typical forty-five-year-old woman has a living mother and a husband and children, so she's concerned about everything from osteoporosis to prescription drug coverage to type II diabetes to childhood obesity and asthma to prostate cancer screenings. All of a sudden, she is fourth on her to-do list for health care. (And if there is a pet in the home, she's fifth!) But for her, it's a very serious matter. She's probably going to find creative ways to go around what many consider to be a very restrictive and impersonal system of health care delivery services and perhaps become more conversant with alternatives like Health Security Accounts (HSAs) and Associated Health Plans (AHPs).

Women will also continue to peruse the benefits packages being offered by different employers when deciding which job to take, and if it's an extra $1,000, $2,000, even $4,000 in salary, they won't bicker over those terms so much as they'll gravitate toward the more meaningful, more comprehensive, more personally relevant health and benefits (retirement) package.

◀ Women Taking Care of Themselves ▶

My greatest concern for women is that they're not doing enough for themselves to protect and fortify themselves and to simply slow down and be content with what is, rather than what should have been or could be. From rising rates of obesity and diabetes to heart disease as the number-one killer among women, the cruel irony is that even as more women are more aware, informed, and educated now, they are also less active generally and less proactive about taking care of themselves.

◀ The Skinny Trap ▶

When we asked women in a survey whether they'd rather be thinner or younger, they all went for thinner. You need look no further than how many billions of dollars in this country are spent every year on diet aids or diet programs and exercise programs that fail to make most of the women buying into them healthier or happier. Women across class, age, and race spectra are partaking in cosmetic procedures; it's become much more acceptable, affordable, and attainable to women of all walks of life. Naturally, to hark back to a nostalgic phrase, "thin will always be in," but youth is what is truly in vogue. Still, the anti-aging movement has become a multibillion-dollar industry, suggesting many women are going for "Option C" (both of the above) when considering whether they should invest in becoming slimmer or looking younger. For years, women tried to shed those last ten pounds. Now, they are trying to erase those last ten years, too.

In a different survey, we asked women if they'd prefer to be thinner, younger, prettier, or smarter, and thinner still won! Imagine that—you can be Mensa material or you can be a size two, and more women chose the smaller waist than the larger IQ. As much as women want to blame the food manufacturers and the fashion magazines for misplaced priorities, they ought to blame one another and they ought to point the finger at themselves. During the height of the silly no-carb craze, it seemed that some women felt more fearful about a slice of bread or a baked potato than they did a terrorist attack. At the risk of intensifying this diet obsession, my message is simple: Lighten up, ladies!

The good news is that there seems to have been a tempering of this quest for perfection. For one thing, it's exhausting. For another, it's unattainable. So why get tired going to a place you'll never arrive? Improvement, good; perfection, impossible.

◀ What Women Really Want ▶

Women seek peace and tranquility—a physical place or even a temporary state of mind each day with no noise or traffic or hassle—nothing beeping, blinking, or bothering them. And in a post–9/11 world, these women still search for a greater sense of control, a feeling of security that they actually have authority and autonomy over their tiny personal corner of the world. On paper, it's never been a better time to be a woman in the United States of America. Women outlive men by an average of 6.8 years, and they make up the majority of the population, the majority of first-time law students, first-time medical students, the largest group of first-time investors, first-time homebuyers—so many of the wonderful achievements and firsts are being led by women, yet they still seem to struggle with this lack of peace and inner solitude, self-awareness, and good old-fashioned happiness.

Stephen Kittredge Cunningham
➤ on Bartending

STEPHEN KITTREDGE CUNNINGHAM *is the author of* The Bartender's Black Book, *which is in its eighth edition and is the definitive guide for professional and amateur bartenders looking to refine their skills. We were interested in Cunningham's perspective on the future of bartending, because in the age of mixology and $1,000 specialty drinks, bartending seems to be evolving into an art form respected and lauded the way great cuisine is. We thought Stephen could give us a good idea of how extreme bartending might become and what kinds of cocktails and bars we have to look forward to in the future.*

I think more people will be choosing bartending as a career. Everybody has had the experience of going into a bar, and the person behind the bar couldn't even recognize a bottle of Port, doesn't know how to make a drink, and doesn't know what is going on in the kitchen. There will be much better educated and trained and informed people in the future.

I attribute it to the Internet, and (I don't want to sound too smug) to the best-selling drink book on the market today. I also attribute it to the global community; kids and adults exchanging ideas all day long—e-mailing, texting back and forth.

◀ Technology ▶

In the future, there will be new customer-screening technology that will make the bartender's life much easier. To keep out underage people, bartenders will be able to check IDs to make sure they aren't fraudulent. There will be databases and facial-recognition technology to check everybody out. The fake ID will be a thing of the past. Of course, the technology will not be immediately available to everybody, but you'll see it in the high-end nightclubs and places that need high security. So that's all going to keep out the underage drinkers, and some of the criminals too, I would think.

There will be drink scans. You give something to the person as they're coming in, maybe a bracelet, and every time they want a drink, the bracelet has to be scanned, so you know where the drinks are going. This will help to keep track of overdrinking. At some point, there will probably be something similar to a Breathalyzer that will help you check people's inebriation level. Perhaps it could be done through some kind of skin, sweat, or saliva test.

It needs to happen. It will cover the establishment's butts. It's horrible how liable they are. Someone can be drinking in your restaurant, go home, fall asleep with a cigarette, and burn down their house, and they can sue you. It will probably be a hardship at first to do all these things, but I think once it becomes more mainstream and they've worked out all of the kinks, everybody is going to think it is a blessing.

They're going to be able to take money and run it under some sort of scanner to make sure it is authentic. They're working on it now. There's nothing worse than a bartender at the end of the night who's got a $100 bill that's not legit. It's often illegal, but it's a very common practice to take that money out of the bartender's pocket.

◀ **The Next Level** ▶

There are going to be new jobs for research and development people who take drinks to the next level. Some places are calling them bar chefs or head mixologists. This will be a managerial, supervisory position that's a lot more involved than head bartender. They'll be changing drink menus and using fresh ingredients with the seasons.

Jell-O shots and alcoholic freeze pops are the norm now. So I wouldn't be surprised if we saw a nice high-end ice cream with liqueur in it, like an espresso and some Kahlua poured over a chocolate ice cream. So why not mix it right in? They've got things now that will vaporize your drinks. Now you can sit at a bar and inhale your drinks. I heard there are people trying to make a pill that will give you the feeling of having drunk alcohol, and another pill that will nullify it, so that you can drive after you leave the bar. I don't think such pills would ever become that popular, except with the experimental crowd. It would be more of a trendy thing, like oxygen bars, maybe in a few places such as Tokyo, New York, Ibiza, and L.A.

The bartending scene will never disappear. There's always going to be a human being behind the bar, not a robot. It's just the retro feel about it—this is what our forefathers did. They walked up to the bar, interacted, and ordered a drink, or they crafted their drink themselves.

◀ **Insurance** ▶

I would love to see people in the service industry get some insurance. It is grossly neglected. In twenty-five years of bartending, I've worked in twenty-plus places. I've had insurance in two—the Marriott and McCormick and Schmick's, because they were national chains. For a little restaurant to get insurance for people is just astronomically expensive. It can cripple a restaurant, just make it fold up. But hopefully things will change. I know some politicians talk about it, but we all want and need to change it.

I fear that bartenders will continue to be scapegoats for irresponsible drinkers. I actually had a lawyer advise me after I had acquired a little bit of wealth to stop pouring drinks for anybody. When there's a lawsuit and somebody wants to sue, they start sniffing around for money, and whoever has it, they'll hit them with it. And I couldn't imagine anything worse than having your wages garnished for the rest of your life for sliding the wrong person a drink.

◀ **Training** ▶

I would like to see a national program to educate servers of alcohol about how to serve it. Some states do it. I had to take a test in August to serve in Texas for one night, and it was a pretty good test. Here in Massachusetts, we have something called TPS, Training Personal Service, where we take tests. But I think people need to be educated and certified across the board. They should go more deeply into subjects like alcoholism and the side effects of mixing drinks with drugs, because these are the things bartenders have to deal with. What do you do if someone is choking or having a seizure? Bartenders usually run to go look for the manager, and maybe the manager knows what to do, or maybe not. If every bartender knew, it would be a wonderful thing.

◀ **Restaurant Design** ▶

One trend that I would really like to see is indoor-outdoor nightclubs. I was in a place in Atlanta called the Compound that was indoors and outdoors. There were fountains, an Asian garden motif with rocks, and Bonsai trees. And then there was a section outdoors with garage doors that opened up, so the whole place was half in, half out back there. And of course everything was wired really well for sound.

I'd like to see better-engineered, more user-friendly restaurants for the staff. I worked in a multimillion-dollar restaurant built probably seven years ago, where they put the bar a huge distance from the kitchen, and the bar was enclosed. If you needed ice, if you needed bread, if you needed a cup of soup, if you needed a pat of butter, you had to leave that bar and walk a hundred yards. I can't believe that somebody sunk all that money into a space and didn't even think about those things. There need to be more people in the business who are engineering the establishments.

I'd also like to see better-informed staff. I want to walk into a restaurant and know that I'm having USDA prime meat, and whether it's dry aged or not. I want to know if the key lime pie is made in-house. And I'd like to see better-informed customers. About 30 percent of the people who receive bad service bring it on themselves. Most of them are clueless about it. And they in turn ruin all the tables' dining experience around them, which is another 30 percent. The last 40 percent is the restaurant's fault (poor seating techniques, understaffing, untimed orders, etc.).

◀ The Magic of Tips ▶

People need to learn how to tip. I think they just don't know the program. The young crowd, the people out there who know what's going on, are usually 20 percenters. But the old school people leave anywhere from 12 to 15 percent, and there are still people, once in a while, who do not tip, which is horrible. They don't realize that restaurant personnel often make below minimum wage, and they totally rely on their tips.

◀ Super-Premium Spirits ▶

Twenty years ago there were probably eight vodkas available in a U.S. bar. Now I could name fifty new vodkas that are better than those eight. Super-premium spirits are a wonderful thing, and I'm happy to say that many are made by inspired Americans. They're going to keep coming out with new flavors, foreign flavors, ethnic flavors. I hope they start going toward organic ingredients—a lot of the flavored offerings don't even use real fruit. Organic/green, that's a trend I would like to see develop. We're very lucky to have the microbrews— the large beer manufacturers are trying either to swallow them or just crowd them out of the market place, and that's really sad.

I recently saw tofu that was marketed to taste like human flesh, and I wouldn't be surprised to see blood-flavored vodka at some point. Dessert drinks are getting more popular. Coffee and tea matching is going to get a lot bigger. Coffee and tea will be matched with desserts. Cocktails will be matched with the appetizers or entrées—even something like a gin and tonic. That will be a new trend. Cappuccino machines are going to end up everywhere. They're going to be in Asian restaurants, Moroccan restaurants—everywhere. It's just so prevalent now. Everybody wants a cappuccino. The meshing of cuisine will become very commonplace.

Alan Dershowitz ➤ **on Law**

PROFESSOR ALAN M. DERSHOWITZ *has been a pioneer in making the legal profession accessible to the general public. He was born in Brooklyn and graduated from Yeshiva University High School and Brooklyn College. At Yale Law School, he graduated first in his class and served as editor in chief of the* Yale Law Journal. *After clerking for Chief Judge David Bazelon and Justice Arthur Goldberg, he was appointed to the Harvard Law School faculty at the age of twenty-five, and at twenty-eight, he became the youngest full professor in the school's history. At Harvard, he is currently the Felix Frankfurter Professor of Law, a chair established in honor of the great justice's work in constitutional law. Dershowitz has been called the winningest appellate criminal defense lawyer in history. Over the course of his thirty-five-year legal career, he's won more than one hundred cases—a remarkable record for a part-time litigator who handles primarily criminal appeals, which generally have a very low rate of reversal. Dershowitz takes half of his cases on a pro bono basis and continues to represent numerous indigent defendants and causes. We were interested in interviewing Dershowitz because his work and writings have been so important to the history of his profession. We also thought that he'd have some interesting thoughts on how technology might impact the law, since technology has been so important to the evolution of his specialty, criminal defense law.*

I think abortion stands for what will be the great conflict over the next ten years. We're literally going to see the greatest religious war—a war between religion and secularism—that we've seen in the world in several centuries. I think we're about to confront a situation that's perhaps akin to the conflict between the Inquisitions and the Age of Reason.

Two trends are moving quickly in opposite directions. On the one hand, we're becoming a country immersed in science, progress, rationality, the computer age, the information age, an age of reason and rationality, and all those wonderful, horrible things. At the same time, we're moving headlong into an age of unreasoning, know-nothing fundamentalism—an age in which we don't want to know, we don't want to think. God told us this, the bible says this, or the bible says that—the conflict is just going to be rampant.

I think that when Bernard Lewis talked about a clash of civilizations, he had it only partly right. He thought only in ethnic terms, of a clash of civilizations between Islam and the West. I don't see it that way. I see it as a clash between reason and fundamentalism. And it's not only religious. I think we see the hard left and the hard right are becoming fundamentalists—secular fundamentalists.

If the fundamentalists win, we're going to see two civilizations in the United States: groups of students uneducated in the ways of science, thinking that science is the devil, thinking that technology is the devil, and other students who are super-educated and super-bright. I already see it among my law students. I only see a little bit, because my fundamentalist students are smart enough to know that to succeed in life, they can be fundamentalists at home, but they have to be rationalists in the workplace. But they are now trying to win over the workplace, and for the first time in modern American history, religion is becoming militant, almost militaristic. We're right. You're wrong. Don't try to secularize our country. We have the right to run and determine everything, they say. And they're overplaying their hand, and so the secularists are perhaps overplaying their hand. There seems to be no middle ground.

It's like the abortion debate today—both sides are totally convinced they're morally superior to the other side. It's not like segregation. Everybody knew in the end that keeping blacks separate was wrong, but they thought maybe they could get away with it. That's not true in the abortion debate. I sat next to someone on an airplane a couple of years ago—worst trip of my life, New York to California. The person purposely sat next to me to try to convince me that, as a civil rights lawyer, I had to change my life and devote it to protecting fetuses. He focused on the fact that six million of my fellow religionists had been killed in the Holocaust, and now six million fetuses are dying; if I had only been there at the Holocaust, maybe I could have prevented it, but now I can prevent this Holocaust. I couldn't throw the person out because he was so sincere. He thought converting me was his chance at salvation. I was his ticket to heaven.

I think that eventually both extremes of the abortion debate will be eliminated by science, and early abortion, like the morning-after pill, will not be deemed abortion by most Americans. On the other side, we'll be able to move up the period when a fetus can be removed from a woman and be viable, and I think on that side the right-to-lifers will win. I think the debate is mostly over. If you can remove the child in the seventh month without damage to the child, the woman doesn't have the right to have a dead fetus; the woman just has the right to have no fetus in her body. So I think we're going to see the debate over abortion narrowed, but the larger debate—over reason versus fundamentalism—will persist, and perhaps even broaden.

◀ **Terrorism and Torture** ▶

This is a similar debate. How do you deal with fundamentalists who think it's okay to kill civilians because, as Justice Scalia put it in something he wrote recently, "To a believing Christian, death is no big deal"? To a believing Christian, death is no big deal, and to a believing Muslim, death is no big deal. How do you persuade a terrorist not to kill children when he believes he'll get seventy-two virgins in heaven? I've often thought that if we can persuade them the text is wrong, and all they get is one seventy-two-year-old virgin, maybe it could have some impact. But we're not going to persuade them by rational, calculated thinking. It's just not going to happen.

I've written a little book on terrorism and torture called *Preemption*. It's all about the new techniques being used to get at crime and terrorism preventively rather than waiting until it happens, and all the major scientific innovations that are coming into play. What happens in the movie *Minority Report* really mirrors the wave of the future in real life, for better or worse. I don't support it, I just report it. And I think we need to analyze it.

◀ Death Penalty ▶

We'll only see a change in the death penalty if its opponents can demonstrate there is a significant possibility that innocent people have been and may be executed. I don't think we're going to see a change in America. It's part of the religious conflict. Basically, religious people favor the death penalty, and many secular people do not. As we've seen, there are so many manifestations of this religious-secular conflict, and the death penalty is one of them.

I predict that the religious right is going to overplay its hand, and the pendulum is going to swing. Is that a good thing? You know I always like to think that the great virtue of America is that it has a system of checks and balances. It's not only a civic system of checks and balances—legislative, executive, and judiciary—but even more important, that religion checks science, science checks religion, the media checks this, and business checks that. There are a hundred checks and balances that operate in our lives on a daily basis, and it would be too bad if religion fell into disrepute the way it has in Europe. In post-Christian Europe today, religion plays almost no positive role in the lives of people, because it overplayed its hand, and now the faster-growing religion in Europe is Islam. Christians don't go to church. Jews don't go to synagogue. But Muslims go to mosques.

◀ Absolute or Relative Morality ▶

I think we're having a conflict and a crash. Do we live in a world of absolute morality, or do we live in a world of relative morality? Law students have to grope with that issue. For those who believe there are ten rules that can be printed, or that human beings come with an instruction manual, life really is relatively easy. Just follow the rules. But for those of us who believe you have to make it up as you go along—that life is changing rules based on changing experience—it's much, much harder, and students really have to come to grips with that issue. And it's very hard for them. They're used to coming from churches or synagogues where they're told: These are the rules; these are the absolutes. Here's the place to look it up. And then suddenly they find themselves living in a very murky world where ethical considerations push in different directions. You have to zealously defend your client, whether he is guilty or not, and that means you're helping to free guilty people in the world. Students have a very hard time with that, and you have to come to grips with that issue. I think that's the hardest one.

◀ CSI: Criminal Defense Law ▶

In the future, criminal defense law is going to be based much more on science. Every criminal lawyer has to know science. DNA is going to be crucial. Lie detection is going to become much more developed, and so in the end, information retrieval and investigation are going to become much, much more important. So lawyers are not going to be able to rely anymore on their advocacy skills. No longer will there be Clarence Darrows who dazzle in the courtroom. Students will win cases on their computers and in the laboratories.

◀ Intellectual Property ▶

Our idea of intellectual property will change, and the greatest threats are going to come from misuses of intellectual property. Imagine what's going to happen when the first real attack on the Internet occurs, and all the bank records in the world are erased, or all the stock transactions in the world are destroyed. Both the benefits and the risks that exist in the world are going to be magnified by information. There are no boundaries anymore. It used to be that physical viruses crossed boundaries, but now intellectual viruses cross boundaries, and the old geographic lines are much more tenuous today than they were years ago.

◀ Assisted Suicide ▶

The conflict over assisted suicide is part of the religious-secular struggle. It doesn't matter so much how laws change in the assisted suicide area, except for a few poor people like Dr. Kevorkian, because states will not be able to control people's end-of-life decisions. You don't need a doctor to help you end your life. You don't need the state to help you end your life. So ultimately, the policies that individuals and families have will govern.

◀ Israel-Palestine Conflict ▶

I think the conflict between Israel and Palestine will be resolved. Ultimately both the Israelis and Palestinians tend to be somewhat more secular in their outlook than much of the rest of the Arab world, and I think it's easier to resolve secular conflicts than it is to resolve religious conflicts. In Israel, for example, as we speak, there is a movement toward the center, and I think we're going to see that happen as well in the Palestinian world. At least I hope so.

TAMARA DRAUT *has written extensively about major economic issues facing Americans. In her role as director of the Economic Opportunity Program at Demos, a public policy center based in New York City, she oversees research, policy, and advocacy on economic security issues. Draut's groundbreaking research on debt has been covered extensively by dozens of newspapers, including the* New York Times, Washington Post, Chicago Tribune, Wall Street Journal *and* USA Today, *and she has appeared on* Today, ABC World News Tonight, Lou Dobbs Tonight *on* CNN, *and* Fox News. *We were interested in Draut's thoughts about the future of personal finances and debt because her book* Strapped: Why America's 20- and 30-Somethings Can't Get Ahead *is a true and harrowing look at how a new generation of Americans has seen its living standards decline and its indebtedness rise. At a time when the culture of consumerism seems more rampant than ever, we wondered what Draut saw happening in the future, and what prescriptions she has for those who want to buck the trend.*

If the last ten years are any indication, it is likely that credit card debt will increasingly be seen as a necessary evil in the future. Over the last decade, people have been turning to credit cards to deal with the fundamental economic reality that incomes aren't keeping pace with costs. It's doubtful that a decade from now this reality will have shifted, unless major new reforms are implemented. People will continue to use credit cards as a plastic safety net.

Our society tends to dismiss credit card use as a symptom of frivolous consumption. But some complicated underlying factors have led to a different type of credit card use, what you might call survival debt. Survival debt is using credit cards to deal with car repairs, job loss, or even a medical expense. The younger generations are dealing with an increasingly difficult economic climate, one that is requiring more debt of all types—student loans, higher housing debt, and yes, credit card debt. Credit card debt is here to stay unless we deal with the increased risk and volatility families face in the new economy, and unless we get serious about regulating the lending industry.

I think we have to have some commonsense re-regulation to crack down on the most abusive and capricious practices of the credit card industry. Right now, the credit card industry has all the power, and the borrower has none. The credit card industry has the right to change the terms of a customer's account at any time for any reason. Some practices that need to be examined include limiting penalty rates and fees; prohibiting interest rate hikes from being applied to existing balances rather than only on new purchases, and requiring some reasonable grace period for late payments so that responsible debtors are not unduly penalized by these current 1:00 or 2:00 p.m. cutoff times.

◀ The Reform of Student Loan Debt ▶

Student loan debt is one area where we are going to see some major reform in the next decade. I think we are very close to a tipping point in terms of the amount of student loan debt the public is willing to accept to obtain a college degree. I'm hopeful that a couple of things are going to happen. First, we're going to see major new innovations in our nation's high school curriculum. There are some interesting pilot programs now, especially around what are called early-college high schools. These schools basically provide students with two years of college between grades nine and twelve. Students leave high school with an associate's degree, which gives them a leg up if they enter the labor market right away or if they continue on to a four-year college to pursue a bachelor's degree. The Gates Foundation is supporting a lot of these model programs all over the country.

A four-year degree has become the minimum ticket required to get into the middle class. This isn't because college grads are earning so much more than they used to; it's because high school graduates are earning much less in today's service-sector economy. So we also have to solve the wage problem by creating more good jobs. It's very likely in the next ten years that we'll have dedicated ourselves to finding ways to combat global warming and, as a result, will see job growth in areas related to the quest for alternative energy sources. In addition to new jobs being created in the energy sector, it's likely we'll also witness an increase in our investment in education at all levels in order to remain globally competitive. College graduation rates have not increased nearly as dramatically as college enrollment rolls—less than one-third of young people have a bachelor's degree. And the United States has lost its lead internationally in terms of advanced education among its citizens. Among older adults—those between the ages of fifty-five and sixty-four—the United States has the highest percentage of people with some college among all countries ranked by the Organisation for Economic Co-Operation and Development. But among young adults ages twenty-five through thirty-four, the United States now ranks only eighth in the world.

Over the next ten years, college will continue to be paramount for getting into the middle class. With the cost of public universities continuing to increase, and federal financial aid growing more and more anemic, I think we'll see a major push to revitalize our financial aid system—ending what I call the debt-for-diploma system that leaves the average college grad today with about $20,000 in student loan debt and keeps too many bright, lower-income students from completing their studies.

When you look at the projections of college-ready kids who aren't going to college for financial reasons, the numbers are just too large—from an economic development standpoint, from a competitive standpoint—and we have to do better. That means lowering the price of college and providing more grant aid.

There is a cliché that knowledge is power, and it is true. If you look at who votes, it's people with college educations. So improving the quality of education in this country—including boosting the percentage of first-generation students who earn college degrees—will also create more pressure for investing in the common good. If you look at the Millennial Generation that is just now aging into adulthood, already they have a more positive view of government. They tend to value collective action over individual gain and individual attention, and I think they're going to take that and harness it into a movement for political reform.

The best personal financial advice I can give young adults is to get active politically and start taking charge of our destiny.

◀ Valuing Family As Family Values ▶

Despite the many stereotypes and myths, the new generation has really embraced family. Gen-Xers—who are now in their late twenties and thirties—are much more family-centered than their Baby Boomer parents were, and I think the Millennials are going to continue that trend. Hopefully as this generation reaches adulthood, they'll continue to push the boundaries in terms of making the United States catch up with the rest of the industrialized world and offer things like paid family leave and subsidized child care.

Culturally, we're going to move to greater parity in terms of men taking more leave and increasing their role as caregivers. Already among Generation X families, we see that men are providing much more nurturing care for their kids. They are adamant about not repeating the model of fatherhood they grew up in. That is only going to continue, and young people are going to take the family values mantra from the old traditional conservative model and really reinvent it and put some muscle behind this rhetoric of valuing family.

◄ Extreme Commuting, Exurbs, and the Middle Class ►

We're going to continue to see the growth of exurbs, and extreme commuting is going to become more common. People will be spending even more time in their cars, which is going to again create more pressures for better social policy in terms of child care and things like that. We might see a glimmer of hope as the first Baby Boomers begin to retire and downsize their housing. We could have an excess housing supply as the Boomers retire.

Hopefully the cost of housing would decline if there's more supply than demand, particularly in areas along the coasts. In ten years, the Millennials will be aging into the prime home-buying demographic. So I think for a short period of time, we may have an excess supply of housing stock.

The other major trend being driven by housing costs on the coast is that the center of gravity, in terms of economic development and political power, is shifting from the Northeast to the new Sunbelt. There has been massive migration into states like Colorado, Texas, Arizona, Georgia, and Nevada. African-Americans are now moving South from the North. All of this is happening largely in search of a lower cost of living and better quality of life. These new migration patterns are going to have huge ramifications and could ultimately disrupt this red state-blue state dichotomy that we have now.

I hope we'll be seeing the growth of the middle class, one that begins to look more and more like the changing face of America. I fear that we will fail to shore up our investments in the public structures we need in order to improve the American standard of living.

And as a result of that failure, that there will be more cleavages along race and class lines than exist today.

Another trend that is just now playing out—its implications will be clearer in ten years—is the enormous growth of the middle class in India and China. As this continues, we could begin to see more benefits of globalization in terms of fewer places for countries with high living standards to outsource for cheaper labor. As living standards rise dramatically in both India and China, I hope they will fuel a ripple effect across the world. This, in turn, could ultimately show globalization as a positive rather than something that has hurt the American worker.

Mitch Earleywine, PhD
➤ on Drug Legalization

MITCH EARLEYWINE, PHD, *is associate professor of psychology at the State University of New York at Albany. He received his bachelor's degree from Columbia University and his doctorate from Indiana University. After years as an alcohol researcher, Earleywine began teaching an undergraduate course on drugs and human behavior. He was excited to share the dangers of binge drinking with college students, but the students were far more interested in marijuana. Eager to avoid spreading misinformation, Earleywine reviewed the relevant research, which led to his book* Understanding Marijuana *and his belief that he could not stand idly by while people went to jail for possession. The research showed that millions of people used marijuana responsibly, and law enforcement officials could use their time more wisely by battling violent crime. By changing their marijuana policies, more and more states and countries could be saving enormous amounts of money. But more important than estimates of costs and benefits, the idea of punishing people for possession just seemed morally wrong to him. We were interested in Earleywine because his research-driven perspective on marijuana makes a lot of sense to us, and his equally passionate worries about the devastating impact of drugs such as meth seem legitimate and important. Our society will continue to battle addiction, but we think it's important to seriously consider which legislation is based on fear and which on fact.*

I t sounds extreme, but a taxed, legal, regulated market in all illicit drugs would be my idea of a chance to really treat this the way it ought to be treated: fairly.

Doug Husak, a philosopher and attorney, has walked through this idea of desert theory, in which each crime should have a punishment that's related to its severity—the severity of the harm it causes other people. It's the same thing with drug possession. What harm does drug possession cause other people? Prohibitionists often say that possession leads to intoxicated driving or aggression or other evils, but those things are already illegal. Folks who are hardcore drug warriors support this horrible underground market, often without knowing it. The underground market has no formal regulations—no way to control purity or add age limits or provide useful information for using drugs safely. If you had a legal market, and people had to come in and buy things of known purity and composition, certainly the negative impacts could decrease. A legal market could also provide materials that listed symptoms of abuse and told you what to do if you had these symptoms. It would then be possible to connect drug abusers to folks who are available to help them if they wanted it.

What's going to happen is, in the next five years or so, things are going to get markedly worse—even for things like medical marijuana. There will be absurdly rough penalties for possession of all illicit drugs, penalties that will put bright young men and women in jail and steal their financial aid for education and destroy their opportunities for employment. Then I imagine the pendulum will start swinging back in the other direction and we'll start talking more about decriminalization. But it will just be drawing the line at marijuana, whether it is criminalized or not. It's a shame, because we've been messing around with this since the late 1930s. I'm afraid that the people who remember it being legal are too old to care about it. It's not like alcohol, where the fiscal backlash is something that people are aware of. But the cash lost because cannabis remains in the underground market is huge. And the drawbacks of a taxed and regulated market in cannabis are markedly smaller than the negative consequences of an underground market.

When I explain all this to undergraduates, they not only understand—they're willing to put time into getting this thing changed. But the guys who I was in high school with are having kids now, and they're freaking out just like our parents did. I'm a little disappointed in some of them; it's a stereotypically paternalistic thing. I'm working on a book now about why marijuana is not for teens. I'm quite impressed with the data that show that early, heavy use of marijuana is not a good thing for teens, but that doesn't mean we should throw them in jail for it. That punishment doesn't follow at all to me logically. Again, the punishment is out of line with the severity of the harm that possession causes other people. I think it would be splendid to have an age at which you could buy marijuana the way there is a legal age for alcohol. You could go to a state-run store and get a couple of ounces a year. It would be kind of a pain in the ass to regulate, but it could keep things under control—it would eliminate some of the forbidden fruit aspect too. It would take some of the thrill of it away. We'd find that teens would view marijuana as less exotic. It certainly has fewer negative consequences than alcohol or tobacco.

I could do my rant on socialized medicine, but in truth I don't think things are going to get much different in terms of medical care and access to ongoing drug rehabilitation. It's sad, but if you aren't rich, access to good treatment for drug problems is severely limited. Another thing that is getting really dichotomized is that there are a couple of companies that are really good about health care, and then quite a few that almost literally say, "You're on your own. Here's your million-dollar deductible." A lot of health care companies toss folks toward twelve-step programs, which certainly can be successful, but people who don't take to them right away are essentially back on the same streets where they first got drugs. I'm afraid it's going to get worse before it gets better. Things are going to get really, really polarized before people finally say they feel "it's not worthwhile to work." Then we'll see. Is there going to be a revolution? Will there be some sit-ins? What's going to happen from there? In my dark moments, I'm afraid. But I see good work out there. My friend Stanton Peele has books explaining how folks can get better without going the twelve-step route. Patt Demming has some great work that can be really helpful. It gives me hope.

Data suggests that from the first use of meth to becoming addicted is even shorter than for crack. The thing that makes it different, too, is its availability. It's made from things that people have lying around. It also seems that almost all the places that used to be known for lush, outdoor marijuana grows have become methamphetamine capitals. If pot were legal, would they be doing that instead? But meth is concentrated, a rapid high, relatively easy to make, something that you're not particularly likely to get busted for compared to having a bunch of plants in your basement and going through all these carbon filters to make sure that the smell doesn't get out. In some sense, the drug war against marijuana has pushed people toward these other drugs that can be made in ways that are less easy to detect. The need to keep your drugs hidden has forced folks to choose the smallest, most potent drugs. Of course, these are the most dangerous ones.

The drug czar would have a cow if he heard me say that, but I don't think he knows many drug users or how people think about this. There is this real commitment among drug users to having an open state of consciousness that's not the result of prayer or purchasing things. When people can choose safe ways to alter consciousness, they will undoubtedly turn to healthier ones.

◀ Drug Education ▶

There is a subset of programs that has been approved by a couple of different organizations. You look at the ones that actually work, and they are much more focused on teens. Chuck Riese has one in the San Francisco area. Instead of saying, "Okay, now we're going to learn how to say no," and telling them these completely bogus tales about how peer pressure leads to drug use, he says, "Well, what happens when you get high?" He brings out the things that matter to them—teens say, "The next day I cough a lot, and I can't play soccer the way I want to," and then the things that really matter to them come up. They don't care about getting cancer in fifty years or increasing their risk for schizophrenia from five in a thousand to seven in a thousand. The problem is that it doesn't feed into the "drugs are evil and any use is abuse" mantra of DARE (Drug Abuse Resistance Education), and so anyone who supports it draws fire for not saying, "Just say no."

DARE has been criticized. The longitudinal data suggest it does next to nothing. They've revamped it. But look at their revamp, and it's the same stuff with different expressions now. Instead of "just say no," they say, "use your good refusal skills," and then students come to me so naive by the time I get them in college that they say things that are just insane. For example: "My friends and I have huffed glue, because we heard that marijuana use leads to heroin." Inhalants are markedly worse than marijuana could ever be. It makes me nauseated.

If people would just spend an hour a week working for peanuts or helping disadvantaged folks—that's part of the issue. And there are these horrible economic things, and misinformation about sex and drugs is being distributed. It's a giant house of cards. If we had real sex education and real drug education in school and schools were worth attending, suddenly a whole lot of this stuff would come apart. If students had small classes with information that they found relevant and exciting, they'd have habits that could buffer them against drug problems. They'd want to read and write and think and learn. They might still experiment with drugs, but they'd be less likely to develop problems. People with lots of interests don't want to be high all the time. They certainly don't want to develop drug problems. Nobody wants to end up a crack whore.

My worst fear is that when people go to work in the future, every day everyone will have to pee in a cup right at the beginning of work. Some of the private high schools have made this mandatory—every student pees in a cup. It is such a strange message about trust and love. What are teens supposed to think under these circumstances?

The way that technology could help us more is to allay some people's fears. Everybody's caught up in drug screening—give me your blood, give me your urine, give me your hair. But what we're really afraid of is incompetent performance. If you're an air traffic controller and you have to pee in a bottle, you start wondering, well, Is Benadryl or Vicodin something they could detect? Can I go to work hungover or exhausted or woozy from cold medicine? A couple of companies are trying the roadside-sobriety-test approach rather than making people pee in a cup. We have pretty good behavioral measures, like making people stand on one foot or stack blocks or do reaction-time tests. These can detect impairment that may arise for any reason. Then people can go home if they're too tired or sick or just can't work. And these tests won't require that someone competent be sent home just for smoking pot the week before.

I'm afraid this predicament is going to get worse before it gets better because of this crazy idea that the new pot is so much stronger and all kinds of such nutty stuff. A number of scientists who have shown that drugs can be used safely always publish in certain journals. They often say, "I can't publish in any of the mainstream journals that people smoke pot without having any harmful effects." And I've experienced that myself. The reviewers nitpick the hell out of you if you say marijuana is harmless, but if you say meth is bad, they overlook some of the same logical considerations.

◀ **Socially Approved Drugs** ▶

I talked to one of my undergrads, who now works for a prominent drug company, and he said that particularly with Ritalin and the stuff they use for kids, there's a kind of brand loyalty. They never come out and say brand loyalty; they say chemicals are for helping you reach optimum performance—but only the ones we give you. That's really the message. Twelve-year-olds can recognize the Pfizer logo now. It's spooky.

◄ Religion and Drugs ►

I'm trying to have some impact with a book I'm writing now. My new book, *Pot Politics,* has a few chapters on religion and drugs. I got Rabbi Elliot Dorf from the University of Judaism to walk through the things in the Old Testament. There's no smoking pot in the Bible, but the issue is not about use, it's about impairment. Commentaries on the Bible, even the Bible itself, emphasize that we need to help people who have problems, not throw stones at people for possession. Chuck Thomas of the Interfaith Drug Policy Initiative walks through what Jesus said, and he thinks he can make a compelling case for more universal approaches. When I was in Mississippi, I saw a bumper sticker that said, "God said it, I believe it, that settles it." And that attitude frightens me, because it's often not what the Bible or any sacred text really says. It sounds like, "I've already made up my mind on this, I will not listen to data. I will not listen to logic. I am hoping that clergy in particular will take the first stab at some of that with the next generation, but we'll have to wait and see."

◄ The Joy of Reform ►

I'd love people to leave with the idea that if you're willing to work toward something you believe in, it feels good. It doesn't have to be drug reform. When I was just filling psychological journals with legal and academic crap, I was really getting bored. Now when I wake up in the morning, I think, Okay, I'm going to go help fight the drug war, and suddenly I'm revitalized. It really does feel as good as all those cornball self-help gurus said it would. I'm blown away in my own life at how big the contrast is. You can make widgets, or you can make the world a better place.

Joni Evans ➤ **on Book Publishing**

Joni Evans *was until recently the senior vice president in the book department at the William Morris Agency. There she represented such authors as Robert Sam Anson, James Patterson, Fannie Flagg, Marcus Buckingham, John Stossel, Ann Coulter, Martin Garbus, Quincy Jones, Dick Morris, and Peggy Noonan. She also served as a publisher at Simon and Schuster and spent many years at Random House, where she was executive vice president of the adult trade division. We were interested in Evans's thoughts about the publishing industry because, as someone who has been both publisher and agent, she has a unique perspective on both creative and business aspects of the book world. With Internet and other media rapidly infringing on the book market, we were curious if Joni had any insight into where the publishing industry is going, and where it should go.*

The publishing industry is bound to change just as the music industry and the television industry have. New technology is transforming our ways of accessing content. In the future, I'd love to see books available in every format—print, digital, online, print on demand, CDs, wireless audio, and so on. Books, the ultimate software, should be available on all platforms. Once digital publishing becomes common, I believe that all the publishing industry and all writers will have an explosion in sales.

◀ **Writers** ▶

The kind of writers that will appeal to audiences in the future will be (drum roll, please) the good ones, as has always been the case.

You can never predict if we'll see the most creative work in fiction or nonfiction. That's what's so great about our business—in fiction, good storytellers, and in nonfiction, informed good storytellers! Just as we couldn't have predicted chick lit a decade ago, it's hard to tell what's coming. But certainly the boom in all new genres—of Christian publishing, the rise of sales among Latino and African American writers, the explosion of young-adult stories—each has invaded the very rigid *New York Times* best-seller profile of old.

◀ The Future for Publishers ▶

The best way for publishers to remain lucrative and grow profits in the future is by getting rid of old systems and old attitudes. Publishers need to stop behaving like venture capitalists (running away the first week the book doesn't sell) and really stick with the books and authors over the long haul. Get rid of the returns system in bookstores (it's like airlines that still use paper tickets). Join hands with search engines to get the books known and accessible. Instead of suing the Googles, work out fair royalty structures, not unlike what music publishers did, so that everyone benefits. And what about market research? Why not test-market a jacket or a title now that the Internet makes it so easy to do so?

Publishers need to stop being so risk-averse and embrace the new technology (And let's always think of the Internet as an *also,* not an *instead of.*)

◀ Technology and Lists ▶

Surely there will be a Google book club in the future, and many more clubs/communities through Internet ratings, online book groups, conversations with the authors and their readers, and who knows what else. Bookscan is already a far more accurate measure of sales than the *New York Times* best-seller list.

What impact will the best-seller lists have? Less of one, I think. The "long tail," as Chris Anderson describes, is stretching longer— the ability to find special-interest books that are not best-sellers. All genres of books are going to become more important than just the best-seller-list books—just as DVD sales and cable television have eclipsed the major networks and changed box office sales and television ratings. When people no longer need to rely on the bookstore for their catalog, when books are available through the Internet, and backlists can be easily accessed, a greater amount of books and a greater variety of books will be available with fewer "gates." Hooray for HarperCollins for putting their book content onto the iPhone. The first giant leap for readers!

In 2006, DEBORAH FINE was named president of NBC Universal's iVillage Properties. In this position, she leads iVillage.com, the world's first and largest online community destination, which, along with Gardenweb.com, Astrology.com, and gURL.com, connects more than twenty-seven million people around the globe each month. Previously, Fine was the chief executive officer of Victoria's Secret PINK. Under her leadership, PINK became a diverse lifestyle brand, setting the stage for the development of new beauty and accessory categories and a multichannel web strategy. Fine was also the founder and president of Avon Future and Mark Cosmetics, where she redefined Avon for a new generation of buyers and sellers. Prior to joining Avon, Fine held executive positions with Condé Nast Publications, including serving as vice president and publisher of Glamour *and publisher of* Brides. *Fine created and executed theweddingchannel.com and Federated Department Store relationship as* Bride's *first online initiative. She redefined the Avon sales model for a new online demographic by defining the Mark brand, its product development, and sales recruitment. She has also held management positions with* Vanity Fair, *the New York Times Company, and News Corporation. We wanted to talk to Deborah because we thought she would have a great sense of women, community, and the future of the Internet.*

Long before I became the president of iVillage, I subscribed to the saying "it takes a village" in both my personal and professional lives. Long-term relationships, from colleagues to consultants, friends to administrative assistants, agencies to—yes—even nannies, comprised the construct of my daily and offline community.

Enter iVillage.com. When iVillage began more than a decade ago, it became clear that perhaps even more important than the content was women's need to communicate with one another. That basic need for a deep connection has held true and helped create what iVillage is today.

The reality of having millions of women in the palm of your hand on a daily basis is both daunting and exhilarating—daunting because of the inherent responsibility of providing those women with the most relevant and credible information daily, and exhilarating because it lets you see the intense power of community.

◀ **The Future of Community** ▶

Today our lives are more fractured than ever. Family members live thousands of miles away from one another, employees telecommute from home, and our global economy demands that we either live in or travel to cities around the world. As human beings, we crave and search out a connection, and technology has made it possible for us to reach out over great distances and form those deep connections, on our own terms and on our own schedules.

Remember back in the '90s, when cell phones were used first by millionaire stockbrokers, then "only for emergencies"? Then, when the advances in technology made using a cell phone cheaper and easier, eventually surpassing the land-line experience by adding fun functionality, like cameras and texting, we became trained to pick up the cell as a first choice for communication.

That's what I see for the future of community. Where once a first-time mom-to-be would go online only for answers to questions, she is now looking to the online community as a first stop for finding that peer group to share the similar experiences of pregnancy and childbirth.

That same young mother-to-be, who may be the first of her friends to be pregnant, has no one in her circle to help her understand what's happening to her body (What's that strange pain? Can I have sex in the ninth month?). Online, she can get support from her peers in a nonintrusive way, rather than from her traditional group of friends, with whom she may not be comfortable discussing certain issues face-to-face.

As another example, consider our Trying to Conceive, or TTC, message boards on iVillage.com. The women there are 110 percent engaged in their topics, spending significant time each day there and checking in throughout the day for updates and news from other message board members. As our tools advance, this level of connection will grow even deeper. Back to the cell-phone example—as technological advances increase ease of use and shift consumer behavior, we experience a richer connection.

Of course the Internet won't replace face-to-face relationships, but it will be among the first sources of support and one of the most effective ways to create community on your own terms. This is perhaps the greatest irony: the tools that fuel communication will continue to be the tools that enable anonymity until the user is fully ready to share her story. In the future, her online community will become one of her most trusted and most valuable sources. In ten years she'll have grown up using the Internet for information, for friendship, for knowledge, for advice. Her online community will truly be just an extension of her being. Her community online may be more important in some ways than her community offline.

Indeed, our ideas of communities will change. You'll no longer have to see someone or touch someone to feel that she's part of your community. In the future, through a group like iVillage and other networks like ours, people will be connected through interests and passions, not neighborhoods. We will see a real shift in so many things. We won't have to depend on geography, or time zones, or even the loyal media to unify us. Instead, we will be more self-sufficient, finding connections to one another through our own interests and concerns. As a result, the advertising we see will become even more targeted, the content we see will become even more targeted, and even the colors and layouts we see will become more personalized.

The explosion of blogs is another excellent example of the strength of online community. Years ago, blogs were self-indulgent creations that, more often than not, cataloged daily minutiae for niche consumer segments. Now, with the proliferation of this medium, vibrant, thriving communities pledge their allegiance daily to one or another blog. Blogs are a home base for many, the first source of news for some. They are this generation's "fireside chat," with an immediacy that other media cannot share. Blogs are increasingly addictive. Some are now as well read, if not more so, than the most venerable of newspapers. In the future, blogs will be the way we tell stories and the way we communicate. I expect to see more people starting blogs as a way to track their lives, the way we use photo albums now. Your blog will be your visual record of your life for your friends and family.

Perhaps the most enlightening example of the power of community was my own realization that as the mother of a child with type I juvenile diabetes, online communities could expose me to infinite realms of information, relationships, resources for fund-raising, and hope. The power of community could enable me to share the trials, fears, and learning experiences, about everything from the latest schoolyard issues to the newest technology and clinical trials and connect with millions of other women who were dealing with the same or similar struggles.

That community enabled my personal "village" to create the largest juvenile diabetes fund-raising walk in my state, three years running. That community enabled friends and family to contribute and post their sentiments about giving. And as recently as last week, that community was able to offer us insight into the up-to-the-minute technology on a state-of-the-art insulin pump for our son that is, fittingly, wireless.

This is the future . . . taking community from the Web's community to a walk for diabetes that raises money to technology that advances a little boy's health. What I see in the future is that people and especially women will expect *more* from their community . . . both online and off. They will want their communities to offer up great information, strong relationships, authenticity about who they are, and they'll also want to give back to the community. The woman of the future wants to be connected but will be demanding of those to whom she is connected. She'll give a lot, but expect that she'll get an equal amount from her community in return.

Mike Fleiss ➤ on Reality Television

The founder of Next Entertainment, MIKE FLEISS *has produced more than 250 hours of prime-time television, including such reality television staples as* The Bachelor *and* The Bachelorette, Trista and Ryan's Wedding, Superstar USA, High School Reunion, Who Wants to Marry a Multi-Millionaire?, *and* Are You Hot? *He has produced several feature films, including the 2003 remake of* The Texas Chainsaw Massacre, Poseidon, *and* Hostel. *With the business model for television changing rapidly, especially regarding reality television, we were curious to hear Fleiss's insights.*

T**he fact is** that the assault of nonstop reality television on viewers is probably over, certainly in the network prime-time business. They oversaturated prime time, and I think that they can't ever go back to reality TV that hard ever again. You have to wait for special, interesting, original shows to come around as opposed to copycatting the hell out of something that's worked.

Reality-show competitions may have peaked, but television is so cyclical that it will come back, just as with *Deal or No Deal*. Before that, you couldn't have sold a game show, but now everyone is out there pitching game shows. It's such a pack mentality, and it will always be that way.

◄ Network Economics ►

The whole network business is somewhat tenuous. It's not what my kids are interested in, really. My son is sixteen and my daughter is thirteen, and they watch virtually no network prime-time television. My daughter will watch *American Idol,* but other than that, they will watch *South Park* and *High School Musical,* and they're on the Internet and playing their video games. It just doesn't seem that the network model as it has been for the past forty to fifty years is going to be able to exist, and I think certainly with reality TV, cable will be its primary outlet. Then every once in awhile, there will be a special show that breaks through into a prime time network. But what's interesting is that the success of a show is so dependent on promotion, and it's the same in the studio movie business. If the studio spends a hundred million or more on a movie, that movie is going to open at number one no matter what it is. It's virtually the same in television, but what's different is that you'll see a network pick up a show that's been big overseas. Whether it's *Deal or No Deal, American Idol,* or *Dancing with the Stars,* they'll wait to see how it performs overseas before they commit to a large promotional budget, and that's something you don't do in other parts of the business.

I've always created my own shows. I've never optioned a format or anything like that, so it won't really change things for me. But in terms of the outlook for the viewer, it's not good. We're waiting for other countries to take bold, creative steps, and then we're following when we're good and ready. And that ain't the American way, you know. Following Dutch formats or French formats, like *Survivor,* or a British format, like *American Idol*—to me that's not very interesting.

◀ The End of Controversial Television ▶

Obviously the loss of television viewers to other forms of entertainment is real and substantial and is going to continue. There's really nothing the networks can do to stem the tide except to make highly explosive, controversial content, which is fighting against the new right wing–dominated mentality. So back when I did shows like *Who Wants to Marry a Multi-Millionaire?* or *Are You Hot?* or *Breaking the Magician's Code: Magic Secrets Finally Revealed,* it was controversial, and that's what allowed them to generate so much publicity and then gather the audience. But now the networks are shying away from the edgier, riskier, crazier, some would say less-responsible programming, and that's going to further hamper their process.

To look outside the reality game and look at scripted stuff, there was a time when the great ABC network that Disney owns—the all American broadcasting company—wouldn't air a show like *Desperate Housewives.* It would be viewed as too sexy for nine o'clock on a Sunday evening. But it feels like the networks will now lean more on sexier, stranger, darker scripted fare than they will on reality TV. I think there is some sort of presumption that if it's really happening, it's worse than if it's just fictional television.

◀ The Internet Connection ▶

I think you can integrate the Internet into television shows, but to have it big and do it in a way that viewers are accustomed to seeing it on television, we're a long way from the Internet being able to support it financially. The model is just not there yet. You can do those little webcasts, those two-minute pieces of downloadable stuff that you watch on your phone. That will all be happening, but it's not going to be produced and written by the top people; it's going to be more underground and grassrootsish, which is cool, but that will be different, and the production values will just be much lower. Of course, now there is YouTube, which I love, but a lot of it is pirated. You know, everyone gets all excited about the 500-channel universe and all the shows that you can put on the Internet, but there is only a certain amount of money to sustain all of that. In a way, the more options you have, the lower the quality.

My favorite time in reality television was when you took radical chances and really did things you were not supposed to put on television. That's when it was great, back in the early and mid-nineties with Fox. You could just experiment, and certain things popped out. I mean even my show *The Bachelor,* which people now see as a wholesome, romantic show, was very controversial at the time. I would just like to see things get back to a place where we took more chances and gave the viewers different things to watch.

Cable documentary shows don't have the same impact as when you put *Survivor* or *The Bachelor* on and millions of people watch it. They're talking about it on every radio station the next day. Everybody can sit around the television and watch it at one time, and go into work the next day and talk about it. That's what television is best at. That's the thing that brings us together. It used to happen all the time in reality television, and prior to that it used to happen all the time in scripted TV. It still kind of does with some of the monster shows like *The Sopranos,* but there was a time not that long ago when you would watch an episode of *Seinfeld,* and the next day at work everyone would be talking about it.

I know a lot of shows do well for their time period performance average, or whatever it is, but the ultimate goal is to make a show that everybody in the country knows about, and everybody is talking about the next day. That's the thrill of it, and that's why, as TV executives have gotten more conservative with their programming decisions, I've gravitated toward making R-rated movies, where you can put whatever you want on the screen. But I think things will swing back to a looser stance in terms of the moral climate within the next five to ten years for sure.

It's important to take chances. If you always play it safe, you're never going to have a big hit. It's true that *American Idol* is a very safe show, and it wasn't a big risk because it was basically just a remake of the UK's *Star Search*. But most of the really big reality shows were groundbreaking—*Survivor, The Bachelor, Big Brother*. Those were bold programming decisions, and I think that if television decision makers forget about taking the major risks, it will be a drag for everyone.

Kristina Ford ➤ on City Planning

From 1992 to 2000, **KRISTINA FORD** *was New Orleans's director of city planning; she subsequently headed the New Orleans Building Corporation, a city agency created to develop city-owned property. Ford has taught city planning at New York University and land use planning at Williams, Bowdoin, and Bard Colleges. She is chairman of the Boothbay Planning Board in Maine, and has written many articles on urban planning, as well as a book entitled* Planning Small Town America. *Her book* The Trouble with City Planning *will be published by Yale University Press in 2009. We were interested in talking to Ford because we felt that in the wake of the Katrina disaster and all that it revealed about New Orleans, it was important to take a look at both how cities are planned and how they should be.*

I can talk most directly about how city planning should change in the next ten years by recalling August 30, 2005—the day when Americans saw New Orleans awash in the ruinous water Hurricane Katrina brought the day before. We saw houses flooded to their eaves; we saw residents who'd escaped drowning by breaking through to their roofs, still waiting for rescue. Most of the city's neighborhoods were ruined, and every one of the 485,000 people who'd lived there was affected by Hurricane Katrina. None more obviously— or badly—than the poor, mostly black Americans we saw stranded and abandoned, even dead at the Convention Center, where they'd sought refuge.

All enormously horrifying to anyone watching. But when I looked at this fine old city's vast destruction, I saw how unwisely New Orleans had used its land. Banking on the ability of the levees to hold back the water that surrounds it, the city had allowed developers to build on reclaimed swamp land, allowed them to construct houses on concrete slabs at grade—all well below the level of the water held back by the levees. When the levees were breached, *all* low-lying residences were flooded, both those built on reclaimed swampland and those built on slabs.

Predictable, yet unheeded. How could this have happened?

There are many reasons, but for the sake of this small essay I'll focus on city planning—the agency with expertise to advise how a city's land should be used, but an agency kept to the side of land use decisions, its advice against unwise development largely ignored. Indeed, the most devastated portions of New Orleans were the large subdivisions built in the eighty years since the city had created a planning commission.

To explain how city planning is kept to the side, I'll describe who city planners work for, then the Byzantine method employed to make development decisions. Although city planners have their offices in city hall, they do not work for the city council—the elected officials who have final authority over land use issues. Rather, city planners work for a planning commission—a group of interested laymen, chosen by the mayor, that meets twice a month or so to consider land use matters. Cities adopt plans that express how citizens want their surroundings to change as new development occurs and then pass ordinances to ensure that land will be developed consistent with the plan. An individual who wants to build a large subdivision presents an application to the planning staff, which determines whether the proposal is consistent with the city's land use regulations. Planning staff then schedules a public hearing before the commission on the application, at which the applicant describes what's been proposed. At this hearing the planning staff offers its analysis and suggests how the commission should act on the matter: approve it, modify it, or (rarely) deny it. Citizens then comment on the proposal. After this often lengthy proceeding, the planning commission discusses all that's been heard and concludes by recommending to the city council—again, the ultimate decision-maker on land use matters—how it should vote.

Even this isn't the end. Within a few days, the planning staff forwards a report to the city council about all that's transpired; a few weeks later, the council holds its own public hearing, listens to the planning staff's report about what's been recommended by the commission, and finally votes. For the council to approve the planning commission's recommendation a simple majority is needed (in New Orleans, four of the seven council members); to overturn the commission requires a larger percentage of agreement (in New Orleans, five of the seven council members).

As I write this description, I can see how overcomplicated it would seem to anyone confronting it for the first time! But the process has more important consequences than its evident overcomplication. Because the planning staff works for a commission—laymen, whose powers are only advisory—the professionally trained planning staff becomes little more than message-carriers from the commission to the city council. In effect, the advice of professional planners is removed from the ultimate decision-makers on planning matters.

◀ Politics and City Planning ▶

Odd as it may seem, this complicated mechanism was intentional. It was devised to protect professional planning staff from political pressure, an objective that dates from the reform era of the early twentieth century when planning first became a part of city government. Reformers focused on urban political machines, believing that politics—and those who practiced it—were corrupt. As a consequence, reformers sought to protect from political influence such good government initiatives as city planning. Hence, the commission.

In addition, when planning first became a profession, the public hadn't yet learned how to use its own political powers in municipal decision-making about how land was used. In the early 1900s, neighborhood organizations were far from becoming the powerful organizations they are now, able to argue effectively about developments proposed in specific parts of a city. The early 1900s was also a time when planners experimented with land use regulation, before mea-

sures such as zoning regulations were found constitutional by the
U.S. Supreme Court. Even as they worked, enjoying a "protected"
status, city planners didn't consider their advice as having a political
component. Planners thought professional logic would be sufficient
to persuade decision-makers.

The world in which land use decisions are made has changed
greatly. Land use regulations *are* constitutional, and neighborhood
organizations *are* powerful political forces in development decisions.
However, the mechanism for protecting planners from political pressure hasn't changed. This observation is consequential to how New
Orleans will be rebuilt, and it's consequential wherever land use
decisions are made in America.

In New Orleans, the practical effect of "protecting planners" was
routinely dramatized while I was director of city planning. A developer would tell me that "he had five votes," but "as a courtesy" wanted
to show me his proposed development. "Having five votes" meant
he'd already lined up enough city council members to overturn an
unfavorable planning recommendation. Another developer would
tell me he had the mayor's support for a project. This meant the
mayor had called enough planning commissioners—his appointees,
after all—to guarantee a favorable vote. In other words, development
decisions were made politically, and the mechanism which would
"protect" planners from political pressure wasn't working.

◀ **The Future of City Planning** ▶

I think that in the next ten years, city planning should become specifically political. Planners themselves should recognize the political
nature of their work. After all, advice about any development proposal requires choosing among a range of individual and community
concerns, costs, and rights—such as those subdividing low-lying,
reclaimed swamp-land. Advice given on these choices is the definition of political activity.

The director of city planning should work for the mayor, and should assign staff to work for individual city council members. The commission should focus on what it's best at: drawing out the public's reactions to proposed development. And the public itself should take a greater political role by keeping track of its council members' land use decisions and making that record an important issue in election campaigns. This last suggestion would be important, since the agenda of city councils throughout America is like that in New Orleans: dominated by land use matters. Of course, to be a supportable idea, changes that increase citizens' political role must include *all* neighborhoods, not just those where affluent residents already make their views effectively known to elected leaders.

These are ideas that need to be carefully worked out to assure they achieve the goal of better and equitable land use decisions. Several other changes should be made to the practice of city planning, but the most important change for city planning in the next ten years is for the profession to become an explicit political actor in local government.

Harry Frankfurt, PhD ➤ **on Philosophy**

HARRY FRANKFURT has spent much of his career exploring the ways in which people think about themselves intellectually and morally, and how ideals and values shape our lives. A professor at Princeton since 1990, Frankfurt chaired the Yale philosophy department from 1978 to 1987 and lectured in the School of Law. His current work centers on everything from exploring the relevance of love, to non-moral goals, standards on issues concerning practical reason and to the distinction between being active and being passive. Frankfurt is the author of four books, including the recent best-seller On Bullshit. *We were interested in talking to Frankfurt, because at a time when religious conflicts and emerging technologies threaten to overtake the agenda, his clarity of philosophy, and in particular his work on exploring morality and the relevance of love, seem particularly important. We wondered what place he thinks philosophy should take in our lives, how we should combat bullshit, and what role he feels philosophers like himself should assume in the world.*

The role of philosophers is to seek clarity and truth. I don't think that philosophers should have in mind a social or political role or think of themselves as public intellectuals or as having the responsibility to do that, but their primary responsibility is to the truth and to clarity and to understanding. I think it's very important to stick to that, otherwise the whole enterprise becomes corrupted and infused with goals and ideas that are inimical to the pursuit of its nature.

I don't think philosophy has ever had a very large audience, at least not an audience that was really committed to following it in any rigorous sort of way. Philosophers have always worked pretty much on their own, without much public support or public participation. I don't think that philosophers should think of themselves as responsible for promoting or advancing social welfare or moral ideals. That tends to lead to the bullshit instead of to strict adherence to the requirements of clarity and of rigorous argument and evidence and so on.

You get dominated by the ambition to help make the world better (and there are lots of people who are devoted to that), but there are very few who, like philosophers, have a specific commitment to these more austere ideals. It is important that that commitment be respected and maintained and not abandoned or diluted by other commitments to other ideas that are also quite valid and important, but to which other people can devote themselves.

There is an appropriate separation here between different kinds of enterprise, and one of the things that I believe has been unfortunate about recent developments in the academic world is that many universities seem to think they have a mission to improve society and to improve the moral character of their students—to teach them to be tolerant and to teach them the value of diversity, and other good things. These are indeed good things, but universities have a different mission. There are a lot of institutions in society that have the aim of improving social conditions. There are no other institutions besides educational institutions, universities in particular, that have the mission of promoting and protecting the respect and concern for the truth and for clarity and understanding. And philosophers should stick to that.

I don't mean to say that philosophers should stay away from or refuse to participate in activities designed to have applications. For example, philosophers have some useful role to play in dealing with bioethical issues. But I'm against the claim that everything philosophers do should have a similarly directed and immediate social value.

Philosophers should play the only role they're really qualified to play in any context, which is to try to get clear about fundamental concepts and to try to examine the arguments that are being used for their rigor and adequacy. The responsibility of philosophy is as it's always been: to speak to the truth and to clarify ideas and to think rigorously. That's its main ideal, and that's the constraint that it should understand itself to be working within, and if it's possible to help improve the conditions of society in this way, then fine, but

there should be no substitution of a social goal for these more austere intellectual goals.

◀ Choosing a Way of Life ▶

One of the fundamental dogmas or assumptions or ideals of liberal
democracy is that people should be free to choose the way of life that
they prefer as long as it doesn't interfere with the choices of others,
and that's good. I'm all for that. One problem is that there is nothing
in the repertoire of liberal theory that addresses the problem of how
people are to be prepared to make those choices. We're going to turn
people loose to choose the kind of lives they like, but they ought to
be equipped in some way to make good or reasonable choices, and
to know what the alternatives are.

   This is a problem that I think the state governments must address
at some point. We don't address it very well. The only answer, of
course, is education. I don't know enough about the educational philosophy of the public school system to have a real grasp of the extent
to which it feels responsible for preparing students for the choices
they have to make in life. I don't think they do much of it—at least it
was that way when I went through public schools when I was a kid.
I'm not aware of anybody trying to prepare me for choosing between
various ways of life. How would you do that? Well, you would do that
by teaching people literature, by making them aware of the possibilities of various kinds of occupations or professions, by introducing
them to the possibilities of certain kinds of experience.

◀ The Secular Mission and the Sacred Mission ▶

All schools, and universities in particular, have two kinds of missions:
a secular mission and a sacred mission. The secular mission is to

prepare the students for their roles in society by teaching them to be good lawyers or doctors or accountants or engineers or astronomers or economists—to acquire the technical skills that are required for a productive life in an advanced society. I think universities and school systems generally do that fairly well. We do turn out pretty good lawyers and doctors and so on.

The sacred mission of the university is to imbue students with an understanding of and respect for the importance of truth and of clarity and of rigor. How do you do that? I don't think the universities do a very good job of that, for one thing. I think they've more or less assigned themselves the role of improving the moral character of their students rather than their intellectual character.

How do you improve intellectual character? I don't think you can do it by giving courses in logic or ethics. I don't think those things help at all, really. The only way you really learn to respect the truth or learn values is by example. That is, by seeing people who are important to you, who are models in some way, behaving in the ways that are pertinent. The burden is on the man or the woman at the front of the class, the teacher, who in addition to teaching students the information and skills that the students will require—the secular mission of the university—has to carry out the sacred mission by providing living examples of the ideals and values that the universities are charged with being responsible for.

◀ The Next Big Impulse in Philosophy ▶

I have a theory. I don't see any evidence that the theory is true, but I keep thinking it's true. Philosophy is in the doldrums these days. There's no powerful intellectual force moving through the field as there was in the days of Wittgenstein or Bertrand Russell, when there was a large creative impulse to which everybody was responding. That isn't happening now. We've got a very highly advanced technical repertoire, and we work on those problems, but nobody knows where they're going, and nobody is deeply inspired by them.

I think the next big creative impulse in philosophy will come from the direction of religion. It's easy to see that a lot more people in our society—and a lot more highly intellectual, highly educated people—are taking religion a lot more seriously than they used to do. You see it around the university campuses. You see kids devoted to organized Christian activities or Jewish activities; orthodoxy has become much less absurd and marginalized. I think in time some of these young people will come to professionalize their interest in religion—turn it into an academic subject and find themselves drawn to theoretical issues that arise out of their practice. Also, moral philosophy has moved in the direction of issues that have characteristically been within the domain of religious thought. People write about forgiveness, loyalty, the meaning of life, and other things that have not been part of the repertoire of moral philosophy for a long time.

For many years, religion has been taboo. It used to be that if you admitted you were seriously religious or observant, people would think there was something odd about you. No serious person in philosophy or in many other fields would take religion seriously or would admit to having a serious interest in religion. To a considerable extent, that has changed. A lot of people around the campuses openly profess and pursue their religious interest, and nobody says boo.

Moreover, there is an enormous literature of religious thought going back thousands of years—books of theology and books of religious thought written by extremely intelligent people. That archive, so to speak, has been neglected for a long, long time, because its content was very unfashionable and serious philosophers, serious students of history and other literature just wouldn't go near it. There are tens of thousands of PhD dissertations and other scholarly monographs waiting to be written about those neglected books. There's a gold mine there. Thus, it's easy for students to find interesting and productive ways of pursuing religious topics; the fuel is there to be thrown on the fire.

The only problem with my theory, as I indicated before, is that there is no evidence that it is going to be true. I don't see philosophers rushing to start talking about religion. It is difficult to see the fading but still living embers of a fire that was once blazing. If my theory is to come true, some very respectable and eminent philosopher has to take the lead to make it legitimate. Nobody will go out on a limb and say that what he really cares about is religion, unless doing so has been made respectable thanks to the initiative of somebody who commands respect, and who nobody would dismiss as foolish. Maybe that will happen, and if it happens then I think there will be a lot of people who follow him or her in that direction.

◀ **Bullshit** ▶

I would like people to be on their guard against all the bullshit, and to try to figure out, as I have been unable to do, just how we can combat it and diminish it, because I do think it is corrosive.

This can happen only if impressive models show the way. They may be teachers, or perhaps political figures. A few years ago, when John McCain was running for the Republican presidential nomination against Bush, he came across as somebody who really had a distaste for bullshit. He never avoided saying I don't know when he didn't know. He was willing to admit that he was quite ignorant of certain things about which politicians ordinarily profess to be experts. He gave the impression of really caring about talking straight, saying what he thought, and it was very exhilarating. I think lots of people in this country are starved for straight talk, starved for the truth.

I don't know why McCain didn't win, but maybe next time someone like that will win. Anyway, my point is that it needn't be a teacher. It might be a political figure. It might be some public figure of another sort who inspires the population with his clarity of thought and with his straightforwardness and with his avoidance of bullshit, and that would go a long way.

You know there was a remarkable event when Jon Stewart went

on *Crossfire*. He called them on their bullshit, and the head of the network canceled *Crossfire*. He threw them off the air. Now that's an extraordinary thing. That's a great achievement for Jon Stewart.

Of course, not all of us are as gifted as Jon Stewart, or are in the kind of position that he is in to show his gift. But it can happen.

Benjamin Goldhirsh
➤ **on Social Responsibility**

BENJAMIN GOLDHIRSH, *still in his twenties, is the founder and CEO of GOOD, a multi-platform media company that produces content at the intersection of entertainment and relevance. GOOD's efforts include print, film, online, and live events, all of which are geared toward educating and engaging today's youth. Active in both regional and international philanthropic endeavors, Goldhirsh is one of the directors of the Goldhirsh Foundation—established by his father, Inc. magazine founder Bernard Goldhirsch before his death in 2003; the foundation supports dynamic social programs, environmental initiatives, innovative medical research, and leading cultural institutions. Goldhirsh also serves on the board of Millennium Promise, an organization guided by the United Nations' Millennium Development goals to end extreme global poverty by 2025, as well as the LA board of the National Foundation for Teaching Entrepreneurship. A graduate of Brown University and Phillips Academy, Goldhirsh lives in Los Angeles.*

My hope is that pro-social behavior will be the status quo in ten years. It will be the status quo that you drive an energy-efficient vehicle, that you care about your impact and your engagement with the world, and that your interests are well aligned. I hope anything existing outside of that will be frowned upon—in the same way that you could say cigarettes have moved into that space today.

My dream would be that everyone starts to give a damn and starts living accordingly with that pro-social sensibility—and that the choices will be available so that they can live that way without sacrificing. But I think a lot of those choices are already starting to come to life, so people are increasingly being given that opportunity, and the more people take to it, the more it moves to the center and becomes the norm. I would love to see pro-social behavior and action, as a whole, extricated from any sort of political or partisan landscape, and to be respected for what it is: that which is patriotic, that which is American, that which is universal.

My biggest fear is we're starting to act too late. I think it's going to happen one way or another. Some people say they fear this is a fad; but I don't think this *can* be a fad, because the stakes are so high right now that there is no alternative but to engage. My fear is that we face huge problems that have already been set in motion, and that we won't be able to get our act together fast enough to combat them. I don't just mean domestically; I mean internationally. There are so many conflicts today that require so much energy and so many resources for a direct response that those resources can't be focused on longer-term issues. My concern is that we can't execute at the pace needed to solve those longer-term issues before we run into them.

◄ The Changing Face of Media ►

In mass media, we'll see more products that will provide micro-entertainment, or pieces of entertainment. And there will be even more ways to digest media. Right now, we've kind of repurposed media that exist from one platform into all these other platforms. But I think we'll start seeing a lot more micro-management of media in these different platforms. And that opens up a lot of shelf space and opportunities for many different people to participate in filling those holes on the shelf.

As far as individual companies go, and what they can do to run more sustainable businesses, there are the immediate and obvious matters of the carbon count and the carbon footprint and going neutral there. But I think to look at their impact only in an environmental sense is kind of skewed and false. I think there needs to be a real, holistic measurement of whether a company is operating on an ethical level. That should include environmental impacts certainly, but it should also include the way they treat their employees, the way they work within their community, the way their products impact their consumer. All these things need to be taken into account along with the bottom line, and somehow be inclusive of the bottom line.

We're moving to a place where the consumer will demand more accountability across all the different components of business, so that people can't just market the one thing they are doing well. They won't be able to say, "Look, we're neutralizing the carbon emissions from our transportation . . . but we're not going to talk about the fact that we pay crap wages and don't give any benefits." That's because the consumer is going to say, "You need to be at your best and set higher standards." I think it's a moving bar, and everyone is trying to do better and better, and the consumer is just trying to move the companies forward. Consumers are going to be the driving agent behind corporate change.

The easiest way to gauge how these changes will affect people within the industry is to look at the people who have been working in the record industry over the last decade—they've felt some serious changes over there. As the gap between the creator of content and the consumer of content closes with technological advances, there is more pressure for people to evaluate how they can add value if they exist in the middle of that space. Simple distribution mechanisms and simple representation mechanisms are challenged by the new models. If you're creating content, there is always a way to succeed, there is always a way to repurpose your content. I think there are different economic challenges, different platforms upon which your content may eventually live, demanding certain realities in terms of the financing of those pieces of content, but there is still a market for content. I think this is a harder business; it gets a lot tighter on every front, there's less fat. So if you're not adding value, you've got to worry about your job.

Of course, this is all great for the consumers, because the consumers get choice and so many more opportunities to pick the content they want and the platforms that they want it on. The consumer all of a sudden can become a producer and a creator as well. I feel there are so many more opportunities now; maybe someone doesn't actually want to be the creator; maybe they just want to comment and be part of the community that's directing the creation. They have so much more influence over what's happening and freedom across that spectrum.

From a professional perspective, we're looking for monetization opportunities and ways to acquire eyeballs given the new distribution means. So there are questions: How do you get eyeballs? And how do you make money? Do you get people to your site? Or do you put your content on other sites? Do you go directly to the consumer? Do you use aggregators? And then once you get those eyeballs, are people paying for the content? Are they getting it for free? Are the monetization opportunities coming from corporate partners? Personally, that is where I think the model leans. People are not going to be so interested in paying for content. HBO slaps that opinion in the face, but I think the model is more like YouTube with some sort of brand integration.

◀ Global Competition ▶

As we start competing in the global marketplace, to think that you're going to have the economies of scale to compete with the industry in India or wherever is laughable. If you're in the commodity business, you're going to need some other way to differentiate yourself from being just a commodity. If you're making TV screens, you've got a whole world of competition right now, so you'd better be on the forefront of technological and social innovation, because those things will be what separate you and put you ahead. You'll be able to say, Look, we make better television screens and we're better for the world, so pay the extra money. And people will pay. That's the fortunate thing, because I think there's a simultaneous interest on the part of the consumer and an interest in the market to make this happen. There's a real drive to see things move forward, and that's thrilling and necessary.

All consumers need to do is stay hungry for this movement and keep high standards. If you look at what's happened to the film industry, I feel as if we got beat up for a while, the studio system basically held us to a very low common denominator of taste. And then the consumers basically walked. They said, We're not coming out, because there are a lot of other, better entertainment opportunities available to us. And that gave birth to all the mini majors, because they saw that the independent films were actually getting traction. So they created Searchlight, Focus, and so on. Consumers have to feel that they hold the sword, and that they have to see their interests served—not just in the present, but in the long term.

This model was really born from the antiapartheid movement. I've heard that Nelson Mandela points to activism on American college campuses as one of the most critical variables in toppling apartheid. He'll say that it wasn't until the students demanded that their college institutions divest from companies that were doing business in South Africa that those companies stopped doing business in South Africa. And as soon as those companies stopped doing business in South Africa, the South African government couldn't stomach the economic impact.

While apartheid was more linear, we have broader, more amorphous issues that we need to focus on. But now we're starting to get some sense. People understand what a carbon footprint is. People understand what fair trade is. So as long as there are organizations that continue to provide consumers with information and an opportunity to engage, all of a sudden we'll have a really interesting, democratic response.

John Gottman, PhD ➤ **on Marriage**

JOHN GOTTMAN *is world renowned for his work on marital stability and divorce prediction, involving the study of emotions, physiology, and communication. Dr. Gottman is the cofounder of the Gottman Institute with his wife, Dr. Julie Schwartz Gottman. The Gottman Institute applies leading-edge research on marriage in a practical, down-to-earth therapy and trains therapists committed to helping couples. No other approach to couples' education and therapy has relied on such intensive, detailed, and long-term scientific study of why marriages succeed or fail. Dr. Gottman is executive director of the nonprofit Relationship Research Institute and an emeritus professor of psychology at the University of Washington. We were interested in Dr. Gottman's thoughts on the future of marriage because of his unique system of predicting, with astonishing accuracy, the success of marriages by evaluating the way couples interact. We wondered what widespread application of Dr. Gottman's system would mean for the way we think about marriage and relationships, and how it would impact families.*

Some state of covenant like "being married" needs to exist as the highest sacred covenant and commitment between two lovers.

I'm not suggesting that being married and being committed to each other form an equation. In fact, in my clinical practice I often find that many couples who marry are not fully committed. The problem is that they often make what might be called conditional commitments. They hold back some condition in their minds, often privately, some deal breaker that makes them feel less vulnerable.

I have often thought that the popular psychology notion of the "fear of intimacy" is wrong. I believe that a fear of intimacy is completely natural. In making a total commitment to another person, as in becoming married, we are something like Alice in Wonderland, who went down the hole after the white rabbit. Alice didn't hang on to the sides of the hole and check it out first. She fell, wholeheartedly, totally vulnerable, fully on her journey.

The only equivalent experience I can think of is when we are present at the birth of our baby. Most of us change in ways that are reminiscent of Alice. When we first see our baby born, many of us do fall like Alice—we are fully and instantly in love, committed, and totally vulnerable to the terror of potential loss.

I think some state like marriage will continue, but most sociologists and historians have commented on the fact that it has been now altered forever. It started as an economic arrangement for producing and rearing children and merging family wealth. Now it has become two people building a life together in complete respect, love, romance, passion, affection, loyalty, trust, shared purpose, and friendship. The new expectations are a tall order for one long-term relationship, especially as we are living much longer today than we ever did before.

◀ Future Dating and Partnering ▶

For first relationships, it's likely that some form of online dating and other rapid methods for meeting people will replace our standard methods. I think that's a very good idea. People need to sample a large number of potential partners before they know what they are looking for. It's my judgment that social science, unfortunately, continues to have very little to offer a matchmaker. That's my view of the research literature; not everyone agrees with me. I think the enormous problem to be solved is that there's a huge positive self-presentation bias in describing one's self to a potential partner. I am unlikely to tell a potential partner that I am grumpy in the mornings until I've eaten breakfast. Failing any systematic way of choosing a partner, people will probably continue to think with "the small brain"; that is attraction and lust will determine a lot of our choices.

Second relationships, re-partnering, and blended families in later life will probably become more intelligently legislated for the welfare of the children. I also think that relationship education and parenting training will become widespread and might even become required by law.

I predict that the divorce rate will reach an asymptote 67 percent. It's nearly there now. But I predict that we will find new ways to combat the divorce rate, if there's research funding for basic research on relationships. Unfortunately, that doesn't look very likely at this juncture. For example, there's very little funding for basic research on sex.

I'd love to see government and private funding for scientific research on relationships, and more widespread application of scientifically gathered advice. But I fear we will continue to equate bad advice with good advice and proceed unintelligently with relationships and families. Afternoon television advice seems to be gaining influence rather than losing it, and social scientists seem mostly to be very quiet about offering practical advice.

◀ Evaluating Relationships Online ▶

One of the ideas we're working on is an online evaluation of relationships. With our Love Lab methods, we can confidently evaluate relationships and make useful suggestions to couples.

I don't know how the ideas that have emerged from our programmatic research will be used. The ideas are simple, and there is a cumulative recognition of their usefulness. I hope these ideas will be stolen by everyone, and that I will be like the guy who invented Velcro. Everyone uses Velcro without thinking of where it came from.

◀ Knowing When Someone Is "The One" ▶

I knew that my wife was "the one." I moved to Seattle and started answering personal ads and started dating a lot of people, and when I met my wife she was just head and shoulders above everybody else. A lot of people don't do that, and they're confused about how to know. I get questions from people all the time when I give talks, and I just say to them, What does it feel like when you are together? Does the conversation flow easily? Do you like yourself when you are with this person? Are you really enjoying yourself? Are you natural? Are you pretending? Are you tense?

My mother used to say about relationships that "every pot has a lid." I think that there really isn't a "one" perfect person for you; there are a range of people that you could have a great relationship with, but you need to know that this person is in the right range; if you have these things going for you, you can really build something. None of these potential relationships will be the same, and all of them will have regrettable incidents to talk about. We can quantify the quality of a relationship, and even create a mathematical model for it, with just the questionnaires. Let's say we can prescribe your relationship—it's kind of like estimating the trim of a sailboat. You can say, These are the characteristics of the ship, and here's what I'm planning to do on this voyage, and that's the wrong ship for a transatlantic voyage; or you can say, Well, you need a lot more social support, and you need to reduce stress a little bit in order to have easy sailing through those waters. You can get different kinds of advice based on your circumstances—say, the cost of making certain changes in your life or anticipating the social support you'll need.

◀ Relationship Education ▶

The state of Illinois has a school program on relationships, and there are a number of people who are really building these programs. Ron Rabin is executive director of the Kirlin Foundation, a foundation in Seattle where they're actually tracking all these educational programs, not only in high schools but in elementary schools. You have to have really gifted teachers to do it.

I hope that in the future there will be widespread research-based marriage and relationship education available to the public that will have high scientific and scholarly credibility, as distinguished from that offered by self-appointed afternoon TV gurus. Relationship education will be available online, in hotel TV rooms, and video stores, as well as books. But increasingly, we will move away from the printed word. We'll learn more about sex itself in relationships and have this information widely available, without religious censorship. This information will begin to be disseminated in schools, which will increasingly focus on social-emotional learning from infancy through adulthood and later life. The emotionally intelligent school will become a reality. Other institutions that concern themselves with the emotional welfare of children and families will also change in the same ways (hospitals, Planned Parenthood, the foster care and adoption systems, the criminal justice system) to foster emotionally intelligent programming. Egalitarian relationships between men and women will become an assumed given. Men will become increasingly involved with the care and understanding of babies. Same-sex relationships will become more accepted, and we will learn from them as heterosexuals and become enriched by this understanding. Cultural diversity will also change relationships, as we benefit from understanding African-American, Asian American, Native American, and Latino relationships and culture.

We know from the work of Peggy Sanday that where there are dangerous environments, family relationships become hierarchical, and you get more of an authoritarian structure regarding the children. But that's changing everywhere in the world. Women are becoming empowered everywhere.

I think we're seeing the dying gasps of the male authoritarian system. Most cultures on the planet are changing, and one really encouraging sign of this change is that more and more men are getting involved with the care of babies. That, to me, is key—it's involved in honoring women and viewing relationships as sacred and viewing women as a source of the sacred in the culture.

◀ Learning from Different Cultures ▶

One thing I discovered when I did this national survey for the *Reader's Digest* was that the Latin American cultures—Cuban, Puerto Rican, Mexican, South American, all these cultures—are really different from African-American or Euro-American cultures in their attitude towards sex. I've interviewed a lot of Latino people, and the attitude of these cultures is *not* that men can go outside the relationship and have affairs. In fact, only the men feel as if they're not really good men and lovers unless the woman is satisfied. She tells him what she needs and what feels good, and he wants to know. That's pretty amazing, and in fact it's even more important when there is a baby. They'll work to keep romance and passion in the relationship even when the baby arrives. I think we can learn so much from these cultures, because so many men I've encountered whose relationships are ailing are saying, Well this is the way I do sex. It's my way or the highway.

Heterosexuals are more embarrassed talking about sex than same-sex couples. Most heterosexuals don't develop a way to initiate love-making, to refuse without it really being crushing. I now do that work with every couple I see in my clinical practice—develop a way of initiating it that works—and give some examples. You can say, How amorous do you feel, on a scale of one to ten? And your partner can use this to say, I don't feel very amorous, about a three, but let's cuddle, or Well, I'm a six, convince me. You just need to be able to talk about it, to sit down and say, Okay, I want to hear what felt good, what didn't feel good.

Gay and lesbian couples do this. They are much less defensive about it. I think because they have been so rejected by society, they've had to develop their own ways of being sexual and their own support systems for it. Heterosexuals, in our very British cultural legacy, have more problems with sexuality. The way we're raised is almost Victorian—to have to mind-read what he thinks, what he feels. Does she really like me? How can anybody really like me? I'm a little fat.

There are many self-image problems that both women and men grow up with. Bernie Zilbergeld died a couple of years ago, and he wrote a book called *The New Male Sexuality.* He had this one drawing in his book that blows men away. It's a drawing of about sixteen different erect penises, and they are so different from one another. Men look at that, and they go, Whoa, I thought I had to be like steel, straight up, 90 degrees; and they look at this picture, and they think, I can be good enough. A survey once asked men whether they thought their penis size was above average, below average, or average, and most men said below average. There's this tremendous insecurity.

The thing about sexuality that Paul Gebhard, former director of the Kinsey Institute, once said, is that it is so malleable, within a person across time, within a couple across time, across people and across cultures—it's just amazing. There's so much difference. If people can start talking about their sexual fantasies with one another, that would be wonderful. "When you wear that thing, I just go nuts. Or when you say this to me or move like that"—if they can just be more open, more accepting, I think sexuality among heterosexual U.S. couples can really change.

◀ **Freedom of Choice** ▶

Part of why there is so much divorce and remarriage is that now people don't have to put up with a bad relationship. They don't have to take getting beaten up or being publicly humiliated or living with sexual coercion or threats. Woman can support themselves, get their own apartments, take care of their children. And maybe the man will be a better father if they're not fighting so much. Now that society is more accepting of cultural differences, there aren't these totally unrealistic expectations on life, and people don't have to put up with a bad relationship. Legislatures had to pass laws in the 1900s that it was illegal to beat up your wife, or to drop her off at a mental hospital and have her committed—that used to be legal.

People should have the right to choose, and we should celebrate love wherever we find it in all its forms. Psychologists have learned that what hurts kids is not the divorce but the constant fighting after the divorce, when they use the kids to get each other. Good science is really key. Let's change these policies so that they're supporting families instead of hurting them.

◀ Honoring Your Partner's Dreams ▶

I think the single most important thing to improve a relationship is honoring your partner's dreams. If I was going to recommend one thing, it would be to know your partner's dreams and find a way to honor them. Couples are also looking for a blueprint for dealing with conflict constructively, and another blueprint for intimacy and maintaining emotional connection. Men as well as women are looking for that. The stereotype is that men want sex all the time, but what I'm really finding as I do my research is that all men want to feel irresistible and desired by their partners. They don't necessarily want a lot of sex so much as to really feel sexy. And I think that women want the same thing. It's not so different. That would be my advice: a blueprint for intimacy, a blueprint for constructive conflict resolution, and knowing your partner's dreams and honoring them.

Laird Hamilton ➤ on Surfing

LAIRD HAMILTON *is known as the guiding genius of crossover board sports, and he is truly amazing in the water. His size—six-foot-three, 220 pounds—makes him seem indestructible. Hamilton has done all kinds of interesting things in the ocean, such as making epic, long-distance journeys on his oceangoing paddleboard and creating the fast forward speed sailing loop. When he was twenty-two, he entered a speed-sailing competition in Port Saint-Louis, France; defeated the heavily favored French champion; and broke the European speed record of 36 knots in the process. Today, he surfs the outer reefs in Hawaii with his friends, after years of working with and innovating different board designs to catch the giant waves. Their pioneering method of tow-in surfing involves getting into a Wave Runner, attaching a water ski rope to it, and towing each other into waves that are too big to paddle into. The craft flings them into the wave at full speed. We were interested in Hamilton's perspective on surfing, because surfing as a sport and a culture seems to be exploding nationally and internationally. We were curious about what Laird thought the next big surf innovation would be and from whom it would come.*

I think it will always come back to bigger, higher, faster.
Do I envision other hybrids combined with surfing in the future? Absolutely. I keep doing all these things with power craft, but I think there's definitely a direction toward more manual and environmentally friendly and independent methods that can help you be a little more self-sufficient. One idea would be a foil system that would allow you to self-perpetuate your own speed. You could physically generate the power to fly on it and ride waves without any assistance.

Rather than huge changes in existing sports, there will be new disciplines that we haven't imagined or seen yet. I think that'll be the most awe-inspiring. My friend told me that I can't let out what I'm imagining, because they'll try to put me in a room with bars. You have to let them out slowly, you can't just open the whole box.

A lot of things will be dictated by conditions. Maybe global warming will create a huge swell that will create an opportunity to do something different and special that hasn't been done before, and might not be done afterward for a long time.

◀ How Equipment and the Sport Will Evolve ▶

In the next ten years, the sheer numbers of surfers will increase and the types of equipment we're using will change. I think equipment will evolve. There are more and more different disciplines within surfing, and I think other disciplines will continue to grow and new ones will appear. Surfing is the parent of skateboarding, snowboarding, wakeboarding, kitesurfing, and windsurfing, and within surfing you have bodysurfing, boogie boarding, waveboarding, small wave performance, big wave tow-in, long boarding, foil boarding, and stand-up paddling.

Stand-up paddling will be a huge part of a new type of surfing. It has a lot of broad appeal—girls love to do it, it's a great workout, and you can go in really small waves.

Obviously tow-in surfing and foil are more specialized, so you have limited numbers but a higher impact visually. For tow surfing, you need a giant, giant wave, and you have to have enough experience to do it safely. There will be some really unique things happening, but they'll be more like visual spectacles for films.

Already you're seeing a huge change. There's a lot of stuff getting built in Asia now, with different construction and lighter weight. At Surftech, they're making molded epoxy boards that are a lot lighter and stronger than conventional material. I think more aerospace products will be available and used at more reasonable prices, and carbon fiber and materials like that will dictate a lot of what equipment will look like. Again, demand will also dictate and determine the kind of funding you have. If there are a lot of people doing it, then you'll have a lot of people making better products.

◀ When the Water's at Capacity ▶

The negative side of surfing being popular is that there will be a lot more people surfing, yet there are not a lot of new surf spots that can be created. To help meet demand, they'll be trying to create bigger and more efficient artificial waves. Also, the more people you have in the water, the more aggression there is and resentment between different types of disciplines. If you go out in a spot with a big board, you catch waves easily. But then a guy who doesn't have as big a board as you is going to have a hard time. He doesn't catch them as easily and he's frustrated. And the bodysurfers out there are even more frustrated. This will only get worse.

We're already going toward regulating, and part of that is working things out ourselves as well. But there might be a precedent of people getting hurt or something happening that leads people to need rules and support. There are so many things going on in the world that I'd hope people spend their time on things other than making laws for surfing.

◀ The Key to Success ▶

I think it's really important that people do things they're passionate about, and there's not any easy route. Everyone wants to take a pill and get a result. But at the end of the day, for anybody I've seen who's been successful with an invention, or in business, or in a relationship, or anything else, the bottom line is that nothing replaces hard work. The way our society is going, if you aren't pretty we can make you pretty, and if you aren't fast we can make you fast, and if you aren't strong we can make you strong. But you're never going to be able to avoid the process of learning, and the work it takes to be successful. You have to be willing to fail.

I think that's the key to success. Failure is the key to success.

Elizabeth Harrison and Lara Shriftman
➤ on Public Relations

ELIZABETH HARRISON and LARA SHRIFTMAN are principals of the public relations, special events, and marketing firm Harrison & Shriftman. Their A-list events have included film premieres for Char- lie's Angels, Bridget Jones's Diary, and The Grinch as well as charity benefits and hotel and boutique openings. Additionally, Harrison and Shriftman have directed and planned product launches for countless Fortune 500 companies. They are coauthors of Fête Accompli!: The Guide to Creative Entertaining and Party Confidential. Harrison & Shriftman has offices in New York, Los Angeles, and Miami, with events around the country, including the Hamptons, Las Vegas, and major film festivals. We interviewed Harrison and Shriftman because they are the best at what they do. Their unique confluence of branding, marketing, and event production offers renewed vision and forward thinking within the public relations industry.

◀ Harrison on Advertising ➤

Since I started doing this fifteen years ago I've seen a huge shift toward the importance of public relations. At a time when TiVo is turning advertising into a different medium, and there's opportunity for the consumer to be a lot smarter, PR and marketing have become much more important. The role of PR is going to continue to grow as people see it impact the bottom line in terms of sales.

Product integration—finding clever ways to integrate product into TV content—is only going to become more prevalent. We have to see what happens to all the reality television. That's not just a trend; I think it will stay and evolve. People are going to have to get more and more creative about the way they integrate product, because the consumer is savvier and savvier about it. It will go either one of two ways. Either people will have to get smarter about it, because the consumer just won't accept it, or it will become so prevalent that the consumer will have to accept it, and it won't be such a big deal. And then one will have to question: How effective is it?

◀ Shriftman on Icons ▶

The definition of an icon differs from person to person. It may be a parental figure, teacher, politician, neighbor, or actress, but the basis is always the same: an icon is someone who inspires. But today more than ever, icons are not just major movie stars. In addition to celebrities, clients want a mix of iconic figures from all disciplines, including sports stars like Serena and Venus Williams, fashion figures like Anna Wintour, music moguls like Russell Simmons, and business leaders like Paul Allen and Bill Gates. When we started our company, athletes and business moguls didn't cross over into the mass market in the way they do now. Today, they're as highly sought after as major movie stars.

When we started our company, *InStyle* had just launched, and it changed the way we think about celebrities. It indulged our fascination with fame by focusing completely on celebrities and giving readers an inside peek at what celebrities are buying—clothes, jewelry, perfume, purses—all the things that they themselves are obsessing over. *InStyle* began putting movie stars on the cover, and in turn the magazine's sales soared, and so celebrities like Julia Roberts, Nicole Kidman, and Renée Zellweger became the new supermodels.

This trend is also apparent in the fashion industry. In the early nineties, there were never celebrities at the Council of Fashion Designers of America Awards, but today events like the CFDAs and Fashion Week in New York, Milan, and Paris are all about the celebrities that are present. We focus on who is sitting on the front row at Marc Jacobs just as much as the clothes that are on the runway!

Music industry and business moguls are also making a bigger and bigger impact. If you look at someone like Russell Simmons, he's crossed over from music to fashion and politics. I think of it as a lifestyle in the way that these icons touch every aspect of our lives. For example, look at the way Gwen Stefani, who began as a musician, is now acting and has created one of the most successful clothing lines, L.A.M.B. Or there's Mary-Kate and Ashley Olsen, who spun their childhood career into a major media conglomerate and are now icons to so many.

◀ Harrison on the New Celebrity ▶

Celebrities are still going to be icons. Business people also are becoming more iconic, like Jack Welch, and in real estate we're seeing all these personalities, such as Steve Ross. I also think that the next generation will be admiring celebrities who are doing more for others, whether it's Bono doing things for world hunger, or Cameron Diaz coming out against cars that are burning too much fuel. The baby boomers were a pretty selfish lot, not necessarily altruistic. The newest generation will be looking for celebrities to take a stand on more than just themselves. It's really interesting to look at Angelina Jolie; with breaking up a marriage and having an affair, you'd think that she would come out the bad guy. But it's certainly not hurting her career. Maybe it has something to do with the fact that on one hand she's done that, and on the other she's saving the world's children and adopting kids.

◀ Shriftman on Events ▶

More than ever, events are a crucial part of an overall promotion, PR, and marketing strategy. I think about events as the public sector versus the private sector. The public sector is Blackberry having a huge party to launch their new phone. But when the chairman of

Blackberry throws a dinner at his home to celebrate the launch, that's a private launch. I see the trend going toward smaller, more intimate, and exclusive parties. The media that goes along with this type of event is very targeted and well thought out. It's about hitting the perfect audience for the product.

It's not just about getting press, it's about getting the right press and getting it in all the different areas—print, television, and the Internet. When we first started, there weren't any weeklies, and today there are six major weekly magazines. And now the Internet has become one of the most effective ways to target an audience. Web sites like YouTube, MySpace, E! Online, and all the different blogs are effective and immediate ways to reach out to millions of potential consumers. The Internet reporter is just as important a contact as anyone working in print. It's all about thinking outside of the box, because on the Internet there are so many opportunities to get the word out—through video, podcasts, blogs, and more.

Events themselves have also evolved. It used to be that we targeted the magazine editor first and then the consumer, but now it's a combination. Everything is about mixing, like, for example, doing a product launch at a new boutique and having the shopping proceeds go to a charity. Everyone wins. We conceptualized the idea of the gifting suite, the concept of taking swag to a new level. Today, beauty and gifting suites are a staple in the industry.

We also started the trend of throwing parties with hosts, other than just fund-raisers. It makes perfect sense for people to go to parties to support a person. And so by adding hosts to an event, you are guaranteed a certain caliber of guests.

◀ **Harrison on Celebrity** ▶

When we started in this industry, you could give a celebrity something, and they would write you back a note and allow you to use their image or their quote in the press at no cost. Now, I think it's going the way of sports endorsements in that every celebrity, no matter what they do, expects to be paid. At the Video Music Awards this year, we saw a trend in celebrities not getting the kind of money they were asking for to host parties, so there may be some backlash. I think we saw that with Jessica Simpson in particular in *People,* where they said, You know what? We're not going to pay that kind of money, and we're not going to put up with those kinds of demands.

A lot will depend on the public's appetite for what they want to read. As long as you have a proliferation of magazines like *Star* and *Us Weekly* and *In Touch,* you know they're just starving for any celebrity knowledge. I don't see that abating. It will continue and grow, and it will also depend on what the corporate appetite is for it, how much people are willing to pay.

Fashion honestly is the last frontier where people are much more content to take a smaller amount of money to offer their name and put their stamp on something. I think fashion designers are getting smarter and savvier about it. I just think it's a more traditional, old-fashioned business, so it will take a little more time.

◄ Shriftman on Fashion Designers ►

For a very long time it was Ralph Lauren, Donna Karan, Calvin Klein, and other high-end designers who were doing the major fashion shows and getting media attention. But the media have changed so much, and so has the fashion industry. Unknown designers are getting media, because celebrities are wearing them, and with the rise of the Internet and blogs, the name gets out immediately. Los Angeles has really influenced fashion in general, because the culture in California is different, and so what celebrities, movie stars, athletes, and musicians in California are wearing is different, and that's what shows up on the pages of *Us Weekly.* In turn, this is translating into the major fashion magazines like *Vogue* and *Harper's Bazaar.* So now we are seeing so many mid-range designers pop up that are not branded in couture.

And this trend is going to continue, because I think the days of people spending insane amounts of money on clothes are over. People are more interested in wearing clothes that are comfortable and stylish than in wearing something that is so extreme or trendy; they're passing on one-time outfits. Instead, expensive items are all about that one "it" piece, an incredible accessory like a killer shoe or must-have bag.

◀ Harrison on Globalism ▶

Celebrity will be driven by the United States for as long as Hollywood is the center of entertainment. But there will be a far greater awareness of the world outside of ourselves. With what's happening in China and India and the Middle East, places like Dubai, the world is getting weirdly smaller. We still get clients who we think are A-list celebrities, but internationally they're still not a global personality. There are these weird pockets of celebrity that don't translate. In the future, that will change as the world gets smaller. There are all these movie stars coming out of China now—do I think they'll be huge? I don't know. Americans are very self-centered. With Hollywood here, I don't see a huge shift.

I'm thinking about how to keep up with it all, and I try to be visionary in terms of where our agency is, so I'm thinking globally right now. I'm thinking about how to set up a satellite office in a place like Dubai. How do I get into China? How do I differentiate myself in Europe? How do I position myself so that I am in the next place where all this is going to be happening?

◀ Shriftman on Brand Strategy ▶

Building a brand is key in today's PR industry. I focus on what the product is, then create an image that encompasses the meaning, and then brand everything from the letterhead to the shopping bags and hangtags. If you think about Ian Schrager hotels, everything is branded all the way from start to finish, from the attitude behind the design of the hotel to the welcome book in the guest rooms.

In order to effectively build a brand, you must have a strategic press plan. Every single thing is planned out, and then you slowly add on each element, from getting the right features to doing media events to throwing specialized events for the consumer. It's important to have a Web site and to keep that updated with what is happening with the brand—for instance, with photos of celebrities with the product. In turn, bloggers pick up on these images and the word begins to spread.

It's important to stay focused on an element in the brand that can really make a statement for the line. You have to look at not only what will sell, but also what is going to be good for publicity. We've learned that what's going to go in a magazine is often different from what might sell in a store.

◀ Harrison on Technology ▶

What will be really interesting over the next twenty, thirty, or forty years is how well we can acclimate ourselves to the speed of changing technology. There's just no turning it off anymore. You're just constantly in this information deluge. I wonder if as a culture we will burn out, because how much can your brain actually process? I do think in terms of celebrity. I think all the different outlets enable you to make a star much more quickly. You see stars now like Eva Longoria; you see a TV show creating major celebrities. You see shows like *Blow Out* with Jonathan Antin creating a hairdresser and a product line. That's a real shift. I don't think we've ever seen that before.

It will be interesting to see how it evolves. I worry about burnout; I really do. Especially in our industry, it's very prevalent. People are their most creative when they have a little time to think and reflect. If we don't build that into our lives, it will hinder us from moving forward as a culture and society.

I've been thinking a lot about how to create a culture that allows people some breathing room and also mentors and nurtures and educates them. We're lousy at that, in our industry in particular. We throw people into situations; we expect them to learn by doing. It's very sink or swim, and there's major burnout. I'm spending a lot of this year thinking about how I can keep people, because in our society we tend to jump from job to job. There's not the same kind of loyalty and longevity. In order to grow brands and do a good job, you need to have people doing it for a while. My initiative to myself and to the company this year is a pledge to really try to make our company a better place to work. Make people less disposable, make people feel important, make even senior level people feel that they can still learn and grow. Find ways for people to profit, but let them feel that they are part of making that profit. I'm trying to figure out a way to make even the lowest person on the totem pole feel like they are an integral part of the company.

➤ on the Latino Population

The visionary founder of Latina, *the first magazine targeted exclusively to Hispanic women in the United States,* CHRISTY HAUBEGGER *is a leading American business figure and opinion maker on Latino issues. Her idea for a magazine designed exclusively for the Hispanic market began to take shape when, as a teen growing up in Houston, she noticed a lack of images and information in women's magazines that related to her experiences as a Mexican-American. After receiving her law degree from Stanford Law School, she set out to create her magazine: a bilingual publication that would serve as a source of information and provide positive images for Hispanic women who, like herself, live between two cultures and two languages. She was also a producer of the movies* Chasing Papi *and* Spanglish *and currently works with Creative Artists Agency. We were interested in what Haubegger had to say, because the Latino population is such a large and growing part of the American future, and its importance and prominence in our national consciousness seems to grow exponentially each year.*

◀ The Coming Boom ▶

If you look at the demographic landscape of this country, in the next ten years, and certainly over the next forty, the non-Hispanic white population will remain statistically flat while the Hispanic population will virtually explode in size. In fact, we're expected to constitute some 25 percent of the population by 2050. Despite what politicians and alarmist news outlets portray, most of that growth is driven not by immigration, but rather by natural increase (the number of births over deaths in a population). If you break it down by compound annual growth rate, the Latino population is growing at a rate of 2.1 percent a year. The aging, non-Hispanic white population is growing at 0.1 percent a year. At some point soon, it will be statistically at zero growth, with the same number of people dying as being born. Then, it will start shrinking, with more people dying than being born, due to a host of factors—but largely because of the senescence of the baby boomers and the trend toward smaller families within America's non-Hispanic white population.

At the same time, there's this incredibly young (median age twenty-six) Hispanic population that's still in its peak reproductive years and also is a group that tends to have larger families. Which is why even though Latinos constitute only 15 percent of all Americans, we're already responsible for 48 percent of the country's total population growth every year. In addition, we are still somewhat geographically concentrated, with most of us living in large urban areas, which means we exercise some disproportionate cultural influence in our nation's media and entertainment centers, such as New York, Los Angeles, and Miami.

◀ More American Than Americans ▶

There's no zeal like that of the converted, and Hispanic immigrants and children of immigrants are more characteristically "American" than other Americans. They totally believe in the American dream— that this is an amazing place and that they're going to have great opportunities.

For example, the young Latino population is twice as optimistic as the general market, as measured by every sort of quantitative measure. In the general market, 40 percent of the group believe that they will do better financially than their parents. Among Hispanics, 85 percent believe this. We're so optimistic, so family oriented. Hispanics think we have better values and morals than non-Hispanics, and believe we're influencing the general market through these values and beliefs.

We haven't even begun to realize the political future of the group. Right now a fifth of white Americans, a fourth of black Americans, and a third of Hispanics are under the age of eighteen. That means that a third of the Latino group isn't even old enough to vote yet. There is this huge population wave coming right behind us, and I think politically we're still totally up for grabs, because Hispanics don't have twenty years of history with one party. We haven't decided who's going to be our political brand yet, but some of the current dialogue would suggest it may be the Democrats. Think about it— Hispanics are twice as likely to go to church every week than non-Hispanics. In fact, we're a churchgoing, hardworking, want-to-own-my-own-business, pull-myself-up-by-my-bootstraps group. That sounds pretty Republican, doesn't it? Unfortunately, a lot of the Republican messaging comes back as, we don't want you or people who look like you here, and I imagine that will take a generation or more to forget.

More important, the biggest threat to our future global competitiveness, in my view, is the fact that education and resulting job opportunities are still largely correlated to or dependent on your ethnic background. We have a huge natural resource of this incredible growing Latino population that is just not going to be able to help us compete globally because we're not allocating resources appropriately. Apparently we don't think it's a matter of competitiveness to make sure that all minority kids get a good elementary or high school education, even though "minorities" are the majority of kids in most large cities. (In fact, when you go to our urban cultural centers in America—the top ten cities in this country—there are only two of them that are not "majority minority," Phoenix and San Diego, and they're hanging on by a thread.)

People debate why some schools fail, but it's usually a concentration of poverty, inexperienced and ineffective teachers, bad facilities and management, and few resources—it's the perfect storm for creating a permanent underclass. (Jonathan Kozol does a great job of exploring this issue in his book *The Shame of Our Nation*.) Consider that Hispanics make up 20 percent of all teens right now. And 40 percent of those Hispanic teens go to one of the three hundred schools that have been deemed the worst in the United States by almost every measure. Just to be clear, the inequalities start much earlier than high school; we've never even fully funded the Head Start program. In any case, we are looking at the fastest-growing population in our nation's history but accepting the fact that most of them will receive a substandard education and that some 40 percent will receive the very worst our system has to offer.

How is this not seen as a competitive issue for America? I'm concerned that within ten years we are going to have a huge, young, uneducated Hispanic group and at the same time, an aging, white group falling out of the workforce that needs to be supported. These two things are moving very quickly in opposite directions. Skilled people are falling out of the workforce, and other people going into the workforce who are less prepared, less educated—or at least that's true for a meaningful part of the group. That huge collision threatens our ability to compete on a global basis.

While this remarkable demographic shift is happening in our country, I worry that we are caught up in a shortsighted political debate. The immigration debate affects a few million Latino immigrants every year. However, there are 42 million of us here right now, and of the 14 million Latinos who are under the age of eighteen, 90 percent (nearly 13 million) were born here.

What kind of Americans will those 13 million have the chance to be? Will they be able to lead us into the future, with a world-class education that allows the United States to compete and win in a global marketplace? Not at this rate. We're foolish to think we're simply debating what kind of immigration policy or education system we want. It's much bigger than that: we need to decide what we want America to be, as a people and as a nation, and then prioritize accordingly.

Tony Hawk ➤ **on Skateboarding**

Tony Hawk is a skateboard legend and the premier ambassador of the action-sports lifestyle. By age sixteen Tony Hawk had become indisputably the best skateboarder in the world. In 2002, Hawk launched the Boom Boom HuckJam, a twenty-four-city arena tour featuring the world's best skateboarders, BMX bike riders, and freestyle Motocross riders. The hugely successful and massively publicized HuckJam tour has sold out in arenas across the country every year since its inception. We were interested in what Hawk saw in the future, because he has been so instrumental in revolutionizing and helping the sport grow. From his innovative tricks to his apparel line to his Boom Boom Huckjam tour, Hawk's brand has permeated both the sporting world and popular culture. In large part because of him, skateboarding's popularity and reach expands exponentially every year. We wanted to know how far Hawk thought this growth would go and what he envisioned for future athletes and fans of the sport.

There are more kids skating these days than there are in Little League. Those are numbers you can't deny.

The biggest change in the next ten years will be perception. Even though skating is wildly popular, there's still this perception, especially in the mainstream media, that skating is unorthodox, a kids' sport, or only for psychotics. I think time will show that skating has a very positive effect on the kids who get into it. It teaches them self-discipline, self-confidence, and self-motivation, and I think we'll see this acceptance and the perception change into something much more tangible.

Skating's still considered more of an underground and niche sport grouped together with all the so-called extreme sports. I think it will outlast that categorization and become just another accepted sport that kids will do as they are growing up. That perception and popularity shift is happening internationally. The biggest change in skateboarding's recognition over the next decade will be on a global scale. It's very likely that skateboarding will be in the 2012 Olympic Games, so countries where the population has never even seen a skateboard before most likely will be exposed to it.

◀ **A Captive Audience** ▶

A project like the Boom Boom HuckJam tour brings all of our sports on tour in an arena format. That was the vision for the tour—not just for me to headline it all the time, but for that concept to live on beyond my skating years.

Even ten years ago, the only way we got into arenas was on the coattails of a concert tour. Today, there is a captive audience for our tour. And they aren't only skaters. I think that's been the thing in the past. The only people who liked skating were the skaters themselves. Now there is a strong fan base that is happy to sit back on the couch and watch the X Games.

In the future, I think the audience for our sport will be similar to the audience for Monday Night Football. I don't know if it's going to be such a team pride sort of approach; I think it'll be more of an overall appreciation for what these guys do as opposed to picking favorites and painting your face. You'll have an athlete—for example a Shaun White—and he'll have a new trick, and the audience's big question will be, "Is he going to try it tonight?"

◀ **Fear of Flying** ▶

When you start moving into ramps that are thirty feet high (as we have with the "Mega ramp"), it's not just about possible injuries and recovery time. The danger level is much greater. But then again, only a handful of people can ride ramps that are that big, and we know the risks involved. There are only two of these ramps in existence, both private, so it's not available for an average skater to try. Although every time that I go out there I think, if someone really gets hurt here, we're not prepared for this. So I think that as people embrace that, and more skaters want to try it, we have to be prepared for the worst.

One of my biggest concerns is people getting into the sport for the wrong reasons—kids start skating because they think it will bring them fame and fortune. When I was growing up, these dreams were not possible. The most successful skaters got free equipment and a $100 check for first place in competitions, which were few and far between. You did it because you truly loved it. And it would be hard to see people getting into it in the future just because they think this is their ticket to stardom, as opposed to their really loving what they do. But I think that skating, at its core, will always be an individual pursuit.

◀ **Future Greats** ▶

Ryan Schekler is one of the top street guys. He is already something of a household name, thanks to MTV and the X Games. He is well-rounded, and he continues to challenge himself even though he is already at a top level. Even though he's already winning these events, he continues to improve his skills, and that's really important for his longevity. I think he is definitely going to be a household name for years to come.

And truly, I think the best-known guy from any of our sports—for years to come—is Shaun White. He is a pro skater as well as being a pro snowboarder, so he definitely has crossover. In terms of his popularity and potential, nobody comes close to Shaun.

Being well-rounded in our sport is really important—knowing you can show up at almost any location in any situation and still perform—and it's something that people don't focus on. If you do dream of being a pro at some point, then you're expected to rise to the occasion and perform, even if you are not feeling good, especially when the conditions are not ideal. It's the most fun, and we love what we do, but at the same time it can be work, because we are professionals. It's our job.

Felicity Huffman and William H. Macy
➤ on Entertainment

Married in 1997, **WILLIAM H. MACY AND FELICITY HUFFMAN** *are both award-winning actors, with a strong reputation in Hollywood as two of today's most talented stars. Macy began his career with roles in more than fifty Off Broadway and Broadway plays and is perhaps best known for his lead role in the movie* Fargo, *for which he was nominated for an Academy Award. In 2003 Macy won two Emmy Awards, one for starring in the lead role and one as co-writer of the made-for-TNT film* Door to Door. *Huffman is perhaps best known for her role as* Lynette Scavo *on* Desperate Housewives, *for which she has won an Emmy and two 2005 Screen Actors Guild Awards. Her outstanding performance in* Transamerica *earned her a Golden Globe Award for Best Actress and a nomination for an Academy Award. We spoke to this couple because they have worked in film, theater, and television, both behind and in front of the camera, and thus have a unique perspective on its future. In a fickle business, they remain tremendously respected among their peers and adored by audiences everywhere.*

◀ Macy on Storytelling ▶

I don't think stories will change much in the future. What we're trying to do is tell the stories that people want to see and hear. And I've based my whole life on the idea that the truth will win out. It's the most fascinating story that you can tell. Even with a blockbuster, part of that film speaks to the human condition, so that we all say, "Oh, my God, that's so true." When you tell a story that is outrageous but true, it works. But when you see stories that are basically not true to the human condition, no matter how many special effects

they've got, they're bores—cheap shots. And you want to see a different movie as soon as you leave the theater. It's like the cliché about
Chinese food—you need more a few hours later. At the end of the
day, it needs to be a story based on an emotional truth. That will be
the key to success in the future, just as it has always been.

◀ Huffman on the Changing Face of Television ▶

Desperate Housewives was successful because in some ways it was
a Trojan horse. It felt and looked familiar—after all, it's about that
American icon: the housewife. But underneath, it was somewhat
subversive, naughty, and a forbidden treat. It broke the rules by *not*
breaking the rules. What the creator, Mark Cherry, did so brilliantly
was to leave the traditional structure in place so that we would watch
it and feel comfortable watching it, but once we were comfortable,
he started to pull the traditional drama and the traditional emotions
apart—not to kill them, but to challenge us and make us view them
from a different perspective. It slowly started changing how we look
at drama, or comedy. When we are allowed or forced to view the
status quo differently, that's when change happens. But it doesn't
happen all at once, or even with just one show.

People are definitely getting more sophisticated, and that means
creators will have to think up new ways of telling stories to keep the
viewers interested. There's so much you can watch today, and that
will certainly continue in the future, but you can also watch reruns
of your favorite shows on cable or on DVD. So creators of new shows
need to make the content all the more surprising and scintillating
just to get you interested. The audience is very sophisticated, sea-
soned, and saturated, so there is an appetite for the new and different. But the stories we want to see will probably remain the same at
heart. At the end of the day we just want to connect to how someone
feels—it's just the package they put that story in might change.

What's great about television is that is so democratic. Everyone's got a TV. I love that about television. It's not elite in any way, shape, or manner. And I feel that it really reflects America because there are so many choices, and we really can measure what America's interested in.

But the business of TV is changing, and changing rapidly. So what we see on TV will probably change. You can look at the movie of the week as one example. I made a good living doing them for about ten years. And for about ten years before that, the movies of the week were a thriving part of television, and then in two years they died. That's how fast things move. In a two-year period many of the networks went from doing thirty or forty TV movies a year to doing zero. That's how fast the economics changed the face of television.

Then there's TiVo and PVRs (personal video recorders). That's going to change everything, because people will have the ability to skip the commercials. And it will change not only the finances of television but the art form itself. Because when you're writing a show expecting commercial breaks, you write it one way; without them, you have to write another way. I once worked with a writer who had it down to a science. It was formatted so that, as he wrote his story, it fit into this format designed for seven-act breaks. Each one was designed to leave people with a little cliffhanger at the commercial so that they would come back. Well, that's all going to change if there are no commercials. I also expect you'll see more programs that are fully sponsored by advertisers without interruption. And while big actors may kick up their heels about product integration in shows, most actors won't really have a choice about it. The problem will be if the advertiser wants more creative control in the future. That could cause a big fight. But it's really just a shift of the fight that exists, anyway, because the arts are always fighting with someone—either the censors or the network.

On the other hand, there are more outlets for creativity these days and that may continue to grow in the future. It was just in the last couple of years that if you wanted to put something on TV, you had three choices. Now all of a sudden, HBO is rewriting the books. And now HBO is running as fast as they can to keep up with TNT and Showtime. And the competition is fierce out there. The good news, for the audience and for the artists, is that there are a lot more outlets; there are a lot more people knocking on my door, saying, "You got an idea?" And that's good for creativity. In order to be successful, you don't have to speak to the entire country. You can tell a tale that's smaller in scope.

◀ Huffman on the Business of Television ▶

I won't pretend to predict the business of television. It's a complicated model and better left (thankfully) to the executives who run networks. But it's clear that TiVo and PVRs are going to change how we watch TV and how actors will have to deal with things such as product placement. There's less urgency now to watch immediately. It used to be that you had to watch an episode when it aired. There was a camaraderie to that. While I love the convenience of watching on demand, it's a shame that we lose that group experience. People know the outcome of a show when they hear about it the next morning on the radio or a friend tells them, so it changes the power of the experience.

As more advertisers can count on people *not* watching their ads, they'll have to rely on product placement. I don't know if people really go out and buy a car after seeing someone drive it in a show, but if it's what helps get good programs on in the future, then so be it. It's clear the business model will have to change. It did in the music industry, and it will in the TV business, but I don't know that anyone is quite sure yet how it will do so.

Audiences today are growing up. Everyone is just getting more sophisticated. And they'll get even more sophisticated in the future. Think about how much TV people watch, and how many shows we have access to. You can watch hours and hours of current television and old television. We've heard the laugh track, the shows with comedians insulting one another, the "yada-yada laugh, yada-yada laugh." We're just too used to it all now. Anybody that's in this business knows they can get you to laugh just by setting up the pattern. If I tell you that you're going to laugh on the seventh beat, and I make you laugh a couple of times, you'll laugh. But after a while, you get bored. And for *Friends* and *Frasier* and *All in the Family*, the laughs came regularly, but it was exquisite writing. But it's so hard to do. For every genius show, we've had a hundred knockoffs that followed the form, and they're just not funny.

I don't think humor on TV will go away. I just think it will have to evolve from where it is now. We'll just have to get more creative about how we make people laugh, which might be a good thing.

I really believe in the audience. I started in the theater, and at the end of the day, we always said, "There's one god, and that's the audience." They're never wrong. You either believe in the audience or you don't. I've done a lot of movies, but *Wild Hogs* is the one that everybody's seen me in. . . . I can't look at the audience and say, "Well, you're wrong because I've done better work or more sophisticated work." If that's what they like, then that's what they like. They're never wrong. There will always be people who have to sign the checks. And they will always be in the driver's seat. So I think it gets better, because the audience is demanding more and more that we give them a good bang for their buck. Everything is based on them. For the actor—nobody cares whether they really feel it or not; it's the audience. They're the ones who buy the tickets. They're the ones who are paying for the whole thing. It will always be for the audience.

◄ Huffman on the Content of Television ►

I think TV is getting better. There's some great TV out there. Sure, some isn't so great, but there's good and bad in every profession. With the explosion of channels, there are so many outlets for stories, and you have to expect that will continue to grow in the future. You can see fantastic little things everywhere—wonderful, weird stories. Wonderful acting. Very interesting storytelling. And with more outlets, more people will have the opportunity to tell their stories in the future and expand how we think and challenge our thoughts.

Reality TV is having a big effect now and will continue to have a big effect in the future. But I find it worrisome. I'm not sure it reflects well on us. Is it necessary? I don't know. People want it— there is a real appetite for it. It's sort of reminiscent of the Roman Colosseum: The enemies were at the gates, people were starving, but there was still an audience for watching people being ravaged by lions. Obviously I don't put a show like *Dancing with the Stars*, where you need some talent, in the same category as programs where they're swapping wives or gossiping and ripping people apart. It's hard to say whether it's hurting society or just sort of holding up a mirror saying, "Here's what's going on and this is what you're hungry for, so I'm giving it to you." So the question is if we want new, surprising, and scintillating now in our reality television, what will we demand in the future?

◄ Macy on Digital Film Technology ►

We'll go to the Oscars someday and see a best picture nominee that was made by some kid in his basement. And it may not be just a kitchen-sink drama. It could be *Star Wars*. The technology has come so far because everything has gone digital. For one of the projects

I'm shooting right now, we're doing on 24p, which is digital. And I'm astounded by the way it looks. And there's so much you can do. Even when you shoot a film, you do all the cutting, all the color timing, almost the entire film on digital. So if an actor's eyes are blue, and we really wanted them green, it's no big deal to program and change the eyes to green in every single frame.

It means anybody can make a movie in the future—anybody. It used to be that very few people had the wherewithal to turn out a film, so one would have to have access to the people who had the money to get a film made. Increasingly in the future, if you have an idea, the technology will allow you to do it, with your own technology. And maybe even win an Oscar. And that's pretty amazing.

◀ Huffman on Independent Filmmaking ▶

Tiny little movies are being made everywhere, which is a fantastic opportunity for creativity. Whether it's for YouTube or for the big screen, everyone should have a chance and everyone should have a voice. But of course whether it's a big movie or a small movie, it has to be a story that really clicks. That's the beauty of the future and the beauty of the technology that's out there right now. But there will still be the kings of Hollywood who control distribution and who decide—to some degree for a while, anyway—what most of us see.

I think most people don't get out to see as many movies as they'd like to. They're busy. It can be expensive. They want to be at home with their kids, so when they go to the movies they want a guarantee that it will be good, and they aren't as willing to take a risk on a small film. They may want a blockbuster, so it seems like that's the way it will go in the future, as we get busier and more skeptical. Of course, the great thing about independent films is that they don't have to appeal to everyone. They are there for a smaller group of people.

Being an old theater buff, it's my feeling that the experience of sitting with a bunch of people watching a story unfold is so delicious that we're not going to lose it. We'll still go to theaters in the future. We do want to sit with all our pals, a hundred fifty of them, and have the surround sound and the big screen. I love movies more when I see them like that than when I do in front of my state-of-the-art, giant TV with the surround sound and I can pause it and go to the bathroom and all that. The theaters may have to get nicer and the experience there may have to get better, but we'll still want to share the experience.

And don't expect technology to make us more creative. There is a reason we haven't discovered Shakespeare on YouTube or suddenly found a wealth of creative talent on the Internet. It's hard! I don't care how good the technology is; it still comes down to a blank piece of paper, fade in. And somebody's got to tell a story. But what's happened just in our lifetime is that it's been democratized, so that if somebody wants to tell a story about a transgender woman, you can make that movie, and it looks like a grown-up movie. I mean, you'll see it in the quadruplex. And it looks just like a movie. Years ago that movie would never be made without a dozen people pulling the strings; but today it can be made. And even more so in the future.

Sharon John ➤ **on Toys**

SHARON JOHN serves as the general manager of marketing for several of Hasbro's key divisions—Boys, Girls, and Big Kids—and oversees a number of the company's blue-chip and best-known brands, such as Transformers, Star Wars, My Little Pony, Littlest Pet Shop, Furreal Friends, Nerf, Super Soaker, and Tiger Electronics. Under John's direction, the company has strengthened its position in electronics for the tween (between kid and teen) market. The successful Tiger Electronics line includes a long list of tween favorites. That same tween insight has brought strong growth to the Nerf brand through its blaster and sports line of products. We're interested in what John had to say, because to us, toys seem to be getting more and more sophisticated. We wondered how technology might impact toy development in the future, and how the increasing complexity of these toys will impact parents and kids.

We **are in a very exciting era**—lower prices and more complex technology provide us with some incredible opportunities, and this will continue to drive development of new products and influence how kids play to some extent. Think about how things have evolved. As recently as twenty-five years ago some of the industry leaders were reluctant to put batteries in some preschool products, because they were concerned about how mothers would react. Today, for many toys and games, it's almost a cost of entry. There is an expectation that a battery, or flashing light, or a chip, provides added value for the consumer and the play pattern.

Technology will continue to enjoy an enormous role as we look to innovate at every turn. The technologies will change and become more sophisticated, and the winners will be the companies that successfully open new categories, leverage brands, keep an eye on lifestyle trends, and focus on innovation in all aspects of business, all with an emphasis on truly breakthrough product development.

There are certain aspects of the toy industry that I believe will remain the same. As an example, the toy industry has always been a highly seasonal industry, and the holiday season will always be of critical importance. Our shipping volume, along with sell-through at retail, is stronger in the second half of the year, and that will continue for our toy and game businesses. Additionally, toys and games remain somewhat insulated from economic volatility. That has remained true over time, and that will likely continue. Parents are generally willing to make sacrifices in other places to ensure that their children have things to entertain them and receive special toys or games, particularly on Christmas morning or during Hanukkah.

◀ Invisible Technology ▶

I think you'll see more and more technology-based toys over time. Today's kids are very savvy about technology, and they educate their parents. The parents are the gatekeepers and may not be as sophisticated about technology—although that is changing as time goes on. Unlike many of their parents, today's kids have grown up with technology—for them it is second nature. There is nothing unique about being on the computer at age three. Due to the increasing sophistication, today's tech toys will be almost invisible to tomorrow's users, because the technology will be taken for granted. Technology will be used simply as a play enabler rather than a category within the industry.

We are currently in a transition period with the consumer. Some people may still buy a product just because it has some kind of buzzer, whistle, or light or simply because they are attracted to the toy because of a tech feature. However, I believe in the near future, technology will be just a transparent enabler that makes the product come to life in a more unique way, makes it more fun, more interesting.

There is already some incredible interactivity in so many of our products that is reflective of the "invisible" use of technology. Some of the benefits of this use of technology center on how it can add creativity to the child's play experience or make the product actually come "alive," while keeping the open-ended nature of play and building on the experience. When done correctly, technology is making toys and games more interactive, and it is encouraging children to interface longer with the product. We have no interest in creating a clutter of "watch-me toys." It's about using technology to create more fun and more surprises; this will result in the child going back to the toy again and again. For example, without getting too techie, we are able to create randomization programs so the toy interacts differently with the child at different times, in different ways or adjust to the way the child interfaces with the product.

Of course, we stress at Hasbro that there will always be room for tactile toys and games that do not live and die by technology, including classic board games such as Monopoly. Sometimes, there is nothing more fulfilling than taking your little brother's last $500 bill after he lands on your built-up properties.

Humans have not evolved so much that they don't want to touch things or have personal interaction. So we will likely always create some toys that are completely dedicated to simple play or even just different kinds of tactile interfaces. This is particularly true, for example, in the infant and preschool area, where physical interface is critical to early development. We believe these toys and play experiences will remain relevant, and we will continually look to bring to market the right balance of products, all infused with *innovation*, not necessarily technology, that will entertain and delight.

◀ **Video Games for Everyone** ▶

Games are inextricably interwoven into how we think about our business. When you look at our games portfolio, it is a who's who of the games that you played with as a child and that remain popular today: Monopoly, Clue, Scrabble, Trivial Pursuit, Sorry, Battleship—the list goes on.

We certainly see gaming as an important opportunity, especially when you consider the incredible game portfolio owned by Hasbro. Of course, the video-game category is likely to continue to grow, but it's also likely to change from the key titles being focused on first-person shooter, first-person driver, edgy-content concepts to more interactive, evolving experiences and more family-centered activities. The video-game business has already moved from one guy sitting in front of the screen to more of an interactive interface with multiple players. I think the next big shift is going to happen in people's homes, where gaming will take on a more prominent role in people's entertainment calendar. There will be planned family time where, instead of watching a movie together, they will break out their favorite game with multiple hand-held units and have a blast.

◄ **Let Them Play** ➤

I hope that we don't forget what toys and games are really about. For the youngest players, it's about kids having fun, being a kid, enjoying childhood, learning how to interact and share with others through toys like Mr. Potato Head and games like Candyland. Toys and games are building blocks. You learn cooperation and collaboration. You learn strategy with card and board games. I trust we will never lose sight of the importance of play. Technology has opened up so many doors, but we should be cautious about the use of technology just for technology's sake.

Our children are far too valuable to forget to let them be kids. Today's kids can be so overstimulated and overscheduled. Without the benefit and balance of both structured and unstructured play, we may run the risk of our children not learning some of the basic building blocks of open-ended socialization that most of us did. Some-times we just need to let them play and have fun.

I think that for the most part, because games and toys are ulti-mately about play, my advice would be not to overanalyze it; trust your instincts. Play is an integral part of being human. You prob-ably know what's right for your kids just by being a loving, caring parent. Your gut can take you a long way. But you should get in there and play, too. Remember what it was like to be lost in your favorite toy or game? You can experience it again with your child and make some special memories for both of you. But in the end, I think toys and games should remain fun and lighthearted, and we shouldn't get overwrought in the analysis of them.

➤ on the SAT and College Admissions

JOHN S. KATZMAN *is the founder and chairman of the Princeton Review, which he started in 1981 when he prepared a handful of students for the SAT. Since then, the company has grown into one of the strongest brands in education, offering classroom and online classes and private tutoring for the SAT, ACT, GMAT, MCAT, LSAT, GRE, USMLE, and other entrance exams. Katzman has become an expert in many areas of education, but we talked to him about the future of college admissions, and specifically the SAT, which has recently been altered to include an essay. We wondered if high school students should expect similar additions in the future, but John predicted a much bigger change. He also gave us insight into the changing economics of higher education.*

I **think the SAT will disappear.**

To truly understand that, you have to understand where the SAT came from. The notion back in the 1940s was that a lot of people were going back to college and we needed some way to train them, but colleges overall didn't want to tell the high schools what they should teach or judge how well they were teaching it. So they needed some sort of curriculum—a neutral measure—and what they decided on was the Army's IQ test. Over the years, people have come to realize that that was nuts. Number one, the test never measured IQ. If IQ exists and if it can be measured, the army IQ test isn't the way to measure it. And number two, the test created its own curriculum. That is, schools would teach whatever they thought was important to teach, and then, as admissions became more competitive, kids would go take a course like ours for the SAT.

Further, the notion that you should create an important test that people shouldn't prepare for is kind of silly. The question is, which test do you want people spending their effort on? Every state has moved and will continue to move in the direction of creating their own test that measures the things the state wants taught—tests like the New York State Regents exam. The states have become more and more serious about measuring, and they aren't doing it to measure how smart their kids are or to ready their paths. They are doing it to measure their schools.

Now we have one set of tests that determines if you're going to get a diploma from your high school and a second set of tests that determines if you are going to go to college. And it makes a lot of sense to have just one set of tests. As each state adopts a high school graduation test, it's making a decision: Do we toss our own standards and adopt the ones embedded in the SAT or ACT, surrendering control to them? Or do we have the state college system accept our state's graduation test as their entrance test? That's where all of this is going to head.

◀ **The New Testing** ▶

The tighter the alignment between the graduation and admissions tests, between what you learn in school and what you are admitted on, the fairer the process is. Because if you study hard in school, you've got preparation for a high school graduation test, or at least you're on the road to it—as opposed to a kid who doesn't have SAT preparation in school and who is at a tremendous disadvantage for the SAT.

Especially for disadvantaged kids, by the time they start the college admissions process, wealthy kids have finished it. If you think about the notion of being a disadvantaged student, some time around the beginning of senior year, you become aware of these tests and you go through this whole process. Everyone else applied early, and they're done. So by replacing the SAT with a high school graduation test, all of a sudden you've taken your high school tests with everybody else the beginning of junior year. And you're told you're not only on the road toward a diploma, but you're college material. And you've already done everything you have to do.

I think this new system of testing will be less expensive and less redundant, and it will speed access for disadvantaged kids. One state will officially change their testing system in this way—it will be New York, California, or Texas. Once one state does it, the rest of the old SAT-based system will fall apart. All of a sudden, you'll have a third national test. That first state will get great press and save a lot of money, and meanwhile the cost of the SAT or ACT will go up because you've taken the largest customers away. If you lose California, 15 or 20 percent of the SAT test takers are gone.

The governor who makes this change is going to be on the cover of *Time*. If you want to become the education governor and position yourself for national office, this is the perfect way to do it. It's just a matter of time until someone truly gets it. It's just a matter of time.

◀ The Economics of Change ▶

Years and years ago, the guy who ran Princeton for a long time projected that education was going to get ridiculously expensive. He said that the economy is based on productivity gains, and education doesn't have any productivity gains. You have a man or a woman with X number of students, and the room has to have a roof and a blackboard. There's technology employed that generally makes that whole thing more, not less, expensive, and sure enough, college education has exceeded the rate of inflation every year by 3 or 4 percent. At this point, it's a couple hundred thousand dollars after taxes. And it will continue to get more expensive.

A couple of things should come out of that. First, there will be all kinds of government subsidies, and those will continue, because there's middle-class entitlement. And there will be the rise of state colleges, which are a lot less expensive than private colleges. And when the squeeze from the baby boom is over, the competition will be fierce on the second tier of private colleges. If you're not going to Harvard, you should go to SUNY, because it's so much cheaper. And finally, online learning, which is still in its infancy and still for the most part terrible. You've got to think that ten years from now, half the classes you take in college you can take online, or that of all the classes you take, you'll take half online. And unless schools and colleges use technology to make education cheaper, as opposed to just having bigger classes, which is only going to water down education, the price becomes simply unaffordable, regardless of subsidies.

Rushworth M. Kidder ➤ **on Ethics**

RUSHWORTH M. KIDDER *is an award-winning former columnist for* The Christian Science Monitor *and author of* Moral Courage, Shared Values for a Troubled World: Conversations with Men
and Women of Conscience, *and* How Good People Make Tough
Choices. *He's also a frequent writer and lecturer on ethics. We were
interested in Kidder's perspective on ethics in the future because he
has so clearly stated the values he feels we embrace now—the five
values of compassion, fairness, honesty, respect, and responsibility
that seem to form core beliefs across the spectrum. We were curious
if he felt those values were changing, and if not, how we need to
preserve them in a world of rapidly changing technology and innovation.*

I don't believe our five core values will change. As you look back
through the histories of religions and social cultures, you find that
people generally move toward a culture that says honesty matters,
responsibility matters, and respect matters—and that wherever you
deviate from that, you run off the rails into dictatorship and tyranny
and ecclesiastical despotism. I don't really think there's much possibility that we are going to deviate from those values, or find some
new undiscovered sixth or seventh value that nobody knew about.
What will change is how we apply these values, and why, and their
importance and significance. We're at a turning point at which ethics
will become more significant to the success and sustainability of our
world than it has ever been in the past.

· · ·

What we are seeing as we move into the early twenty-first century is an unprecedented capacity for technology to leverage ethics—to make our ethical decisions far more important. That's largely because one single unethical decision can now produce world-class calamity and mayhem in ways never seen in the past. Up through the twentieth century, of course, it was always possible for dictators, despots, and people of great accumulated wealth to lay waste to great parts of the world. You could devastate entire cultures and commit genocide, but it took a huge amount of effort organized by powerful people over a period of time, either malevolently or ignorantly.

Now, however, you can see globally catastrophic results produced by kids, almost instantly and without much thought. Take the Love Bug virus, which was launched by a couple of young people in the Philippines and created an estimated 5.5 billion dollars' worth of global damage. Or take the Chernobyl nuclear meltdown, caused by a couple of plant operators performing what the Soviets called an unauthorized experiment and creating the largest industrial accident in the history of the world. Neither of these things could have happened in the nineteenth century, or even in the early years of the twentieth century. The reason is obvious: the technology wasn't there.

This technological leveraging plays out in much slower, subtler, less noticeable ways. One of the most serious legacies of the industrial revolution in the early nineteenth century was economic dislocation—the ways entire communities changed, the ways the entire sense of what it meant to be a member of a culture or a religious group altered irreversibly. Such changes brought with them enormous ethical transformations to families, to governments, and to the ethics of the entire cultures.

The same thing played out on a slower scale, perhaps, in the early twentieth century, in the presence of two huge technologies: the automobile and the television. The very architecture around which we design our communities is now shaped by the fact that we have automobiles. Drive through communities that were formed a hundred years ago, and you see a lot of front porches facing the road. Drive through new communities, and you see a lot of back decks— because nobody wants to sit and look at a lot of cars. In a way, we've traded public neighborliness for personal privacy, and we're simply not as involved in community as we were when we sat on the front porch and people walked past and stopped and chatted.

What's ahead? We're now in a position in which the coming technologies are capable of producing astonishing transformations in our ethical structures. Let me focus on one of them: radio frequency identification tags, or RFID.

◄ RFID ►

RFID was first viewed as a replacement for the barcode on the backs of consumer packaging. No one saw it as more than a simple, innocent upgrade. Plant a little radio frequency chip in every jar of jam, every book sold, every package of Gillette razor blades, and you can track where that product is. It's very helpful for product recall. You know exactly who bought it, when it was bought, and where it was shipped—hugely valuable information as you move products around the country. You no longer have to stop at the gate of the warehouse with your semi-trailer and have somebody unload and check that every box is still there. You simply drive through the gate, and there's a scanner that picks up a signal from every box inside. In the next few years, we'll go grocery shopping, fill our cart with whatever we want, and walk through the door without stopping. The whole thing will be billed to our credit card, at great convenience to us, efficiency to the grocer, and lower cost all around.

Once this starts happening, you can count on one thing happen-

ing: that somewhere, in some computer around the world, a profile about you will slowly be built that shows everything you've ever
bought. We may not think of that as identity theft. But remember
that, if you want to know who someone is, one of the best ways to
find out is to look at what he or she buys. As a result, things will be
known about us that we do not even know about ourselves—about
our choices in everything from magazines and medicines to liquors
and lottery cards.

That opens up wonderful possibilities for helping us in security
measures. Wouldn't you want to have known that a guy named Timo-
thy McVeigh, who was never a farmer, had suddenly bought tons
of fertilizer? What did he want that for? Had Homeland Security
known that, some intelligence analyst might have said, "Watch out,
this guy may be building a bomb." And with that, the Oklahoma City
bombing might never have happened.

But there's a downside. Several years ago, I was at Bentley College, talking to a class of five hundred freshmen. Most of them were
late—because, as they came through the lecture-hall door, each one
had to stop and sign in. I said, "We'll be able to make this easier, you
know. In the next ten years, you're going to have a radio frequency ID
tag as your university identification card. Just keep it in your pocket
as you walk through the door. You won't have to sign up or anything.
Every door in the university is going to have a scanner, so they'll
know exactly where you are at every point. Isn't that a great idea?"

They weren't so sure it was.

"Why not?" I said. "Are you planning to do something nefarious
and dishonest, and you don't want to get caught?"

No, they said, but they were still squirming. Then one student
nailed it.

"Look," he said, "suppose I'm a member of Alcoholics Anonymous,
and every Thursday night I go to room 305 in the basement of the
physics building for a meeting. And every time I walk through that
door somebody knows, and they know that's where the AA meeting
is. I don't want that information out there in any form. I'm trying to
recover from something."

He's right. There are some very good reasons for people to say, "I'm not sure I want to be tracked in that way."

But can't we impose restrictions, and refuse to use the technology in this way? Theoretically, yes. But here's a chilling fact: As a race, we have no history of developing a technology that we then choose not to use. Every technology that we develop will be pushed into uses we've never seen for it. We may think that necessity is the mother of invention, but it's also true that invention is the mother of necessity. If we invent something, we're going to find a need for it. I would suggest that there is only a negligible probability that RFID will never be used in ways that allow us to track the movements of innocent individuals against their wills. The ethical questions raised by that fact are both absolutely staggering and perfectly foreseeable. We don't have to wait until this technology is in place in order to say, "Oh, look, we've created an ethical problem."

What we most need, and what we are coming toward slowly and in peculiar ways, is some capacity for what I've come to call moral futurism: the capacity to look over the horizon and anticipate the ethical issues that will arise, so that when we finally get the technology developed, we've also thought enough about it to figure out how to deal with these dilemmas.

◄ Corporate Ethics ►

Fortunately we're in a situation where the corporate world is very rapidly coming up to speed on ethics. Corporations are at various levels of doing so, and some are better than others. But I doubt there's any serious corporation out there that now sees ethics as utterly irrelevant.

Unfortunately, many corporations still define *ethics* as *compliance*. But the tide is shifting. In the wake of Sarbanes-Oxley, we're beginning to worry that we've overemphasized regulation at the expense of genuine, values-based ethics. The Federal Sentencing Guidelines, for example, now make it clear that ethics matters, not just compliance.

Compliance, after all, is simply obedience to the law. Ethics, by contrast, is a proactive sense of integrity. It's the sense that says, "Look, values matter. We have an obligation as an organization to pay attention to ethics and to create organizations that are honest, responsible, and fair."

Fifteen or twenty years ago, if you wanted to talk about ethics within organizations, you went to hospitals because they were the only ones that had something called an ethics committee. These days, there are many more venues for ethics, and the public receptivity is greater than in the past. While that's a good sign, we need to couple that trend with some of the standards of future studies.

Future studies is not trying to predict the future. It's trying to lay out alternative scenarios: if A then B, and if A minus then B minus, to the point that you can begin to track future possibilities with some degree of success.

I think we need that discipline as we've needed it never before, because technology is developing at an exponential rate. My concern is not that we have an unethical culture. We don't. We have a culture that in many respects is more ethically attuned than it has ever been. It may surprise people to hear me say that, but the fact is that I don't know anybody in this country who owns slaves. I don't know any women who can't vote. We've made enormous ethical progress over the last few centuries. The point is that the development of our ethics is rising at a very much lower rate than the development of our technologies, and the gap is getting bigger and bigger as we move forward.

◀ Creating an Ethical Person ▶

Corporations are paying attention to ethics in part because they're encountering potential employees who are in a kind of a zone of ethical neutrality. They're neither ethical nor unethical, and they'll blow either way depending on whether it is in their advantage to cheat or not.

Good cultures of any sort—corporate, government, educational— can take people who come in, work with them, and gradually make them better. Good families do that, too. If there's one more thing that will take people out of morally neutral positions and rocket them to a much clearer sense of ethics, it is the act of childbearing and parenting. It's astonishing how people who have lived in ethical ambivalence suddenly change once they have children for whom they must be responsible.

◀ **Genetic Technology** ▶

In the field of genetic technology—designer babies and so forth—we do have a leg up, because of a brilliant insight that took place with the creation of the human genome project. The developers of that program basically required that five percent of the funding for the human genome project be spent on the so-called ELSI questions— the "ethical, legal, and social implications." Their point: Don't wait until you've done the laboratory research and then suddenly say, "Oh, my goodness, look at the social and moral collapse we're encouraging." Think about ethics ahead of time.

The downside of that requirement is that the bulk of that money, by far, has been spent on legal and social implications rather than on the ethical, even though the ethical implications are enormous. By ethical, I'm clearly talking here about those things that lie beyond the regulatory and legal side. Should MDs get involved in the genetic forecasting or genetic design work for building a better future generation? Or should the individual MD say, "I'm sorry, that's just not something I'm going to do, given all we know can go wrong with genetic engineering"? Genetic engineering, after all, can be as simple as the Chinese government's one-child-per-family policy, which, in ways they never foresaw, has led to an enormous genocide of female babies. Is that really what you wanted to do? Did you want to create a culture where, whenever a girl baby is born, it gets left out in the cold to freeze? That is what has happened, because they didn't think about the ethical issues when they tinkered with the social and political policy.

As for the human genome issues, there may be all kinds of ways that society can benefit. But the truth is that regulation always lies behind ethics. It will always take five or six years for the latest invention to be regulated if need be. And in the interim, the only regulation is self-regulation.

◀ Worst-Case Scenario ▶

The apocalypse, as T. S. Eliot said, arrives not with a bang but a whimper. Is it possible that the coming whimper will be a return to communism without our even knowing it?

The fatal flaw of Soviet communism could have been foreseen in 1917, had we been sharp enough to spot it. It was the fact that in order for communism to work, everything had to be legislated. Once the moral basis of a culture was stripped away and replaced with a mere legal basis—which is what the Soviets did—absolutely everything had to be regulated from the top. How are you going to enforce that? The only way the Soviets could enforce it was by hiring between 15 and 30 percent of their workforce to spy on the rest. Those people did nothing productive whatsoever, created nothing of value. They were simply spies and enforcers.

A while ago I asked a corporate CEO, "What would happen to your company if you took 15 percent of your people out of productive work and just made them spy on all the others?" He was horrified. "That's the whole profit margin, right there," he said.

But that's where the global economy will go if it can't self-regulate through ethics. The only alternative is to impose regulation through law. If we turn away from ethical regulation through law, and the government has to bear the cost of regulation through law, then we'll have to have increasing numbers of people doing nothing productive. We're already seeing that trend in some of the worst excesses of Sarbanes-Oxley regulations. That's the far more damaging downside than any great public eruption, or even another Chernobyl or 9/11, because it gradually freezes up every kind of economic activity.

◀ **Energy** ▶

What is the collective ethics of the United States at this point, when 5 percent of the global population is absorbing 25 percent of the world's resources? That number has been floating around for some years, and people have been staring at it and saying, "Isn't that interesting." It's becoming more than interesting right now, as Brazil, Russia, India, and China begin to need so much of those resources because they have so many people. How do we sort through these ethical issues?

We've basically sold the consumer public on the need for automobiles. In Western culture, at least in the United States, we've created a structure whereby one cannot negotiate the world without a car. There are very few places, such as New York City, where cars are so expensive to keep that people have found ways around them. What do you do about the ethics of gasoline at ten dollars a gallon? A friend of mine is working on hydrogen fuel cells, and he and a few folks in that culture are saying it's a chicken-and-egg question. You have to have hydrogen stations before you can have hydrogen-powered cars, but who's going to want to set up hydrogen fuel stations before there are enough cars to make it work?

In other words, a restructuring of the ethics of energy probably isn't going to happen simply by private enterprise. There will have to be some governmental impulse to do it. But the predictions suggest that the public may not be willing to put pressure on government for these kinds of changes until gasoline gets to ten dollars per gallon. In the meantime, when prices approach that figure, rising to eight-fifty and nine dollars a gallon, what are we going to do with the people in rural Maine, for example, where the ability to get to work depends on driving? There's a lot of rural poverty in Maine. What are we going to do in that situation, as the economy of those people simply collapses, and we get pretty close to a state of anarchy because there's no way for people to move around? They've been as cut off from their jobs just as effectively as if they'd been locked out by their employers and told they couldn't work there anymore. How are we going to negotiate that? How are we going to think about the ethical responsibilities that we have to one another when government can't get itself ramped up to act?

One of the great dangers is that we've allowed ourselves to fall into a kind of bipolar world of the socialist left and the reactionary right. And we haven't put a lot of sophistication in the political thinking between those poles. As a result, the people most deeply committed to social justice are the ones most apt to say, "Look, this is absolutely unfair, these people in rural Maine have been handed a very difficult situation." Those who say that are almost instinctively programmed to imagine that government is the answer, and that if government doesn't do something, nothing will happen. On the other side are a whole lot of people who tend to distrust government but are deeply interested in personal responsibility. They don't necessarily respond to the plight of those people who are struggling, because they feel it's up to those people themselves to remedy their situation by finding other work, or moving, or figuring out a new transportation system.

I think we're going to have to come to an entirely new blending of those two sides of the political picture. The answer has got to be individual ethics, because government ethics will never catch up fast enough.

The bottom line is that we've come to a turning point in terms of petroleum. I don't think prices are going to recede at this point. I think there's simply too much demand out there. So we either can do all kinds of wrenching things to produce more petroleum, or begin seriously to shift our gears and find other sources of energy. I'm told that we're already at a point here in Maine where, if you live more than about a third or half a mile off the electricity grid, it's worth your while not ever to connect—just go solar, use wind power, build your own energy-sufficient house. The technology is finally at a point where you can do that.

There may come a time where energy self-sufficiency becomes a hugely popular goal. That will have all kinds of benefits to society. But what will that cost in terms of the dislocation, as we unhook ourselves from a gridded world and retreat into a culture of isolated individuals? The metaphor is a profound one. I think the question of energy is going to create huge changes in technology and in sociology, and when that happens, the ethical issues always get ramped up.

◀ **The Promise of Youth** ▶

I'm convinced that we're looking at possibly the best generation of young people that we've seen for a number of decades, maybe a century. I don't think the change is going to come from the top. I think the change is going to be brought on by the young people themselves, almost despite the teachers who have been educated in the construct of ethical relativism. Many of them have outgrown it, many of them see through it, but there are still many in my generation who are knee-jerk relativists. I get the sense that this younger generation is taking us in very different directions. There's been some interesting work done on this generation, the millennial generation, by people like Neil Howe. It's interesting to look at questions asked over time, so you can look at the profiles of answers to the same question. One of them was a statement made to eighteen-year-olds: *I have no difficulty getting along with my family and with my parents, yes or no?* As I recall, in 1974, 45 percent of the young people said yes. By 2003, 85 percent said yes. This is absolutely astonishing.

Neil and his colleague William Strauss have been asked to consult with the U.S. Marine Corps on recruiting. What they've found is that a lot of tough old gunnery sergeants, working in recruiting offices in strip malls around the United States, have always been accustomed to having burly, tattooed eighteen-year-olds show up and enlist. Now, apparently, these same kids are coming in, but with their mothers. The recruiting officers are saying, "What's *she* doing here?" And the prospective marine says, "She's my mom. I like my mom. I mean, this is a family decision, isn't it?"

There are questions of responsibility, and respect, compassion— all those things are deeply embedded in a sense of working in the community, and not just thinking it's all about you. The next generation is saying, "Yes, it's about me, but it's also about something else."

◀ **Ethical Leaders** ▶

I think we're hunting for those paragons of excellence out there, and we have a few that we revere. Every once in a while the Gandhis, the Vacláv Havels, and the Nelson Mandelas appear in the political realm. I've been doing some interviews with the CEOs of highly ethical corporations and asking, "Why did this happen? How do you create and maintain an ethical corporation? What makes the difference?"

A lot of these companies are not the big ones. Instead, they've been down in the trenches doing wonderfully ethical work for decades. I think those companies have special appeal to the next generation of employees looking for leaders of integrity. They're looking behind the current roster of sports figures and media stars and pop idols. I think things are shifting. That's a risky statement, and I could be proved wrong. It may just be my inherent optimism.

Young people aren't saying they don't want to be successful; but they're saying they want to be successful within the parameters of doing good things. That, I think, is the real change.

◀ **What We Need to Do** ▶

What's needed can be translated into two words: *moral courage*. We can talk abstractly about these five values, and we can develop very sophisticated methodologies for making good decisions when our values come into conflict. But if in the end we know what action we need to take, and we don't have the guts to go there, it's no different from having no values at all and making no decisions. It produces a society that is indistinguishable from a society that is morally neutral and unwilling to think ethically. That's the penalty we've paid for a culture of unanimity, a culture of uniformity. We've paid a price in individual courageous decision-making, and we've got to get back to that willingness on the part of our elected officials, on the part of our government, and especially on the part of individuals in their own homes to be willing to take those kinds of courageous stands, whether it's in raising a teenager or in taking a public stand about something that's not right.

Greg Lynn ➤ **on Architecture**

With degrees in philosophy and architecture, **GREG LYNN** *has been involved in combining the realities of design and construction with the speculative, theoretical, and experimental potential of writing and teaching. He is the author of six books, which combine his interests in contemporary and popular culture with the rigors of architectural theory and history. Lynn teaches at both UCLA and the Eidgenössische Technische Hochschule in Zurich, Switzerland. He is also principal of LA-based Greg Lynn Form, which has been at the cutting edge of computer-aided design in the field of architecture. Most architects make paper drawings, then use design software to visualize those with walk-through images, but Lynn's practice is paperless. He starts with computers, using programs developed for auto designers and film animators, and finds new shapes, twists, and forms. The shapes he favors: isomorphic polysurfaces, or blobs. We were interested in what Lynn had to say about how buildings will be designed tomorrow.*

Architecture is interesting to people in a way that it hasn't been in a long time. There is tourism designed to go see buildings, which there always was, but it's a bigger deal now. People follow architecture and the personalities of architects and designers in a way that many have never done before. More than half of that interest is focused on mid-century modernism. When this is burned out, which will be very soon, it will be really exciting if people refocus on contemporary architecture. My guess is that in the next ten years, this is going to happen. Modern architecture is going to become a historic phenomenon for collectors, and once this happens, things will open up for contemporary architecture.

◀ **Creative Collaboration** ▶

Contemporary architecture is already strong; I think it just needs to get more into the public consciousness. Another thing that is happening now is that architects are collaborating with and in conversation with automobile designers, fashion designers, graphic designers, painters, sculptors, and so on. For a long time that connection was broken, and I think it is probably reconnecting due to shared use of and expertise with technology. These kinds of links are getting stronger and stronger. And I would predict that in the next decade, those are going to continue to get more intense and creative in terms of exchanges. I know in terms of my own experience, I started working with painters and sculptors, because I did a little show of three-dimensional prototypes, and instantly I became the mechanic for the art world. Painters and sculptors would call me up and ask, If I want to do a thing in this size, in this material, can you tell me how to do it? And what was a purely functional relationship actually turned into a creative one.

The same thing has happened in the other direction, with aerodynamic and automobile design—I will call friends in those fields. When I wanted to do a titanium tea set, I went to some aerospace people I knew, and all of a sudden we started doing stuff together with recently declassified, very high technology. So it goes in both directions. I think the architects are reaching into higher tech and more engineering-related fields. Motion picture people are calling all the time asking the same questions that you're asking me now. When Spielberg and Alex McDowell did *Minority Report*, they went out and interviewed five or ten architects. They wanted to know about design as well as technical things, like how to create computer-driven CNC-manufactured, vacuum-formed wall panels with three-dimensional relief. I think that's going to get more and more intense, because we're all using the same software, so there's not a big distinction between a piece of aerospace software, architectural software, or

Hollywood movie software. It's all the same platform. And places like LA, London, and a few others have all those industries right next to each other. That's been happening for the last ten years, and I think it will happen more and more.

◀ Technology and Computer-Based Innovation ▶

Automobile design is ten years ahead of architecture in terms of when it integrated the computer, and it is ten years behind architecture in terms of aesthetics. The funny thing is that it was the architects who started all of the technical stuff. In the seventies, architects were doing all the visual interfaces and using computers for modeling. They figured out how to use computer software for simple, repetitious drafting tasks, but they never figured out how to use it to sketch. Meanwhile, architecture became a hot, provocative design field. The car designers are looking at and being inspired by architecture right and left, but so far there isn't much dialogue. The automobile designers and the aerospace designers figured out how to use digital technology as both an engineering and an artistic medium.

Now the architects are taking some of that stuff back. I was an early adopter of software in the design process. I'm on that first wave, and I'm probably the oldest person around who, from the very first sketch, does everything on the computer. I do frequently use a pen and paper, but my sketches look like computer drawings. Basically, I am creating in software—that's my medium. It's not like I do a model and then have a room full of people digitize it, which is what most designers and architects still do.

But in ten years, not only my generation, but the generation of my students and ex-employees and other people like me are going to be using the computer in a more integrated way. I think that has really concrete aesthetic consequences. Architecture's been about planes and lines, because we build all of our models out of cardboard sheets. But when you can build a model of something you can document and engineer, you can then figure out how to build it on a bigger scale. If you can't build a model of it, it's pretty hopeless. I think everybody realizes that, and architects now are becoming very skilled with a lot of digital media.

I think there are two, maybe three components. One is that I'm using mathematics that is based more on things like calculus to describe buildings—and that is managed digitally—whereas before if I drew a volume I would want it at its biggest scale. I would want it to be 120 feet long rather than 122.7 feet long, only because I would need to subdivide it. With a computer, it becomes truly an aesthetic decision. It's more a question of proportion and aesthetics, of how repetitious elements relate to each other.

Architecture is a funny industry, because the steel industry, the metal facade industry, the glass industry, are all globally industrialized, and they have been industrialized for a long time. So if you want to make every piece of the building different in steel, there's zero premium on it other than doing the fabrication drawings. You can have everything the same, or you can have everything different; it doesn't really matter, because you're dealing with a factory that is set up to do a different job every day. When you get into things like masonry, formed concrete, framing, and local labor-intensive things like that, it's very regional craft- and union-based, and that's less forgiving. It's a real mix of those two kinds of technologies. It will still involve a lot of hand-built, craft-based stuff, but this is mixed with the highly industrialized approach to fabrication. It's very global, too. You can buy your steel from Canada one year and Germany the next and Japan the next. Buildings are composed of a weird combination of globalization and local construction mixed all together.

The bottom line, though, is that the construction industry is way, way, way ahead of the design industry. This is the big irony that everybody is just now figuring out. For a long time, people would say those are some crazy shapes, but aren't you going to have to build it out of some new kind of plastic? Frank Gehry has made a great contribution by discovering that because some things are so industrialized, there's no big expense at all in building these amazing forms. The critical task, really, is how to document them. How do you give instructions to the people on the site? How do you give instructions to the fabricators? And more and more architects are getting savvy about this.

I think the software companies especially are really keen on that and understand what kind of impact it could have. So in the next ten years, I think the big thing is that everyone is going to understand that architecture is not utopian designers waiting for new materials, but it's in fact an industrialized industry with all this potential that hasn't been tapped yet. As architects gain the design skills, they will tap more of this potential.

◄ **Robotics** ►

The big expense turns out to be the real estate these robotic machines occupy, and where to put all the study models. We have had a large CNC router for six years, and now we also have a robotic laser cutter and an ABS plastic rapid-prototyping machine, so all of our model building is accelerated. If we used to build one or two models during the duration of a project's design and documentation, we'll now build ten or twenty.

It's a totally different model of work, but the craftsmanship that used to go into model building has gone into preparing the design for those tools, and what that does is close the gap even more in terms of construction. For example, one thing that's kind of a signature style of mine is intricately tooled textures. This is just because when we got the cutting robot, I realized that you needed to take a three-dimensional surface and translate it into the path of a tool. It's as if you have to draw a continuous line that describes a complex curved shape. This translation from a shape to a cutting path happens automatically, with translation software, if you want it to. You can take your shape and drop it in a piece of software, and it will make a tool path. We started playing around and said, Why don't we make this tool path part of the design problem and figure out a new way of getting a textured matte finish on things like corduroy? By taking advantage of this tool, we not only save time, but we have a new creative expression. It opens up a whole new territory for expression and decoration.

It's kind of like the turn of the century when everybody started to use cast-iron and steel. The first phase was, Well, let's figure out what styles go along with these new manufacturing processes. I think that for the next decade or longer, you're going to see architects and designers playing around with these tools like artists. We're talking about wall panels, not components of an airplane. The airplane designers are calling and asking us about design anyway, so the engineering and the design are related, not separate problems. You can make a wall into a perforated screen; you can give it texture; you can introduce color; you can put images on it. There are a lot of things that an architect will see that aren't necessarily implicit in the tool, but it is lying there latent, waiting for a designer to tap into.

So I think you'll see a lot of bizarre and experimental stylistic things going on as more architects start to use these robots. It's happening already. A lot of these firms are doing some very fresh but also decorative things by using these cutting tools. Jacques Herzog, Rem Koolhaas, Ross Lovegrove, even the designers and architects who were married to minimal modernism ten years ago are going technological and florid.

Every couple of weeks I get hit with some new amazing tool, and there's all this amazing stuff out there. I'd like to see the price come down for the things that exist, and I'd like to see the people who are doing the R&D get their stuff on the market. Both of these things are just a question of time.

◀ **The Future Classics** ▶

Primarily, because architecture is so public, the thing that I really want is for the reception of the work to change a little bit, because right now everybody sees computer-based work in a kind of sci-fi, shocking way. Wolf Prix's is great, because it's unfamiliar, beautiful, mature, and exotic. But I wouldn't say it's the norm. I don't think exemplary projects like this will ever be the norm, but they should be today's classics. I think in the next ten years, you will start to see some things produced that are classics the same way that the Eames house is a classic. These will capture the moment and the technology and the genius of a designer and put these together to make something that's really a classic baseline for contemporary design. I think that in the next ten years, this will happen.

The architectural scene is so international. Where it is happening doesn't necessarily have to be where it is getting built. Part of the reason I moved to LA was that I just got a sense that things were happening here, and I think in fact that's the case. A number of architects that really don't have any proclivity toward digital technology at all found themselves the leaders in it just because they happen to be here where a lot of it was being used for other reasons, such as in the movie and aerospace industries. I always think about where there's a good place to hook into, and it's always the places that have those fields—a good pop culture scene, a good high-tech–aerospace or car-design scene, some good industrial designers and architects. That scene is only ever going to be a few places. But I would guess that's where you'll find people producing whatever the next classic is going to be.

◀ **Finding Inspiration** ▶

When I think about what people are going to like in architecture, I also try to think about what they like in industrial design. What do they like in fashion? What do they like in art? Then the question is how to get architecture to those levels. There are always great architects, but to get architecture to a place where it has something to say to industrial design, and fashion and everything else creative, is where architecture really gets good. There are a couple of recent exhibitions, such as Mood River Exhibition in Columbus, worth looking at. Sometimes it's the International Biennale of architecture. Then there are the magazines, where you see people trying to put all these design fields together. Those are the places I try to send people. For example, I like to read *Tokion* to see what the architects, automobile designers, and fashion designers are saying to one another. These magazines and exhibitions are all pretty ephemeral, and only people passionate about design hear about them before they're gone. You know it's magazines and exhibitions and conversations between friends and acquaintances that matter.

Judith Martin, aka Miss Manners
➤ on Etiquette

JUDITH MARTIN'S *Miss Manners newspaper column—carried in more than 200 newspapers in the United States and abroad—has chronicled the continuous rise and fall of American manners since 1978. Readers send Miss Manners not only their table and party questions, but those involving the more complicated aspects of life—romance, work, family relationships, child-rearing, death—as well as philosophical and moral dilemmas. Mrs. Martin writes an additional Miss Manners column for the Microsoft Network. In addition to her most recent books,* No Vulgar Hotel: The Desire and Pursuit of Venice *and* Miss Manners' Guide to Excruciatingly Correct Behavior *(Freshly Updated),* Mrs. Martin has written ten other Miss Manners books and two novels. We were interested in Mrs. Martin's thoughts about the future, because in an age of rapidly accelerated lifestyles and technology, personal interaction seems less of a priority, and the gentility that was once mainstream seems to have been replaced by many with a desire for efficiency at all costs.*

Manners tend to be cyclical. When they get so complicated as to be burdensome, as, for example, in Victorian England, France before the revolution, and recent Japan, there is a reaction against them. "Why can't we just be natural?" people ask. Gradually they disregard the etiquette rules they find most irksome and begin behaving as their feelings of the moment dictate. They become heady with freedom. It seems as if a wonderful new era has dawned. But soon they start noticing that life is becoming increasingly abrasive. Still claiming the right to push others aside when they are in a hurry, they are furious at being pushed aside. Enjoying the spontaneity of not having to commit themselves to plans involving others, they howl about the imposition when others fail to keep appointments with them and answer their invitations. So they find themselves interested in making others behave—not as those people judge best, which does not take others' feelings into account, but according to some generally agreed-upon rules. Etiquette returns. Eventually it gets over-complicated, and the cycle begins again.

We are now in the midst of reacting to the derision of etiquette in mid-twentieth century America. When I began my column in the late 1970s, the very word *etiquette* had fallen out of use, except to make fun of previous generations who were thought to be so inhibited that they were incapable of knowing, much less acting upon, their own feelings. Now everyone is talking about etiquette—which is far from saying that everyone is practicing it. There is still the vain hope of retaining one's freedom while putting restrictions on others. The natural passing of etiquette from one generation to another (although the particulars are ever-changing to meet changing conditions) was broken, and professionals now teach it remedially. Yet those who deplore the state of manners forget about the monumental advances over the last decade or two—the extension of courtesy and dignity to huge groups of people who had long been denied this basic human respect and were routinely insulted and ridiculed with impunity.

It is of course my hope that people will finally reach a sensible middle ground, realizing that if they want to live in peaceful and possibly pleasant communities, they must give up just enough freedom to avoid antagonizing others and must teach their children to do the same. Given the history of manners, however, I am not so foolhardy as to predict this.

Trish McEvoy ➤ **on the Beauty Industry**

TRISH MCEVOY'S *modern approach to beauty has inspired a loyal and devoted following, from stay-at-home moms to Hollywood's leading ladies. She founded her business as a New York City makeup artist and skin care specialist in the mid-seventies. McEvoy identified a void in the beauty market—women had all the makeup they needed to look their best, but not the proper tools for easy, effortless application. Taking matters into her own hands, McEvoy created a line of professional-quality brushes, and her trademark half-face technique removed the fear of makeup application for her clients, who could achieve the same beautiful makeup results at home as they did at the cosmetic counter. Simple designs, clean modern shapes, and functionality give McEvoy's creative beauty solutions enduring quality—from skin care, cosmetics, and fragrance to her signature makeup planner and cosmetic palettes. We were interested in what McEvoy had to say about the beauty industry, because she's always been an innovator for her emphasis on real beauty for real women. Her philosophy seems especially compatible in a world where appearance is everything, but no one has time to attend to it.*

The future in beauty is customization when the industry offers makeup and skincare options directed at individual consumers. As time increasingly becomes more valuable to the beauty industry's consumers, they'll want products to be multifunctional. Skin care and skin care ingredients will continue to evolve as new research is done. We'll continue to see treatments that were once only offered in doctors' offices being targeted for effective home use.

When new products are developed, it is usually in building-block steps. By enhancing the performance of products we are currently using, new products will be developed on the knowledge that we have gained through research and customer feedback. Antiaging, preventative, and correcting products will continue to be areas of development. Skin care will no longer be an exclusive category of treatment but one that is woven into the choices of color. Multifunctional time-savers will become more popular. I feel strongly that multipurpose products will impact the future, for example, the mixing of skin care with color. The focus of the future will be a move toward products geared to prevent, enhance, and rejuvenate.

◀ Professional and Consumer Education ▶

Professionals will continue to invest in training and education. Their knowledge needs to evolve and be current so that they will be able to customize products more according to the clients' individual needs. There will be more of a focus on educating consumers and listening to their need for change. The importance of shared information to enable consumers to shop in any environment, from a department store, a beauty boutique, or on the Internet, will become more of a necessity.

Listening to our customers is everything. Staff will be armed with the information to answer all our customers' questions. The future offers the convenience of an online shopping experience, supplementing the precious connection with clients.

◀ The Evolution of the Beauty Concept ▶

Beauty will be about the individual and her community of friends and less about what a celebrity is wearing. It will be more about individual needs and concerns. Our ideas about beauty will be shared with other women who have mutual concerns. Women who love makeup will come together through the Internet, in-store experiences, and makeup parties. Beauty will be more lifestyle driven and less about what is dictated. Beauty will not be one look for everyone, but rather specific and customized for the individual. Men will become aware of how color can benefit them. They'll feel comfortable by learning the corrective benefits of makeup and skin care.

The shopping environment will be cozier, so women feel as comfortable as possible. We'll see big chains looking to make smaller, more boutiquelike versions of themselves to create more intimacy. These types of environments will create a bond between the brand and the consumer, ultimately making customers more satisfied because all their needs are being met. Consumers will be more educated, demanding products that suit their lifestyles.

◄ The Human Factor ►

My wish is that we will continue to be more aware of the human factor in our world, understanding that doing the right thing for the greater good of others is most important. We'll need to continue to protect the earth's resources as they become more and more precious; refilling anything and everything will become more popular out of pure necessity. And finally, my personal wish continues to be the achievement of global harmony.

Elon Musk ➤ on Space Exploration

ELON MUSK, *who grew up in South Africa, is the chairman and CEO of Space Exploration Technologies (SpaceX), considered the leading private space exploration company. Musk is developing a family of rockets intended to reduce the cost and increase the reliability of access to space, ultimately by a factor of ten. When we sat down with Musk, we were impressed with his passion for work and his conviction that travel to Mars, and perhaps other planets, will be both possible and imperative in the future. Musk's goal for SpaceX is that humanity become a multiplanet species. Musk also cofounded PayPal, the world's leading electronic payment system, which was sold for $1.5 billion, and he cofounded Zip2 Corporation, which sold to Compaq for $307 million. Musk is only in his thirties, and with that kind of track record, we're convinced that he'll succeed with his space transporation venture. It could mean that we might be living on Mars in the not-so-distant future.*

The long-term ambition of SpaceX is to play an important role in enabling humanity to become a multiplanet species.

I'm hoping we're able to put the first people in orbit within the next five years. Before the next NASA vehicle is ready, I think there will be a period when we're providing the only American manned access to space, moreover, providing that service to NASA at a cost that is at least a factor of ten less than the space shuttle.

Within ten years, I hope that SpaceX will have sent someone beyond Earth orbit, perhaps at least a loop around the moon. Conceivably, we'll even be ready to launch someone to the surface of the moon, or in a wildly optimistic scenario, to the surface of Mars.

•   •   •

◀ Why Private Companies Matter ▶

In the case of NASA historically, success was putting people on the moon at the cost of probably several billion dollars per person. There's no way to establish a self-sustaining civilization if you spend that kind of money per person. You need to create a significant population base to become self-sustaining, and you can't spend trillions doing so.

It is common knowledge that the private sector is far better than the government at doing things cost effectively. Just as we don't expect the government to be the primary operator of passenger aircraft or cars, we shouldn't expect that the government will be the primary operator of rockets and spacecraft in the future.

◀ The Founding People of Mars ▶

No rocket has ever been built in which all the stages can be reused. This issue of reusability is really the issue—imagine if you had to buy a new car every time you drove, or a new airplane every time you flew. The cost would be enormous and out of reach for almost anyone. We would still be riding horses and traveling by ship. So reusability of rocketry is critical, and I think SpaceX is on track to build the world's first reusable rocket, which will be a massive and world-changing breakthrough, if successful.

The cost of this is really fundamental to our ability to colonize space. NASA expects to pay two or three billion dollars per person to put astronauts back on the moon, and at least twice that to get someone close to Mars. However, at five billion dollars per person to get to Mars, we will never, ever become a multiplanet species. If we can do so privately for fifty million dollars a person, or eventually a thousand times less, for five million a person, you can really just do it. You could probably even do it just on a private basis, for people who want to be the founders of a new human civilization on Mars, just as people in Europe spent their life savings on a one-way boat ride to America. Governments may also want to send representatives from their country, and at five million dollars a person, they could easily afford to do that.

The average home price in many parts of California is over a million dollars today, and likely to climb over the long term. If we can get to a point where the cost of moving to Mars approaches the median house price in California, then I think there will be enough people who will buy into that to go. It will be a very productive crew that goes to Mars, very industrious, so the place will build up like gangbusters.

Of course, on Mars you can't waltz around without protection. You would need to live in a contained environment, but that's not necessarily a terrible thing. Frankly, most people live in a contained environment on Earth for 90 percent of their waking and sleeping hours. I mean, there are very few brief moments between the door of my house and the car, and the door of my car and the office when I am actually outside and not contained. Actually, from a pragmatic standpoint, life will not be substantially different. It won't feel different on a day-to-day basis.

But I think societal development would be quite different. Whenever a new society forms far away from the old society, you tend to reevaluate the way things should be done. That's what happened after people moved from Europe to the United States. It really wasn't so far away, but you needed an ocean separating the old culture and sociopolitical environment in order to have something new develop, as it did here.

I think it would be somewhat similar to that on Mars. I think there will be a substantial increase of the cultural wealth and breadth of civilization by having a multiplanet species. It will also set us firmly on a technical path toward spanning multiple solar systems.

◀ **Citizens of the World** ▶

I think it will be a longer period of time before we have pleasure vacations to Mars. It's quite a chore, because you have to wait for planetary alignment. The bottom line is that it's a two-year family trip. A trip to the Orient in the nineteenth century was a two-year experience, so it's not fundamentally different than that. We will find ways to make that trip time shorter—less than a year, I think, based on developing technologies. That's a plausible thing in the future.

If a self-sustained civilization is growing on another planet, it will change the psyche in a number of ways. It may prompt people to be less parochial. People may stop thinking of only themselves. If you look back in time, people were very clannish, they were only inter-ested in their little clan. And so, perhaps by inhabiting more planets, people will stop thinking of themselves so much as part of individual countries as they think of themselves as part of planet Earth.

I might go to Mars someday. I'd like to see my kids grow up first before risking my life going to Mars. Maybe twenty years from now I'd do it.

Marion Nestle, PhD
➤ on Food and Nutrition

MARION NESTLE, PHD, *is the Paulette Goddard Professor of Nutrition, Food Studies, and Public Health at New York University, in the department she chaired from 1988 through 2003. She is also professor of sociology at New York University. Her degrees include a PhD in molecular biology and an MPH in public health nutrition, both from the University of California, Berkeley. Her research focuses on food and nutrition policy, particularly as they relate to dietary advice and food consumption. She is the author of* Food Politics *(2002, revised edition 2007),* Safe Food *(2003), and* What to Eat *(2006). We were interested in what Nestle had to say, because her recommendations and expertise seem particularly important at a time when obesity, poverty, and bioterrorism threaten our well-being more than ever.*

I **think three trends will develop** in food and nutrition in the future. First, there will be concerns about the increasing prevalence of obesity, its consequences for the health of children and adults, and its costs—personal and financial—to individuals and to society. Second, we will see an increasing public interest in the ways in which food production influences health, the environment, and the quality of life for animals as well as people. And third, there will be mounting public pressure on food companies and the government to provide safer and greener food.

Dietary guidelines ought to address obesity in a much more direct way—by advising that we eat less of the calorie-dense foods, meaning junk food and drinks. Because eating less is bad for business, corporate political pressures on government will continue to influence dietary guidelines that are expressed as euphemisms.

Food companies will increasingly use health to sell their products. Since virtually all foods have some nutritional benefit, companies will use research on single nutritional factors to justify health claims for their products. Unless current trends are reversed, which seems highly unlikely, practically all supermarket foods will bear health claims in the near future.

◀ **Competitive Eating** ▶

The greatest economic driver at present is the cheap cost of basic food commodities, which in turn leads to overproduction of food and further reduction in prices. The United States already has 3,900 kilocalories of food available for every man, woman, and child in the country—roughly twice the average need for the population. This makes the food industry exceptionally competitive; companies have to sell food products in an environment that is already way overabundant. Because companies must report quarterly growth to Wall Street, they are forced to make decisions based on short-term targets. In this sense, business imperatives trump health considerations.

Companies will influence nutrition and health in the same way they always have—through billions of dollars in advertising and marketing, of course, but also by making a product that will sell, regardless of quality; by lobbying to make sure that no government agency or nutritionist ever says anything negative about their products; by attacking critics; by arguing that food choices are solely a matter of personal responsibility; and by targeting children, minorities, and foreign populations as new areas of promotion.

Supermarkets are caught between high-end stores like Whole Foods, which target an upscale, health-conscious consumer, and low-end stores like Wal-Mart, which focus on keeping prices as low as possible. Although health-conscious consumers constitute a small fraction of supermarket shoppers, the "healthy and green" fraction is increasing rapidly, and every large food company is paying close attention. Supermarket chains are already going into organics in a big way, and this trend is certain to continue if the organic standards remain credible.

As industrial companies, both conventional and organic, pressure the USDA to weaken their organic standards, consumers will want foods produced "beyond organic." They will ask for local foods that are produced sustainably, and they'll reject foods shipped long distances. Rising costs of oil are likely to accelerate this trend.

◀ Technology and Biotechnology ▶

Technology will enable food companies to make products reduced in fat, trans fat, saturated fat, salt, and sugars, and with added vitamins, minerals, antioxidants, fiber, cholesterol-lowering substances, or other components with druglike properties. These products, classified as functional foods or nutraceuticals, will be developed specifically to take advantage of relaxed standards for health claims on food package labels.

Biotechnology will continue to encounter public resistance, unless companies use it to make products that consumers need or want. It will most likely be used to produce functional foods and nutraceuticals. Its most useful effects so far have been in pharmaceuticals, such as recombinant insulin.

Biotechnology's greatest potential is in developing plants that can flourish under climate conditions typical of developing countries, but there is little financial advantage to companies to conduct such research. Its negative effects are best seen in largely unnecessary products, such as recombinant bovine growth hormone, or in environmental contamination of organic crops.

◀ **Prescription for the Future** ▶

The increasing centralization and consolidation of food production increases the vulnerability of the food supply to contamination by unsafe microbes and toxins whenever companies cut corners on safety procedures. The Government Accountability Office has argued for years for a single food safety agency to coordinate federal safety issues. This is a good idea, one worth working toward.

I am heartened to see so much public interest in production methods that protect the environment and the health of farm workers and animals, as well as consumers. May this trend continue!

My advice always is to eat less, move more, eat fruits and vegetables, and don't eat too much junk food. I'd like consumers to vote with their forks for seasonal; locally grown; organic (and beyond organic), sustainably produced foods.

Consumers and professionals can prepare for the future by working as hard as they can to achieve a food system that places the highest possible priority on nutrition, health, and environmental protection.

John Passacantando ➤ **on the Environment**

A onetime conservative, **JOHN PASSACANTANDO** *holds degrees in economics from Wake Forest and New York Universities and served as executive director of the Florence and John Schumann Foundation, doling out grants for campaign finance reform work and environmental issues. He then founded Ozone Action, an anti-global warming group, before moving to Greenpeace in 2000. In April 2001, he led a group of about a dozen activists, who locked themselves inside the main entrance of the Environmental Protection Agency, leading to his arrest. The action came less than a week after other Greenpeace activists scaled a water tower in Crawford, Texas, during President George W. Bush's visit. We were interested in John's thoughts, because at this time of global warming and rapidly developing technology, it seems obvious and important to focus that technology on protecting our environment.*

We're becoming aware that the calamity of global warming is upon us. Big pieces of the giant ecological systems are coming apart, and we'll likely experience similar amazing, awesome pieces coming apart in the ocean systems as well.

And this will be from global warming, from overfishing, from lots of things. We'll then see the emerging challenge for us as a society and as individuals. We had an adolescent approach to our world, despite all the warnings. That's classic teenage behavior; God knows this is the way I was when I was a teenager. Denial of the obvious. Believing you're immortal. It can't happen to us. And now it is on us, and it will over the next several years be on us with a vengeance. Katrina and Rita, these superstorms, were really just the omens of what's coming.

That's a very scary realization. When you first get that information, that's when you make a key decision about what kind of human being you're going to be on this planet, because there is a part of you that's going to want to just say screw it, I can't do anything about this. This is too big for me. This is somebody else's problem. So you go from denial and then very quickly to despair. But there's a moment in there when you say, wait a second, I have an obligation and my society has an obligation to deal with this, with as much grace and courage as we can. We have to make a determination about how we'll respond. Ultimately, what we are like as human beings, and then collectively as a society, is determined by how we respond to that.

◀ **How We Respond** ▶

There are lots of precedents, because it's not the first time society has been hit with a huge challenge. This one is pretty amazing, but take World War II. Hitler is marching across Europe, and there are people throughout the United States in denial. They don't want to believe that stuff about the Jews and the ovens and the trainloads of people. You think it must be propaganda; you don't want to believe the stories, but you're reading it in the papers. You simply don't want it to be true. You don't want your kids to go. You don't want your life to change. You don't want these things to happen, and then when it's upon you, there are other people who just say, Look, the Germans are too strong to stop—just take German lessons.

But you ultimately had the magnificent response from many societies, especially America, which said, We'll fight this. We are going to reorient our entire economy. Women are going to work in factories; every able-bodied boy is getting shipped over to Europe or to Asia, and they are going to fight to their deaths if they must, and we are going to stop this menace. We are going to make a new world.

That's a great mythology. That's a mythological and beautiful response, despite the fact that we didn't fix it. There are estimates of 20 to 30 million people who died, so it's not as though we got there in time. It's not like slavery was ended just in the nick of time—there was 500 years of carnage. But still, as a society we were able to find the courage in various individuals, and then ultimately as a society, to engage in a way that had grace.

I can't make a prediction. I can say I'm hopeful. And I refuse to be pessimistic. We see we've got this enormous and horrific challenge of what we have done to this planet, and what we are doing every day. Our industrial system is just growing. The Chinese economy is growing. The Indian system is growing. But at the same time, we're having this awakening. We're starting to get it. It has taken about thirty years. I've been working on global warming for fifteen years. I've been struggling to tell the kinds of stories that are mainstream now.

The media have finally grabbed it: the cover of *Time,* back-to-back *60 Minutes* pieces, leading ABC, NBC, and even Fox news pieces. The president says we're addicted to oil. I mean, he's still running the oil industry's agenda, but he admitted we are addicted to oil. We have to credit him for how hard it is for him to do that. It was the world's opening statement at Oilman's Anonymous. Here's a man whose every campaign has been paid for by the oil industry, whose whole trust-funder livelihood has been funded with oil money, and he said, we are addicted to oil. Well, he is doing that because he sees he is in trouble, and he sees the numbers. What he did was hard. Of course, we needed him to do it seven years ago, but for God's sake he did it. And so there's a chance. And that chance is what is so cool.

◀ **Technology** ▶

To me, technology is nothing more than an extension of ourselves. Technology leverages us as human beings, so if our behaviors and our intent are bad, technology makes them 10 times worse. If our intent and behavior are good, then we have environmental technologies that are cleaning things up, making things more efficient, enabling people to do videoconferencing. Technology is simply a reflection of us, the way a hammer makes somebody's arm able to hit something harder. It's just a lever.

When good intent is there, we'll get environmental changes. Hybrid cars are the tip of the iceberg of what can be produced by that intent. But if there is ill intent, technology can leverage horrible acts. Our weapons technology can enable this country to kill lots of Arabs for their oil. The Internet is, of course, the greatest example. You can get lifesaving medical advice on it, and al-Qaeda can organize terrorist strikes on it. It can be one extreme or the other. Just like an AOL account.

◀ Politics and Policy ▶

There's a good chance that Americans are not going to elect another extremist president. I don't want to be partisan about it, because Greenpeace pressures everybody; in fact, we never endorse candidates. But Bush was an extremist, even by Republican standards, and my sense is that the next president will be a moderate. Whether Democrat or Republican, it doesn't really matter to me. And he or she will be favorably disposed to lead in some modest way on stopping global warming. The important thing may be the opportunity of what it could mean in terms of jobs for the next generation, who will be building superefficient homes and factories and appliances.

And if that gets drilled down to the level of congressional districts, then we'll have an opportunity for a moderate next president to turn to Congress and say, My God, this is not a political issue—we have got to lead the world on this. So the House won't be led by what we use to call flat-earthers; it will be led by people who want to responsibly engage and deal with global warming and put the country on a track where we just use renewable green energy. To work it will have to be Democrats and Republicans.

I think that the Democrats will start to lose their grip on the environment as an issue. It will be at least in part stripped from them, because they have taken it for granted. They don't like to talk about it much when running, because they're afraid of alienating people, but the environmentalists have nowhere else to go, so they stay with the Democrats. I think the Republicans will see now that the religious right is moving and starting to engage on global warming. You'll see Republicans begin to make some efforts to grab leadership on this issue. Many Democrats have spoken in platitudes about caring about the environment, yet most are vulnerable to Republicans running with the issue on their own terms: using business solutions and tax breaks and such. We'll end up with both parties working this issue, which is what Americans need, and what the rest of the world needs.

Ultimately, we don't care which party wins. We don't want calamities like Katrina and Rita and severe droughts and severe flooding and the spread of infectious disease and the bleaching of our coral reefs and the melting of our polar icecaps. We don't want to lose the polar bears, and we don't want to lose our neighborhoods. I don't care which party solves it, but we are going to need leadership, not platitudes, from both.

◀ **Genetic Engineering** ▶

Greenpeace has fought hard against the spread of genetically modified crops, the mixing of genes across species, and to a great degree we've lost in the United States. I'm afraid it's simply driving some of the ancient genetic codes out of existence. Some other countries are sort of wavering, but we have a very strong hold in Western Europe.

I'm told that some of the companies are actually more interested in doing very sophisticated gene work within these species, a more sophisticated version of what farmers have always done: picking and nurturing the best seeds. Cross-pollinating plants with slightly different characteristics. And if that ends up working, I think it ends up being a real plus for all of us. Because you're able to find crops that are more resistant to drought or certain pests, but you're not scrambling God's genetic universe. That's the stuff that's just so arrogant. You just know you're set up in the first act of some kind of Greek tragedy. You know in your gut it's wrong. Humans shouldn't be doing this. We've got Godlike power with nuclear weapons and damn if we didn't use them on each other. How long will it be before we abuse our ability to make new species?

If we can have more resistant crops and more crops to combat the extreme poverty in third world countries without rolling the dice on this great mystery that is out there, then that's the best of both worlds.

◀ **Global Warming** ▶

We know the oceans are warmer. We know that global warming is making them warmer, and we know that warmer oceans supercharge storms, and we know we have just seen a fraction of what is to come. We know it is becoming more and more difficult to find the oil, even if we weren't worried about global warming, so is it a hard prediction to say that there are going to be wars over oil? We're in one—the war in Iraq is really an oil war. We know WMD was a big fib. So we are in this oil war, and now we are threatening another oil war with Iran.

What does an oil war mean? It means a daily death toll. It means living in fear. It means rewiring an economy around the military as opposed to making beautiful, super-efficient products, beautiful schools, great instruments, great medical breakthroughs. It's about learning how to kill people more effectively, so that's where our wealth is now going. And of course our next generation's wealth, because we're doing it on debt. Just take that and magnify it, and then if you want an even greater warning, then just read the history books. Read Gibbon's *Decline and Fall,* and see where a mighty empire, the Roman Empire, ends up: in utter disillusion.

Some would say that's such a dark analysis. "This is America. Come on." But this is where we're headed if we choose not to act.

◀ **A Tenuous Future** ▶

We view ourselves as so secure in this country, especially if you're middle class and up (not if you're poor; that's a completely different perspective). There are good jobs to be had. You go to the grocery store and the shelves are full. But realize just how vulnerable these systems are. If you shut off the oil, the whole system shuts down. The grocery store shelves are empty in three to four days. At some point there is a difficulty with getting fresh water, because it is being pumped to you. You find this in extended electrical outage. Wow. What happens without that clean water? What if we can't get the groceries? What if I can't get the gas to get to the groceries? Suddenly you think, I don't have any vegetables planted in the ground. And I don't have a well. Suddenly it just closes in on you.

So you go from what you think is the most independent and powerful and empowered society to one that is absolutely as dependent as an infant. The way we run this economy is amazingly dependent on all these pieces working on a fairly exquisite level, and oil is a huge piece of that. There's been an acknowledgment of this going back to Truman, and then reiterated under Nixon, Ford, and Carter, but it really does come down to the convenience of oil, and the influence of the big oil companies sealed the deal. That's why we are where we are.

These guys are doing lip service now, saying, hey, the oil companies really manipulated us, they manipulated the prices. I mean, just in the last energy bill they gave the oil companies tax credit. Right now they're embarrassed. They say we want it back. And that was simply a giant quid pro quo for campaign donations. The oil companies give these guys crumbs, Democrats and Republicans alike. Two-thirds to Republicans and about one-third to Democrats. Crumbs. And then they get these amazing benefits.

But there is a beautiful spotlight on them right now. A beautiful spotlight. But the spotlight should be on all of us. We individuals are part of a society that is emerging from its wild adolescence. And now we see the costs. Shall we just take the wild ride straight to the end, stealing oil from around the world and throwing our ecological systems into mayhem, *or* do we choose to live like good tenants of this place? Do we choose adulthood? It's pretty damn exciting to live in a time when that question is being asked and it's unclear what the answer is going to be. This is a wild ride, and engaging this challenge is one of the most graceful things we can do as humans.

Robert Rey, MD ➤ **on Plastic Surgery**

DR. ROBERT REY *specializes in minimal scar plastic surgery. He completed a plastic surgery fellowship at Harvard Medical School's Beth Israel Deaconess Hospital, focusing on breast and cosmetic surgery. In pursuit of his craft, Dr. Rey has also attended other top American educational institutions, including UCLA School of Medicine, Tufts University School of Medicine, and Harvard University. Dr. Rey has conducted academic research in both cosmetic and reconstructive plastic surgery and has been published in some of the world's most prestigious medical and plastic surgery journals. He has expertise in the latest techniques in liposculpture, breast lift, breast reduction, brow lift, endoscopic face lift, nose improvement surgery, ear reshaping, laser eyelid rejuvenation surgery, neck lift, male surgery, tummy tightening, lip enhancement, Botox, and collagen. Having watched Dr. Rey on the television show, Dr. 90210, which looks at the real-life world of plastic surgery in Beverly Hills, the most competitive place for plastic surgeons in the country, we were interested in learning Dr. Rey's thoughts on both the technology and the social implications of plastic surgery.*

What types of plastic surgery procedures will become most popular? How will plastic surgery change in the next ten years? That's very simple. We are moving toward less and less cutting. Cutting is so Neanderthal, if you think about it. I'll give you an example. In the old days when we did just a brow lift, we would split your skull open, and we peeled the skin across your face. Today, we do brow lifts through a little tiny hole. We slip in a camera. It's all done this way.

We used to do the faces of older people with a big slit, an overpulled face. Today we have a procedure called Featherlift, which is a permanent lift done with just sutures placed throughout your face, done through little tiny, tiny incisions. It's a great, great face-lift, or we can do it endoscopically as well. Just a little camera placed in here, and we lift your whole face through two little slits here.

Today, we do the same thing with Botox, which is just a little injection. Now, even better, you can have a face-lift done with a thing called thermage. It's radio frequency waves from a little machine that basically heats up the collagen, heightens the molecules in your face, and gives you a wonderful face-lift that lasts ten years and tightens up very nicely at a fraction of the cost. There's a laser now that will tighten up your face, tighten up your eyes at a third of the price. A little redness, and you are all set. It's like a face-lift. So, we're moving towards lasers, radio waves, less cutting, cameras—and that's just the face.

We used to get a piece of cadaver skin, make two slits on the back of the lip, and put in the cadaver skin. Imagine kissing someone with a piece of cadaver skin in their lips to poof them up. Today, over-the-counter lip plumpers, such as Lip Fusion, have become so good. Chemically they inject collagen molecules into your lip with over-the-counter lip plumpers.

So we are going the way of less and less cutting. You used to enlarge breasts using a big huge cut on your nipple or a big cut in your armpit. These cuts were horrendous. We used to make holes in the chest that were barbaric. But we're trying to make them prettier, not uglier. Today, I do the breasts through the belly button, and you can't find a scar. And the day will come—it's almost like *Star Wars*—that we'll just wave something next to your face, press a few buttons, and a change will be made.

◀ **Cost and Ethics** ▶

Plastic surgery will become increasingly affordable. It already is today, compared to thirty or forty years ago, when plastic surgery was just for the affluent. Now plastic surgery is available to everyone, which of course brings ethical issues as well, because if it is that affordable and it is that available, will people abuse it?

Recently they did the first facial transplant. Wonderful. I had several patients when I was back in training who tried to commit suicide using a shotgun to the face, but shotguns are too long, and at the last minute they'll tilt back. A shotgun will blow off their face, but it won't kill them, so these people were literally missing the entire face—the forehead, eyes, maxilla, nose, mouth, everything. So a face transplant is a life-changing operation.

On the other end of the spectrum, surgery can be abused, and that's the ethical dilemma we're going to run into more and more in plastic surgery. We're going to get to the point where we can make basically the perfect human being, and what are the ethical implications? That day is not too far away.

What type of plastic surgery procedure will be the most popular? Liposuction is at the top of the list. I think we're ultimately going to conquer the battle of the bulge through better foods, so I don't think liposuction will continue to be at the top of the list. First, it's going to be breast augmentation, and second, I'd say breast-lifts, and then face-lifts. I think breasts will be top of the list, because we're going to continually make a generation of women who are breastless and buttless. Breasts and butts are made out of fat tissue, and the more women exercise and diet, the more androgynous they'll look.

Will the purpose of the plastic surgery change? Plastic surgery is going to become more about building people's self-confidence than about reconnecting fingers and transplanting facial burns.

◄ **The Market for Plastic Surgery** ►

At this point, 94 percent of our patients are women, but that's not true for every country. I just came back from South America, and about 13 percent of patients there are men. I think men are going to get more and more comfortable with the metrosexual. They're recognizing that there is a lot of competition in the world, and not only from a business point of view.

The world economy is becoming globalized. In my lifetime, I have seen an exponential increase in the competition—exponential. Today to get my daughter into preschool is more competitive than it was for me to go to Harvard some twenty years ago. I think competition is going to push people more and more into getting plastic surgery.

So many executives are coming in and saying, Dr. Rey, I really don't want to be here, but I'm a mid-level executive, and I've got this young guy just chomping at my heels, and you've got to look good. You're kidding yourself to say that a pretty Coke bottle doesn't sell Coke better than an ugly bottle. The same thing is true for humans, obviously, and that pressure is going to continue. The American Society of Plastic Surgery shows that about 55 percent of Americans accept plastic surgery now. About ten years ago, it was just 15 percent.

It's going to get to the point where people say, I went to the gym, I went to a night class, and tomorrow I'm seeing my plastic surgeon. It's going to be all in the same breath.

◀ The Plastic Surgery Scene ▶

We're moving away from the hospital. I rarely set foot in a hospital anymore. I do it all in surgical centers. We're moving away from the institutional aspects of medicine, and we're moving to a friendlier, more homelike environment. Will we end up at the home? There are laws that I don't foresee changing. There are some very stiff penalties for doing that kind of thing at home. I mean, for me to go down to Pepperdine and see patients at the Pavilion Dorm—that's going to be a trick to pull off.

My patients are mostly eighteen- and nineteen-year-old women. Last year, the most popular gift to graduating high school seniors was plastic surgery. Even for us plastic surgeons, that's a very troubling statistic. One thing that really jumps out is that they are having breast augmentations at seventeen. Breasts are not fully developed at seventeen, so in the process of putting in this implant you're damaging the growth center of the breast. One thing I find is that people in their forties, thirties, and twenties are still a little hesitant about plastic surgery. But the young set, the teens, it's become a normal part of life—go to high school, go to college, get my breasts augmented, get married, have my tummy tucked.

◀ **The Beauty Ideal** ▶

Will our concept of beauty change in the future? I think history has shown conclusively that there is a universal beauty that transcends culture and transcends time, but short of that the specifics of beauty are constantly changing through history. Will a youthful appearance continue to be prized? Yes, unfortunately. As we become more and more secularized, as we lose some of those moral values that have historically been associated with religion, we'll become more carnal, we'll become more obsessed with the body, and there will be more and more worshipers of youth. That's not a positive tendency, because it's self-destructive, but that's where I think we'll be going in the short term.

Are there trends that I don't like? Yes. We can change anything now. We can make everyone look perfect. We're going to make everyone look the same. Already, as you walk through stores here in Beverly Hills, there is the look that you can see at the Playboy Mansion. It's like they all come out of the same mold. There is an ethnocentrism built into the standards of plastic surgery. Basically I was taught to make people look like a Western standard. You see all the top models from all over the world—they all look like American girls. We're going to create a homogeneity. It's very disturbing. That's a problem. We are not really bending backward to allow for racial differences. We give lip service to it, but really we're making everyone look like a perfect Scandinavian person.

My take on life is that we are here to improve ourselves. We just have eighty years to make the best of ourselves, so we improve our brains through education; we improve our spirits through religion; we go to the gym. The Scriptures address the body as a temple, and so we keep it tidy and we take care of it. I think to some degree it is okay that we make ourselves as good as we can be in every possible way. However, everything in the extreme is damaging. We have an obsession with looks and creating the perfect children and cloning. We're going to get to the point where we can change everything and anything. The fact is that ethics will always lag behind science. Theoretically, ethics should be ahead of science.

◀ Media and Message ▶

Will television shows continue to broadcast plastic surgery procedures? I don't think so. I think they have two or three years left. Then we're going to move toward wellness, and I think that's where the future is going to head. Will plastic surgery become a much better or a more common procedure? No question. It will become much more widespread.

What I see increasingly is that people are so secularized. They don't realize that a lot of beauty is internal. In the future it would be very nice to have a plastic surgeon right next to a priest. To have Zen right next to collagen. I think we are ignoring where real beauty comes from. We've lost the human touch in medicine. I think we're going to get the human touch back, because we can cure just by embracing somebody. I think we are going to get back to the warm doctor of the bygone years.

I tell patients, Listen, we've got to clean out the inside. Beauty starts from the inside. I know it sounds very corny, very PC, but it's not really. I have patients who walk in here who are perfect—nose perfect, breast perfect, butt perfect, belly perfect, perfect girls—and

I look at them and they're ugly. There is some darkness that revolves around them that's repugnant.

I think we're going to rediscover that religion not only feeds your soul, but it makes you beautiful. Going down to the soup kitchen at Christmastime makes you beautiful. When nobody is looking, helping that mom with two kids at the grocery store—that makes you beautiful. Go home and give your mom a call—that makes you beautiful. So I encourage patients to do the things that make you beautiful inside, and then I can take it from there. When you're beautiful on the inside, I can make your outside beautiful; but if you are dark on the inside, I can't make you beautiful, no matter what I do. I think we might see a marriage of Zen and plastic surgery, a marriage of religion and wellness. I think making beauty start on the inside is going to come back to medicine.

Steve Ross ➤ on Yoga

STEVE ROSS *has been a yoga instructor for more than twenty years. Called Yogi to the Stars by* In Style, *he is the host of* Inhale, *an early morning yoga program on the Oxygen network. He own and teaches at Maha Yoga in Los Angeles and also holds retreats worldwide. He has appeared in numerous publications, including the* New York Times *and* Vanity Fair. *Ross focuses on finding joy in the mind, body, and yoga practice, as described in his book,* Happy Yoga. *Since the rapid pace of modern life and exponentially growing technology seem to portend very little time for reflection or the search for joy in the future, we wanted to hear Ross's thoughts on transcending it all, and on how one of America's favorite forms of exercise is going to grow and change.*

Yoga will change dramatically in that people will delve into the deeper aspects, such as meditation, so that it is no longer about the superficial cultivation of the body and the body image that is so dominant and pervasive today. Asana practice has become extremely commercial and superficial. I'm not invalidating that, it's just where some people are. For me, asana is merely a foundational practice and the real juice, the real power in yoga is what comes after that foundation.

It really boils down to a shift in consciousness. What characteristics that will assume is hard to predict, but I think ultimately there will be more spaciousness in people's minds—less compulsive thinking, less addiction to seriousness, and more celebration. When this happens collectively, this world will be a much better place to live in. I think there's always going to be some tension between the individual and the powers that be. But if one is conscious and independent, it doesn't really matter.

◄ The Search for Joy ►

The created universe expresses itself in polarity. The yoga world, like everything else, reflects that. So, there is rigid yoga and there is fun yoga. Yoga has become like religion in the West, and there are many fundamentalist yoga practitioners who feel that their style is the right way and every other way is wrong. Then there's the other group, who feel that yoga is a celebration for the joy and fun of it.

I personally resonate with the latter view. True yoga is about bringing yourself into a state of union with the source of all and everything. This source is described in the yogic texts as absolute love and absolute bliss. Making yourself and others miserable in the name of efficiency or correctness is going in the opposite direction. If one is doing yoga truly correctly, one should become happier in all aspects of their lives. However, in the yoga community that I'm aware of, it's the opposite—people are becoming more obsessive, anal, and insane. I often get criticized by people with that mentality, which means I'm doing the right thing. After all, to be threatened by happiness is extreme dysfunction, don't you think?

Chanting is a way to get people in a celebratory and blissful mood. It opens the heart, and most important for people in the West, it stills the mind. I also do a lot of meditation and teach deeper aspects of yoga to the few people who are genuinely interested.

◄ The Source of Enlightenment ►

It seems to me that the vast majority of all the gurus, yogis, and enlightened beings in the universe come from India. Many people are disenchanted with the Western model of reality and the structures that support it, whether they're religious, political, or social. The climate is ripe for a deeper, more global understanding and awareness to take hold. I think we're seeing this now. Our challenge is to embrace it without allowing it to be diluted and commercialized.

I'm completely against having yoga regulated, because it's opposite of what yoga is about. If you go to India, there are hundreds of different styles of yoga, but when you come to the United States there are six or seven, and they all claim their style is the only true yoga. Some say it doesn't really matter if you bend the knee and push your little toe down, and another one says it matters completely—it's all really subjective. People have to use their own intuition and discover what works for themselves.

◀ Yogic Hybrids ▶

Some people who come to my class stay only for the first half, the most physically strenuous portion, and leave right afterward. There's nothing wrong with that, it's merely what some people want. The more mature someone is in their outlook, the more they pursue the deeper, more fulfilling aspects of yoga. For example, the body is a perishing object, and everyone is aware of this, at least unconsciously. When this fact surfaces to the conscious mind, you may ask yourself why you're putting so much time and attention into something that's not going to last. In other words, what is truly significant is consciousness, which transcends the body and mind. This rarely gets addressed in most yoga classes. After all, this is the United States, and most people are very new to this—they're babies, so they just don't know any different.

◀ Knowing Where You Are Right Now ▶

I have no clear idea where we'll be ten years from now, because so much depends on the collective consciousness of humanity. As far as changing yourself, the most important thing is to first be clear about where you are right now in this moment. You must accept yourself exactly the way you are physically, emotionally, mentally in this very moment. That is, you're sitting in a chair, you're breathing a certain way, you have a certain feeling or sensation in your heart or stomach, and so on. The more you can bring your attention to this moment, the more alive you become. With practice, this becomes a more constant experience, and change happens naturally, without effort. It requires only observation and attention. The reason people suffer is that they indulge their non-attention and act out their conditioned behaviors and therefore overlook what they truly are. It's possible to release past conditioning. You get to a point where you're so conscious that when a pattern or conditioning arises it doesn't catch you unawares, it no longer bothers you—it becomes merely phenomena rising and falling in your awareness. That's real freedom. Only if you're free on the inside is there any possibility of external freedom.

The Rosso Twins ➤ on Tween Culture

Thirteen-year-old twins from England, BECKY AND MILLY ROSSO *now live in Los Angeles, where their acting careers are taking off. After being discovered in the audience during a taping of the Disney Channel's number one hit show,* The Suite Life of Zach & Cody, *Becky and Milly Rosso were given a nine-episode arc on the series as the characters Jessica and Janice. In addition to being featured in numerous tween and teen magazines, the Rosso twins will star in a new major motion picture with MGM entitled* Legally Blondes— *the third film in the* Legally Blonde *series. The girls are also recording a debut album with Hollywood Records. As the Rosso Twins are just now beginning to create their careers and their stamp on the entertainment industry, we thought they could tell us about how their generation will have an impact on entertainment and trends.*

Tweens today are growing up in a very fast moving and high tech world. Today's tween acts more like a teen of five years ago, and we expect that ten years from now, tweens will be even more sophisticated and savvy. Part of this maturity comes from the media, part from society, and a great part from the Internet. The Internet plays a large role in tweens' everyday lives, since it's used for homework, games, instant messaging, fan sites, competitions, movie and concert reservations, and even online shopping. In a lot of homes, tweens know more about computers than their parents. They can navigate Web sites and software better than adults, and they often make choices for the family when it comes to what to buy online.

More and more homes are getting computers as the prices go down, and even the kids who don't yet have computers at home can learn computer skills at school. Tweens are exposed to adult subjects at a much younger age than in past generations, as viewing regulations and dress codes have been relaxed. We expect that as kids have more exposure to computers at younger ages, they'll be even more precocious. They'll be connected to a global universe of trends, friends, issues—what is happening in the world. By the time they're tweens, they'll be ready to be heard.

◀ With Maturity Comes Responsibility ▶

Tweens today are more aware of personal safety concerns, as well as poverty, pollution, global warming, and health. In ten years, we think that tweens will be even more educated on global issues. We expect they will feel part of a worldwide culture that works together to help less fortunate people. From IMing to texting to Club Penguin, we're much more connected to other tweens and are used to feeling like part of a group. We hope this attitude will allow us to be more unified and work together to solve problems in the future.

We also expect that tweens will seek out positive role models. Some celebrities are already raising awareness of global issues, and off camera, they work hard to help to improve the lives of millions of people. They also encourage people to recycle and use the world's resources wisely, and although many other celebrities seem to be able to get away with some bad behavior, tweens are increasingly sharp and want their role models to be responsible. They'll respond to someone who shows that it's cool to try hard at school and be conscientious. These role models will make it uncool to be disrespectful and unkind and behave badly. They can show by example that if we live healthy lives, work hard, and help other people, we can find happiness. Some actors are already choosing movie roles based on inspirational stories, so that entertainment is combined with a good message. We hope they carry on doing this as young people especially are very influenced by these movies. Of course, these role models may come from any field, as long as they have a good message and unite to influence people to be good citizens.

◄ Entertainment Goes Higher Tech ►

We've grown up with technology such as computers, TiVo, and Leap Frog, and we expect entertainment to become even more interactive. Sometimes adults give tweens a bum rap and say that they have short attention spans, but we think that's unfair. In reality, it's the entertainment itself that is getting shorter and more stimulating. We think tweens will want to watch more interactive shows, especially on their computers. Tweens would love to be given choices about the plots, even choose the endings. It would be cool to be able to choose the outfits that the actors wear! We think that in the future, tweens will still want to watch a lot of comedies, where they see other tweens in situations that they can identify with.

◄ A Global Tween World ►

Finally we feel, and hope, that tweens will spread a sense of unity in the future. Shows will be broadcast around the world at the same time, so tweens in every country can watch the same shows, even the same commercials. This will connect tweens to one another and make them all feel part of the same community. This will also extend to music, fashion, and everything in popular culture. Tweens in South America will have the same posters in their rooms, listen to the same music, and wear the same jeans and sneakers as their peers in Australia, China, and Europe. We already have relatives in England, Argentina, and Australia who listen to the same music as us here in California. Our cousins in England have similar hairstyles and use similar expressions, because so much is already global.

We think that even though fashions and trends change with every generation, and there are big advancements in technology and communications, at the end of the day, tweens around the world, always have and always will want the same things. They want to be loved, they want to belong, and they want to be happy. We are very excited about what the future holds, and we can't wait to see what's next!

John Rother　➤　**on Aging**

JOHN ROTHER *is the group executive officer for policy and strategy for the AARP. He is responsible for the federal and state public policies of the association, for international initiatives, and for formulating AARP's overall strategic direction. He is an authority on Medicare, managed care, long-term care, Social Security, pensions, and the challenges facing the boomer generation. He is frequently quoted in the news and regularly presents at conferences and congressional briefings. John Rother is an honors graduate of Oberlin College and the University of Pennsylvania Law School. We were interested in what Rother had to say, because as the Boomers enter their sixties it seems the idea of being elderly is changing. With people living and working longer and the price of health care escalating, we were curious about what Rother thought the biggest changes might be.*

When you're talking about older people because of the boomers and the changes they'll bring, both in numbers and in terms of preferences and desires and purchasing power the damages will be profound. In ten years, we'll have a third to half of that big demographic boomer wave retiring at least from their principal job, so that's really going to be the big impact in the shorter term.

I think the two big drivers of change in the next ten years are demographics and then technology, and they intersect most clearly in health care. Demographic difference is not just the numbers, but that people are going to be better educated than in previous generations of older people. They'll have more purchasing power and higher expectations. They'll want more control over their own lives, more choices, and more options. Being more educated is associated with wanting to express yourself more as an individual, and that translates into greater social tolerance. All these things are going to happen in the next ten years as a result of this big generation getting older. Then you put into place the unpredictable: the revolution in technology that not only computers but cell phones and Blackberrys and everything they have already brought.

◄ **Health Care** ►

I think the big news in technology going forward is likely to be related to health care. We're already seeing some real advances in imaging and the ability to diagnose at an earlier stage, and so that could be very important in terms of keeping people healthy and finding cancer, for example, much earlier. That's good news. Another technology area is pharmaceuticals. It's much harder to predict, but let's suppose in ten years we have a way to either cure or control Alzheimer's. That would make a huge difference in all kinds of ways, not the least of which is our whole idea of what it means to get older in society—if you take away dementia, the public image of aging would be completely different from what it is today. These are unknowns, but a cure could really have a profound impact if it has to do with one of the big diseases.

The cost of prescription medication is a huge issue, and it's as much a political issue as anything else. Other countries have addressed that and have negotiated with manufacturers to get lower prices. We are the only country that hasn't done that. It's a big issue and likely to get bigger, yet it's very hard to predict whether we'll take action, because it depends on whom we elect.

Another area where technology has potential is in health technology and the electronic medical record—the ability to have anyone who treats you have access to your health information and for you as an individual to have better access to decision-making tools and keep track of your own health status. That has some really big potential for both saving costs and improving care.

The pattern of disease has changed and is changing. It's much less about acute episodes and much more about chronic illness and disability. And if you look at where we're spending the money in health care today, it's more and more on people with those chronic conditions. Diabetics, people who are hypertensive, people who have arthritis. Most people have more than one of those as they get older, and our health care system for older people needs to become a system that can help people better manage and respond to their health. That's not what we have today. Chronic disease management is one of the big challenges for health care, and technology can be part of that, but it's really going to require an overall reengineering of our health care system.

The majority of older people will have access to these new and important applications of technology. The adaptation and use of this kind of technology by people in their fifties is already high and growing fast.

Another demographic fact, though, today and ten years out is the diversity within the population, and in making all these generalizations, it is always important to point out that there will be people who won't be in line, and who aren't going to have money, and who are going to be alone in the world. And that problem is not going away. What we're talking about is the middle class, the majority of people, but there is still going to be a significant minority who are going to be vulnerable and require some attention from us all.

◀ **Long-Term Care** ▶

People are generally fearful about long-term care. What we're going to see is people finding alternatives to a nursing home and having not only a desire to live in their own homes and stay independent, which will be achievable for more and more people, but also a desire to be more in charge of their own lives, even if they do become disabled. Instead of having an agency send people to your home and having to be a passive recipient of care, older people will be more involved and more in charge of seeking out and actually hiring the people they want to care for them, therefore maintaining more control over their lives. Obviously, not everybody is going to be able to do that, but most people are capable of doing it. It just seems so preferable and much more consistent with the values of the boomers than our current system.

It will become more of an accepted practice that instead of a home-care worker coming to your home, you would get a check every month and arrange for whatever care you felt you needed. It would be a very different way of meeting these needs, and one that I think most people would welcome.

◀ End-of-Life Choice ▶

The thing we find that people desire, especially our boomer members, is more control over their own lives. They don't want somebody making these decisions for them. I actually think that is the way it will play out, where whether or not you are subject to very intense care designed to keep you alive at the end of your life will be something that you or your family members have more and more say over. That means some people will choose not to receive all that care, and others might choose to. That is our pluralistic American religious tradition—not trying to impose values on everyone, and respecting the fact that people have different values.

◀ Sixty Is the New Forty ▶

Our idea of old age is already changing. We kid around that sixty is the new forty—people's self-image has changed. I think we're going to see that more and more. People who we used to think of as retirement age see themselves as still having a lot to offer. They still want to be engaged in life, doing things that may not be a full-time career but rather new ways of working, volunteering, traveling, and grandparenting. We're going to see a period of ten to fifteen years after retirement when people are really going to be much more active and engaged in their communities and in the economy than we've seen in previous generations.

I don't think too many people want to work fifty and sixty hours a week until they're seventy-five. They want the opportunity to take on different and perhaps more flexible work, and some of that work will be paid, and some will be unpaid. Today the age at which most people retire is sixty-two. I think that will go up, as much as anything because of health care insurance. For many people, it's going to be very difficult to find health insurance until they're on Medicare at age sixty-five. This will be a big change from current behavior and from the early retirement trends of past generations.

But it is also a change in the economy, so another prediction for ten years out is that we'll be living in a much more do-it-yourself financial environment, where instead of having a pension that you can count on, most people will be trying to live off of their 401K plans or other kinds of personal savings. That is going to be difficult for some, and it's probably going to be an obsession with the boomer generation, because they're going to have to worry about things their parents didn't have to worry about.

One of the things we find is that most people really want a greater sense of community, because it's other people that provide so much of the satisfaction of life. I think we're going to see new waves of people trying to achieve that community. Some of it may actually be physically going back to a dorm-style of living or another geographic community, but a lot of it is going to be electronic and hooking up online with people who have similar interests and outlooks to your own.

◀ Tragedy or Triumph ▶

It would be a national tragedy if we had all these people who have so much to offer, and we didn't have better ways for them to stay engaged and productive in our society. It would also be a national tragedy if health care costs were to run up in an unsustainable way and the response to that, rather than reengineering the system, was to have some kind of arbitrary budget cuts that resulted in people of modest means being unable to afford the health care they need. And it would also be a real loss of the potential of some of this new technology if it's so expensive that only some people could afford it. Then you don't have the social benefit that it could provide.

The biggest thing to be careful about going forward from my perspective is probably health care, because that is where so much money is now, and where opportunities to do better are very great indeed.

The best-case scenario is three-fold. One is that we actually recognize the continuing contributions that the boomer generation can make. In both the private sector and the public sector, we can make opportunities available for people who want to stay engaged and contribute, because we know that people say they want to stay engaged and continue to have flexible work opportunities, and they have trouble finding them. Number two is the potential that comes from improving health and health care. It's not like we are going to see suffering and illness go away, but we could see it delayed substantially for most people, and so that's extra good years that I think are worth a lot.

The third thing is the potential of technology to keep people in touch with one another, to facilitate individual self-expression, to help people get in touch with the services and support that they need. We're really already seeing a lot of potential for technology to improve the quality of life, and I think we'll see a lot more going forward.

Atoosa Rubenstein ➤ **on Teen Culture**

ATOOSA RUBENSTEIN *started Big Momma Productions, Inc., in 2006. Before that, she served as editor-in-chief of* Seventeen *magazine, the premier teen title in the United States, with 13 million readers each month, and as the founding editor of CosmoGIRL!, Hearst Magazines' successful teen spin-off of* Cosmopolitan. *In 1998, Cathleen P. Black, president of Hearst Magazines, decided to create a new teen title and asked Rubenstein to develop a prototype. Within forty-eight hours, she presented a product that was so compelling that Black offered her the job of editor-in-chief on the spot. Rubenstein was only twenty-six years old, making her the youngest teen magazine editor in Hearst's history. Under her editorship, CosmoGIRL! more than doubled its initial rate base of 500,000 in 1999 to 1.25 million in 2003. CosmoGIRL! apparently struck a deep chord with its female teenage audience. Rubenstein has been featured on lists of super-achievers, among them the coveted Crain's New York Business's "40 Under 40" and Folio's "30 Under 30." CosmoGIRL! was named Start-up of the Year by Adweek in 2000 and one of Advertising Age's top five magazines for 2001. We were interested in Rubenstein's thoughts about the future of teen culture, because she so clearly understands how to communicate with teen readers.*

In the future, I see the magazine being the period at the end of a conversation. Ultimately I see it as the product of an online community. Every magazine will have its own tribe based on a psychographic and a thought leader. That community will exist and evolve and grow and communicate on a day-to-day basis. And then once a month, if that's the frequency, a product will be born of it: a magazine. So it's a little bit the reverse of what it is now, which is the magazine acting as the beginning of the conversation.

When I first went to *Seventeen*, I would always tell my boss, What you paid a hundred eighty million dollars for is the word *seventeen*, meaning our rights to use that word digitally. Right off the bat, one of our strategies was to make it mostly reader-generated content. Was the Web site 100 percent set up to get us exactly what we needed? Not quite. So was some of the content we had to seek out. For instance, we had to find guy writers. Any guy articles in *Seventeen* are either from girls themselves or guys themselves. That's a major shift, because for the past sixty some-odd years, *Seventeen* was a set of editors sitting in their high tower telling readers what they needed to know and empowering them with information. But we turned the magazine into a conduit for the readers' conversations. People ask me, "Why did you move your editor's letter to the middle of the book?" I did it because I thought it was too odd for the conversation to *start* with me. I wanted the conversation to start with *them,* through their letters in response to the last issue. And I think that things are only going to go more in this direction: with the Web being the place your tribe meets every day, and the magazine being your community project.

◀ How Thought Leaders Will Make an Impact ▶

I think paper magazines will always exist, because they create a different experience. The question is, how do you make that experience more high impact and relevant? First, by allowing readers to create content themselves, and second, by empowering the magazine editors to be really high impact in what they add to the mix. For me, whether it was with my team at *CosmoGIRL!* or at *Seventeen,* we don't consider ourselves to be "working on a magazine." When I hired people, I always said, If you want to work at a magazine, go somewhere else. This is a *project.* For the most part, magazine jobs have been sort of fun gigs for girls who like to shop and have fun.

But at *Seventeen,* it's really a laboratory. We were always studying on a micro *and* macro level what is impacting our consumer. We were constantly surfing her wave. I think that model is going to have to continue evolving, as these girls become women and need their magazines to be as finely tuned to their ever-changing needs as possible.

The other thing that's really important is not to just commoditize the magazine. It used to be that all editors, and editors-in-chief in particular, had writing or journalism backgrounds and would just sort of gather information. In my opinion, today and especially in the future, editors of magazines and brands are going to have to be thought leaders. It's not just about whether you're well read and a good communicator; it's about having something to communicate, having a point of view, being strong enough to have a tribe. I believe that things have gotten very tribal. I experienced it when I was at *CosmoGIRL!,* and again at *Seventeen.* When we do new brand initiatives, whether they are television shows or books, it's more stuff for our tribe. I think you need to be able to warrant having a tribe—because not everybody can be a tribal leader.

The idea of a thought leader is very important to me. I think that's the future celebrity—people who have something to say. When we did our contest on MTV, Miss Seventeen, that's what it was about. The show did really nicely for teenage girls. It wasn't necessarily *The Osbournes* for MTV, but the girl who ended up winning sold a lot of magazines. And I think that happened not so much because of her show, but because she had something to say. I think these real people with important things to say will rise to be the real celebrities.

I really believe the next Oprah will be born on online video. I don't think she'll come from television. People don't want to sit down and watch an executive producer's idea of what that day's content should be. They want to decide what their entertainment will look like. Oprah is obviously such an important voice to Americans, but not as much to young Americans, and I think that young Americans need an Oprah. They need somebody to inspire them—and to give them advice.

◀ Customizing for Individual Readers ▶

I think customization is going to continue to be really important. Maybe it will be that when you sign up for a magazine, you can specify, for example, "I'm Latina, please include the Quinceañera section," or "I don't want that—I want prom," or "I don't want that—I want sweet sixteen," or "I want beauty that applies to the bronze skin tones and not the others."

When I first came to *Seventeen,* there was the unique opportunity for us to communicate style information in a way that's most relevant to teens today, because the rest of the magazines really weren't focusing on that. Customization was one area we found tremendous success in. For example, every time we talked about color cosmetics, we broke it up into five skin tones, or we'd discuss different hair textures, including relaxed and curly—every possible hair type. And we do the same with fashion, helping our reader fit her exact body type and style. And the more we do that, the more useful the readers are finding our magazine. I do think that, hopefully, in the future, with technology, magazines will be able to create enough content so that girls can customize and get exactly what speaks to them.

The most successful features were the cheapest to put together. Why? Because we weren't paying writers and fancy photographers. We were using real girls' photos, their words. It seems like a big endeavor, but if you have the right digital setup and the right sort of content management system, which is essentially what your site becomes, then I don't think it's that crazy.

◀ Real Content for the Real World ▶

I think one shift we'll see is far more real content. And I don't mean real just in the obvious way—the real life stories and how we used

real girls as models. I mean real dialogues, not the caricatures that
advertisers feel comfortable with—and especially as the online community becomes stronger, because we know there's a lot more flexibility online and more of an appetite for raw and real stuff.

Seventeen had a tremendous controversy a couple of years ago
when it showed pictures of a vagina in a health story. The pictures
weren't there for any lewd reason—it wasn't like a *Cosmo* how-to
story. Yet people were really in an uproar about it. Magazines will
need to reflect more of what kids are actually experiencing. I think
these more explicit conversations will continue, and the content
in magazines will continue to be more surprising than what we're
used to.

The only differences between *Seventeen* and *Cosmopolitan*, the
magazine where I started my career, are three things: First, its readers are still in school. Second, they're still living at home or in some
sort of parentally subsidized situation, like a dorm. Third, they're
having sex, but sex is still "oh, my gosh." It's not like they've been
having sex for years and it's no big deal. Outside of those three
things, *Seventeen* readers are very much the same. So in order to
really communicate with readers in a valid way, I think the voice
and tone of the stories in the future will be the kind that raises
parents' eyebrows. If anybody's parents really knew what they were
doing, they would be horrified. But I think parents are going to *need*
to be prepared to be horrified. It doesn't mean their kids are bad,
it just means there's going to have to be honesty in order to protect
them.

◀ A Pill for Pink Lips, and Fast Food Surgery ▶

I do think this generation, unfortunately, is more comfortable taking
pills. In my opinion, ADD is so highly overdiagnosed, and I think it
will make kids more open to experimenting with pills. For example,
you'll take a pill and your lips will look pinker. And we definitely see

the tolerance for plastic surgery continuing to increase as it becomes safer and cheaper—almost like fast-food surgery.

On the fashion side, we're seeing girls viewing themselves as celebrities, and their proms, Quinceañeras, and homecomings are their red-carpet moments. It's almost as if the red carpet is going from E! to your hometown. Teens are spending a ton of money on themselves, and I think it's partially from growing up seeing their peers as some of the biggest movie stars. Britney Spears started it, then Lindsay Lohan, and the list goes on.

◀ How the Bases Have Changed ▶

Today it's easy for boys to get porn—they all have it—which means that guys expect different things from girls both in terms of sexual performance and appearance. Girls are talking about getting the "bare look" when it comes to waxing. I'm not talking about just a bikini wax, not even a Brazilian, but totally bare, because guys are looking at porn—and so are girls, for that matter.

You have to remember that this is the generation of kids who heard the president of the United States say that oral sex is not sex. It was a huge topic of conversation just as they were coming of age. I see the new third base being anal sex. It used to be oral sex, which, in my opinion, is turning into second base. When parents hear anal sex, they think, Oh, my God, deviant sexual behavior. But you know what? This is what's happening. Do we want to help kids be informed about it, so they are not putting their health at risk? Or do we want to turn a blind eye?

Also, parents are aware that their kids are online, but they're not as aware of the ramifications of their kids' online activities. Most important, it's breeding a false sense of intimacy with virtual strangers. I think that's going to contribute to more sexualized interactions—not necessarily more intercourse, but more highly sexual situations that kids might get themselves in on a day-to-day basis.

◀ **The Mini-Adult Adolescence** ▶

Adults think of adolescence as being a time of bliss, a time to grow up and learn lessons, and they often use the phrase, when I was your age. . . . That is going to have zero relevance to the coming generations of teenagers. These are the kids of 9/11, of Katrina, of the tsunami. I have tremendous fears about technology and its effects on youth, but in a sad and sick twist of fate, all the horrific things they're having to go through are really what's going to create the most powerful leaders.

In the future, adolescents will really feel the weight of the world on their shoulders. They are—and they're going to continue to be—more and more like mini adults. They're going to have to take matters into their own hands. I see this affecting the minimum age at which we do things—the driving age and the drinking age will go down. There will be less and less of an obvious gap between the teenagers and the adults.

I think of my generation (Generation X) as the most apathetic and embarrassing generation ever, completely uninvolved in the world. Think of where that has gotten us with the environment, the state of our government, obesity, health and fitness, and nutrition going by the wayside. I'm hoping the new generation will give birth to activism, specifically environmental activism, political activism, and health activism, by which I mean not just health care but rather activism surrounding nutrition and fitness.

Cathy Schulman ➤ on Film Production

CATHY SCHULMAN *won an Academy Award for Best Picture for the probing race drama* Crash. *Schulman attended Yale, studying playwriting. She moved to Los Angeles to work at Sovereign Pictures, helping with such international productions as* Cinema Paradiso *and* My Left Foot. *Schulman then became co-director of programming at the Sundance Film Festival and was later asked to join the Samuel Goldwyn Co., where she worked in acquisitions and production, becoming involved with* Much Ado About Nothing *and* The Madness of King George. *In 1998, former CAA head Michael Ovitz wooed Schulman to his newly formed Artists Production Group. Schulman continued making films at Bull's Eye Entertainment, maker of low-budget, high-quality features, including* The Illusionist *and* Crash, *a financial hit and an Academy Award winner. We were interested in Schulman's thoughts, because of her breadth of experience. As a producer who has worked both inside the studio system and independently with great success, Schulman offers a unique perspective on where film is going, and who will succeed.*

We are facing a future in which there will be a much greater need for content, and much more access to content over multiple platforms. I see both an opportunity and a challenge in that. The good news is that more content means more need for producers like myself and producers in the next generation coming up behind me, to make film content for distribution by means that we're not even used to being relevant.

Sometimes more means more opportunity to do more, but it also means that the need to distinguish ourselves is going to grow exponentially. We are already seeing a glut in the marketplace not only of movies, meaning too many movies every weekend, but too much content everywhere and too much marketing everywhere, and it's a blur. We're already in a world that requires pictures to self-distinguish, and by that I mean to be worthy and notable in one way or the other.

The thinking in the last decade was that the louder you could be, the more marketing you could do, and the bigger spectacle you could make, the more your film would show up in the marketplace. And I think we're seeing a trend toward that not working, a failure in the notion of blitz media marketing. In turn, we're starting to see that the things that are breaking through are those that are worthy of conversation, that are more didactic, that are perhaps even controversial at times—things that can really stand out.

There was always the theory that one had to make specialized movies that would create word-of-mouth buzz. But the primary reason I think specialized film needed that word-of-mouth was that you couldn't afford to do huge marketing campaigns, so you needed people to talk about the material. And it used to be good enough that, if you made a good movie in the specialized arena, it would get word of mouth, which would mean that more people would go to see it. That's not good enough anymore. It can't just be a good movie to get word of mouth, it actually has to be worthy of discussion, worthy of controversy, worthy of note. *Crash* is the perfect example. This movie was 100 percent rejected by the Hollywood establishment vis-à-vis being financed through normal channels—rejected as a screenplay, rejected as a co-financing possibility, rejected as 20 minutes of footage, rejected as 40 minutes of footage, and rejected as a finished film.

The fear was, Oh my God, it's too out there, too controversial and oddball. And the irony is that the controversy was exactly what made it work. With increased content comes an increased pressure to be interesting.

I also think it's going hand-in-hand with a much more socio-political trend, which is that we're in a world marketplace, and people are very interested in the experiences of other people. I think it's interesting, this whole notion that we are all Internet-connected—it's giving people access to one another's stories and creates sort of an increased curiosity. So not only do you have to stand out, but it's worth it because people are becoming interested through increased access.

◄ Storytelling Specificity ►

It's a quest for specificity.

One could look at what's going on and say the dumber the comedy and the bigger explosions, the better it works. But if you actually analyze the theatrical marketplace and the releases, many, many movies are not working. The reason is that they are bland and boring and not interesting and not specific.

Let's take an old-fashioned romantic comedy: Boy meets girl, boy loses girl, boy thinks of a clever way to get girl back, and runs on the train platform and says, Please, please be mine. That is what we did for years. Audiences don't want that anymore. And why is that? Well, take a look at reality television. People are seeing a lot more of supposed real-life storytelling and messier endings. Communications are so intensive by Internet, by phone, by everything else that this notion of going into a dreamy place, as you would with a novel, isn't the way we live. I think there's going to be more and more interest in real stories and real lives. We are definitely in a time where truth is stranger than fiction. It's hard to come up with stories that are as interesting as what's actually going on with the people living in this world. And as you start to analyze and make stories about the real people, there's actually a politic in that. As you excavate the lives of people and experiences that they're having in all different aspects, you start to get into something that's a bit of a consciousness, rather than being mindless.

◀ **The End of Producing** ▶

Marshall Herskovitz, the current president of the Producers Guild, said recently at the annual producer's meeting that the job of the producer is under attack. I'm extremely fearful that the job of producing will not be able to support itself through the next ten years. There actually may not even be an economic equation that makes being a producer a viable business any longer.

There has been long-term a growing lack of comprehension and insidious disrespect for what a producer does. Since I started doing this twenty years ago, and up until now, I still get the question constantly—What is a producer, anyway?—and I can't figure out how to answer it in a way that breaks through the apparent confusion. Look at the job of the producer: It's your job to find the material, to somehow get it under your control. That's the first place where you need money and overhead, people to troll around looking for the material, the ability to read through material—it's a needle in the haystack kind of a prospect to begin with. And actually securing material is an expensive proposition. No one is paying you so far in this, right? Then once you've done all this work of pulling pieces together and starting to develop a story idea, or taking it into a screenplay, or putting some talent pieces together—all of this putting these things together, and there's still been no kind of transaction. Lots and lots of time, with no financial remuneration.

Then you set up the picture with a financier. Recently in an arbitration, we were in this hearing and the judge said, "Everybody just stop. I need someone to help me with a definition. Can someone just explain to me what it means to set up a movie as a producer? I raise my hand and say, of course, I'll do that, judge, that should be simple. And I started to explain, and the judge basically got as far as understanding that now you've taken all this time and you've put together a piece of material and you've convinced a writer to write a script or an outline, and maybe you've got some talent interested. And then you take all of that quote-unquote capital, and you bring it to a financier, and they give you nothing for it, but you sign over 100 percent of the rights. The judge kept saying, "Where is the transaction? How did the value of what you built get turned into something that you get in return? Like, you make a sock, someone pays you so they can wear it." And I found myself so in a flutter trying to explain this, it became comedy the whole place was laughing, because it is a nonsensical transaction. In the old days, there was something called a development payment, which the studios today have sort of collectively decided not to pay. There's no money in that transaction, either. Now they own everything you've done, and what you've got in return is that they might make the movie on their terms if they choose to at some point.

You've pre-negotiated the fee, but they have the right to renegotiate under the circumstances affecting their ability to finance when they choose to maybe do so. When it's done, it's not under your control—if it's done.

Producers used to be covered by overhead deals, but the studios have figured out that the producers have no way to make their movies without financing, so why not wait around for the product without contributing to the time and effort it takes to prepare the product? Producers are going to have to come to the studios to give it over for free at one point anyway, so the studios think, why pay for the privilege?

So I fear there will be no way for anyone who isn't frankly a millionaire or dilettante or both that will be able to actually carry the torch of a job that's taken years and years throughout the history of American and world cinema to perfect. And the best movies are the best-produced movies. That's just true, it's not because I'm a producer that I say that, it's because it's true. The thing about producing is that it requires this insane synchronicity. I mean, you are the person in charge of this thing from the minute that the lights are turned on in this project to the minute that they are turned off, when it's finally finished its distribution cycle. And that can be many, many years, and during that time sometimes more than a thousand people come into contact with this material, and you're supposed to keep some kind of synchronicity and balance and leadership and diplomacy happening. Then when it's all done and you actually make the movie, you have to hope that you don't get distributed on the weekend that the president decides to have an affair with his intern and all interest goes in another direction. The point is that this is a tricky job and it is under assault. So what do we do about it?

◀ The Grim Financial Reality ▶

I'm extremely hopeful that we'll be able to turn the Producers Guild into a real collective bargaining organization that could win back the earning rights of producers. I think what's important to remember is that when the members of the Producers Guild decided to begin the Truth In Credits campaign, it was done because producers were trying to figure out how to get paid. Because most producers work on low fees, and there is no economic structure for their work, and when the movie finally goes, the credits are being bartered. The producer has to share with managers and actors and directors, and what happens?

Here's an example. Let's say you got a $200,000 fee that you've waited two years worth of work to get. And then the reality of getting the movie made is that you've now had to attach two managers, one actor, and four foreign-tax-shelter people to your producing group. It's not as if the equity financiers say, Oh, let's take the $200,000 fee and multiply it by eight people, and we'll give you guys a million six. They say, Take the $200,000 and we'll divide it by eight. And then for that small pittance, the actual producer, the person who's doing the job, has to sign a service-rendering agreement with said financier saying, I'm all yours for the eight months it takes to make this movie. And then, usually because it's very expensive to shoot in this country, they ship you off to Hungary with the $20,000 pittance you've now earned over the two and a half years you've worked on this movie, and you can't do anything else while you are there.

This is why the Truth In Credits campaign began. The theory was that if we could win back the producing credit, if being a producer meant one thing, and an associate producer meant another, and an executive producer meant another, that we could also get people paid for their job. So my dream for the future is that producers will come together, that the studios will jump on board, that the equity financiers will jump on board, to create some kind of system of protections like the Writers Guild, or the Directors Guild, or the Screen Actors Guild, that will allow producers to be paid for their work so that they can continue the job of making good and self-distinguishing content that can stand the test of time.

◀ Socially Conscious Filmmaking ▶

I have a dream for the future that filmmakers will take on the responsibility of being socially conscious storytellers. It doesn't mean you can't be entertaining, but I think there is really a way to reach people through this medium. There's more of a willingness among audiences to embrace this kind of expression now than ever before. And I think we have to challenge ourselves to make movies with a conscience. That's a hope for the future, and something I'm personally devoted to.

Another producer, Lawrence Bender, and I have become sort of the flag-waving, socially conscious filmmaker/producers, and we were talking about how our lives have become part activist, part filmmaker, and a lot of our other colleagues are doing the same thing. In promoting *Crash,* I spent much time doing grassroots meetings at the NAACP. Producers can be useful tools for the studios to do their grassroots work, because someone needed to be able to talk about the politics of the film. The same thing happened to Lawrence on *An Inconvenient Truth,* and I'm doing a movie right now on the crisis in Sudan.

The producer or the filmmaker as activist is a really interesting goal. Filmmaking started in a political way, and I think we're at a place right now where there is a willingness to move toward that again—not because I want to make boring movies that are educational and didactic, but because we have an opportunity to open up minds, and I think we have a responsibility to open up minds. The world really needs that kind of a future.

I think we have to keep that in mind a little, because we have an opportunity to stop some of the madness. I do believe and dream that we can all join hands and do a little more of it. It doesn't have to be everything we do, but some of it would be good.

Nancy Schulman
➤ **on Children and Early Education**

NANCY SCHULMAN is the Director of the 92nd Street Y Nursery School program in New York City, which is considered one of the best, most substantive early education programs in the nation. She is a renowned teacher and the co-author of Practical Wisdom for Parents, *a parenting book with a cultlike following that offers advice on everything parents need to know about young children. We felt that Schulman's long experience in early education might make her able to accurately assess the impact of technology on kids today compared to those in the past, and to predict how that might change both education and children in the future.*

My hope is that some of the basic premises of how young children learn will still be at the forefront of early education in the future. Children learn by doing. They learn by hands-on experiences, by engaging with materials and ideas, by using language and interacting in a very direct kind of way. Because technology is such an important part of our everyday lives now, I imagine that ten years from now or over the next ten years, it's going to be even more of a factor in people's lives, both in the way we communicate and in the way we interact, and that is going to have a palpable effect on the lives of children.

But my fear is that some of the things that we know to be true about how young children learn will be undermined as computers determine more and more of the way we interact. We've already seen that in the past few years the largest growing market for computer software is in the zero-to-five age range. As a result, children are being exposed more and more to digital technology, which is, in fact, counterintuitive to how children learn. If a child wants to learn about the properties of a material, its shape, or how it works, he does so by playing with it and manipulating it. When it's translated into a two-dimensional experience, he is not using all of the senses, which are necessary to interpret the world. I think that early childhood schools will have to protect the tangible, real-world experiences that enhance learning. As the pace of life continues to move more quickly and children's lives creep into a cycle of over-programming and constant stimulation and activity, we will need to rethink how to simplify children's lives so that they can focus and learn from the kind of direct experiences that affect their lives in an immediate way.

◀ **Stimulation** ▶

Teachers have been concerned recently about the fact that young children, who used to come to school to be stimulated by new ideas and to have new experiences, are now coming to school overstimulated. We are trying to pull back a little bit, to simplify things by not putting too much on their plates and in their lives. We see children at younger and younger ages who are taking foreign language lessons, tennis lessons, or instrument lessons, but who have fewer self-help skills like dressing themselves and going to the bathroom independently—basic things that children need to know to take care of themselves and feel confident in the world. We're spending more time trying to counteract the sort of insanity of a three-year-old who is learning to play soccer, but who doesn't yet know how to wipe his bottom.

At some point, I hope that there will be a backlash and that people will gain a better sense of really what children need to feel competent—a sense of independence and responsibility for themselves. To a certain degree, adults can control how much they want to do or not do in their own lives. You can choose to have more or less activity in the course of a day. But children don't have a choice about that. In fact, they're looking to the adults in their lives to manage their level of activity for them. Contrary to what it seems, most children don't have limitless energy. Their reserve runs down. If they're trying to do a thousand other things, they have less energy to focus in school. You end up seeing children who have been so bombarded all the time that they don't have enough time to play and be creative.

When children are over-scheduled, they have a harder time holding on to basic information, and the cumulative result is more anxiety in the lives of children and their families. At school, we see that children are less capable when it comes to sticking to prolonged activities and dealing with frustration. They have a harder time being inventive, problem-solving, coming up with new ideas and new ways of doing things. When left to their own devices, they are less sure of themselves when they need to take a chance or a risk. Learning is about risk-taking—trying something you've never done before. Children are less likely now to be open to something new or unfamiliar to them, because they have been overly directed and have become too achievement-oriented too soon. When everything is rushed and children's lives become too fast-paced, they don't have enough time to become self-sufficient and self-confident as people.

For better or worse, school has taken on a bigger and bigger role in taking on responsibilities that should be the parents' job. If you're at work or at home tethered to a computer or Blackberry, you have less focus and time for children. When you're used to always multi-tasking, you end up feeling unproductive when you're doing only one thing, like reading a book to a child. Children need undivided attention from adults—not every minute of every day, but often. What has happened is that simple everyday things that have typically been the role of the parent, like teaching a child how to put on her coat or socks and shoes, has become much more the responsibility of the preschool teacher.

◀ The Two Most Important Goals ▶

The government needs to provide greater support for parents in terms of quality childcare and quality early childhood education.

Most of the studies that have been done have shown the importance of strong early education in the lives of children, and many families have turned to private schools for high-quality early childhood education, but the reality is that private programs can be unaffordable. At the same time, they offer many qualitative benefits, so our hope is that within the next ten years, the government will be more supportive of high-quality educational programs for young children and their families by making them more available to people of varying economic means.

Also, early childhood teachers' salaries are quite low in this country. If you want to improve the quality of schools and draw better qualified people to this line of work, it is essential to increase the salaries and benefits and the level of respect of teachers who work in this field.

Those are the two most important goals for the next ten years. Recently, I've interviewed people for teaching positions who had gone into other fields but found them unrewarding. They always wanted to work with children, but never did, and they end up finding their way into a teaching career through the back door. It's wonderful to see this, because they come to teaching as a real choice, even if it means taking a salary cut. But there are great benefits in doing a job where you can make a difference in the life of a family and a child. Teaching young children is a career with incomparable rewards, despite the compensation.

◀ Friendship and Community ▶

I think what children learn from coming to school at a very young age is how to be part of a community, and how to be part of the world outside their homes. It's not just the friendships, but the community of the classroom and the community of the school that benefit children. They learn that they are part of a world beyond themselves, and that there are rules and expectations within that community.

The world is not always going to accommodate them—they are part of a group. Some children come to school for the first time without ever having had any real expectations of them, who have never heard the word no, or who have been accommodated their whole lives, and they really struggle with how to be part of a group. School can help children learn how to take turns, how to delay gratification, how to work through frustration. Without those experiences, you can have the sense that you are alone in the world and you don't feel competent. When children learn that they are one of many, and that what they say and do has an effect on others, they become more successful in all they do.

◀ A Recipe for Good Schools ▶

How do you make good schools? It's not one style or philosophy, but there are many common things that create a high-quality experience. Most important, a school must have an educated faculty who understand young children and have good communication between parents and teachers. Everyone needs to be working together on behalf of the child. There are plenty of schools that do that, and it can be done well in many different ways. But there are a few essential ingredients. There must be a high ratio of adults to children. The facility and materials should be clean and safe. The program should be interesting for children and thoughtfully planned.

Also, parents can help reinforce many of the things we teach their children; they can help teach them colors, numbers, letters, and shapes, and they can read to them every day, and they should. But you can't teach children how to be part of a group with shared expectations for everybody unless you send them to an early childhood education program. It is essential for children to develop an understanding of social dynamics—how to be a friend, how to make a friend, what it means to be part of a group. In order to be ready for the next school experience—kindergarten, first grade, second grade, and third grade—children must know how to follow a teacher's directions and to listen as part of a group. Children can't truly be ready for academic learning without these important skills. You can learn all the letters of the alphabet before kindergarten, but if you can't listen or follow directions, you won't learn. That's why early childhood programs are essential in preparing children for the next step.

◄ **Getting in** ►

Part of the problem with admissions is that people are on a success-track mentality. They tell themselves, if you get your child into the right preschool, you can get them into the right elementary school, and then the right high school, and the right college. But that isn't the way it works. It's written about and it's talked about, but it's not really what children need or what really ensures success.

I recently spoke to a partner in a law firm who told me that when they hire young lawyers who have been on this success track all their lives, they come to the workplace with very few life skills. They don't know how to solve problems, take initiative, or be flexible in their thinking. Their parents have micromanaged their lives from the day they were born, so that they really don't know how to deal with obstacles on their own. They haven't experienced any real frustration and haven't developed the ability to overcome it—all things that you need in a workplace environment. She said that in recent years, young people starting jobs tend not to be very resilient. They have had all this opportunity during their lives, but they come out the other end a bit burnt out and a somewhat fragile.

Getting in to the right schools isn't everything. Parents need to allow their children to experience a few failures and learn from them and move on to be confident in themselves and feel capable.

These same advances have also given consumers and potential business partners unprecedented power to see through the walls of organizations and evaluate not just what they do, but *how* they do it. Economic decision-making at every level—from a consumer's choice of fast food to the financial market's determination of credit-worthiness—is increasingly shaped by consideration of not just what a company does or makes, but by the newly revealed *character* it displays in all its actions. One misstep in conduct can often cause severe damage to both a company's evaluation and bottom line.

The circles of relationship of both individuals and businesses around the world have grown exponentially, and our ever-growing ability to easily uncover deep information about those with whom we are dealing will continue to make those relationships more rich, nuanced, and involved than ever before. And we can never go back. We will never be *less* connected, *less* transparent, or have *less* information available to us.

◀ Hyperconnectivity in the Future ▶

It follows, then, that as the world becomes hyperconnected, those that make the strongest connections will succeed over time. If you collaborate more intensely with your co-workers, you can win. If you reach out and inspire more people throughout your global network, your productivity will skyrocket. If your company keeps promises 99 percent of the time and your competitor keeps promises only 80 percent, you can build the trust that becomes a critical advantage in the marketplace. If your interactions with others deliver a more meaningful customer experience, you can engender a loyalty that brings them back again and again.

From relationship marketing to brand promise to mission-based corporate governance to leadership by inspiration, we see this underlying truth beginning to inform much of what business now believes is important, and it will become more vitally important in the coming years. I've come to believe that the innovations of the twenty-first century will come not just in new products, services, or business models and strategies, but in new ways to create value and differentiation—innovations not in *what* we do, but in *how* we do what we do. The tapestry of human behavior is so diverse, so rich, and so global that it presents a rare opportunity: *the opportunity to outbehave the competition.*

Outbehaving the competition is not just about customer and partner relationships, it's also about the ways organizations create cultures that call forth the best in people, that create climates of trust and certainty, that allow people to be bold, take chances, and innovate. Acting consistently, keeping promises, saying what you mean and meaning what you say, and other *how*-based approaches to organizational conduct can create working environments that unlock creative risk-taking, from which springs the innovation and progress necessary for twenty-first-century success.

The best, most certain, and most enduring path to success and significance in the dramatically new conditions coming to dominate the way we act and interrelate lies not just in raw talent and skill, but also in behavior over time. Those companies and individuals who can see, realize, and make manifest this idea in all they do will both excel in and shape business (and life) for years to come.

Liz Smith ➤ on Gossip

Known as the Grande Dame of Dish, LIZ SMITH *is possibly the most famous gossip columnist in the country and the highest-paid print journalist in the world. She started out at New York's* Newsweek *as a proofreader and became a newspaper columnist in 1976 for the* New York Daily News. *She has also worked for* Newsday, NBC-TV, CBS Radio, *and the* New York Post. *In 1995, she won an Emmy for reporting. Her column runs in more than seventy newspapers, she has a twice-a-week column in* Variety, *and she makes regular appearances on E!'s Gossip Show and Fox's Fox & Friends. Smith's famous parties raise money for Literacy Partners, and she's written two memoirs,* Natural Blonde *and* Dishing. *We wondered if the many blogs and Internet columns about gossip were changing the nature of the gossip columnist's role, and if Smith thought that our escalating access to information would change the way we build icons and celebrities.*

G **ossip has never changed.** It is entirely dependent on human nature. It just now has a larger audience because of mass media. And it will probably only be disseminated more rapidly and widely because of the instant idea of the Internet, e-mail, and so on. Technology will drive gossip just as the print and photo media have driven it since their invention. But gossip and celebrity worship always existed. People were gossiping in caves, and they went right on gossiping in enclaves and families. As lyricist Alan Jay Lerner wrote in *Camelot*, "I wonder what the king is doing tonight." People are always wondering what the king is doing, or whoever passes for the king, and they also like to gossip about their lovers, spouses, children, in-laws, and neighbors. You can't change that.

I would love to see print media endure and flourish in a healthier manner, but I wonder. I think it will always endure to some extent.

There will always be people who want to hold a book or magazine or newspaper in their hands. But the wonders of technology are multi-fold and continue to astound us. The only way it would stop would be if there is some environmental or physical problem in the old world that interrupts electricity and communication. We certainly don't hope for that. An international cataclysm, a nuclear war worldwide, an asteroid hitting earth—any one of those events could change the gossip media celebrity culture for quite a long while.

For now, there is already an absolute plethora of bullshit, manufactured photography, and speculation passing for gossip, and it will probably increase, because there is a demand for it and people will pay for it.

You could stop the taking of pictures, the intrusions into private life, the nonstop gossip, and speculation about celebrities only if somehow you stopped the democratic idea and interfered with free speech. This already happens in more backward, underdeveloped societies or more religious ones, but in America, the sky's the limit. People can say what they want and print what they want—the laws of libel and slander in America are quite limited.

Our icons in ten years will be the same that we celebrate now—movie and TV stars, sports stars, great and low actors, and people famous for being famous, as well as a certain low-grade interest in true scientists, world leaders, real artists: in other words, the people we substitute for what once passed for royalty, or leaders, or forceful pioneers (I'm thinking of Lindberg, one of the first American celebrities). People are always looking for their betters, or what passes for their betters—people who are richer, better looking, sexier, more athletic, more famous than themselves.

Let's just hope that our future icons will not turn out to be dictators and tyrants. This is the cult of worship now, for instance, in North Korea. We don't hope for that kind of celebrity worship. It's better if we stick with the old tried-and-true ideas.

Michael Stoops ➤ **on Homelessness**

MICHAEL STOOPS, *now the executive director of the National Coalition for the Homeless, spent four years as a Volunteer in Service to America (VISTA) volunteer working with migrants and Native Americans before he started to work with the homeless in the early seventies. He got involved with the homeless through the influence of his family and his church and because his grandfather died homeless on the streets when Stoops was very young. Stoops is one of the founding members of the National Coalition for the Homeless; he joined the staff as the director of community organizing in 1988. In early 2005, he became acting executive director. We were interested in Stoops, because we're so appalled by the escalating rate of homelessness in our country. At a time when celebrity focus on worthy international crises across the globe seems to be happily gaining momentum and support, there seems to be a lack of similar focus on domestic poverty. It's not a sexy issue, but as Stoops told us, homelessness only threatens to get worse if we don't make a concerted effort to improve the situation.*

Homelessness is not a new issue; it has been around for the last twenty-five years. I think Americans have unfortunately grown accustomed to homeless people being on the streets, and that's why we walk by real live human beings without even acknowledging their existence. Homelessness continues to increase in this country regardless of who occupies the White House. This steady increase in homelessness is because we have not attacked the root causes of poverty in this country or around the world.

In this country there are three root causes of homelessness and poverty. One is the lack of affordable housing. Two is a lack of jobs that provide living wages. Three is the lack of universal health care. We've been working over the past two decades to raise awareness and understanding, and one by one we're influencing the American people and trying to convince them to demand that their public officials make a commitment to ending poverty in this country. The Live 8 event over in Scotland and around the world talked about ending poverty in Africa, which we support of course, but we should also make a commitment to end poverty even in the industrialized nations. We do have the resources to do it; we simply lack the political will.

In this country, many advocates have been talking about ending homelessness, and we've been able to get a number of cities around the country—more than 200—to develop ten-year plans to end homelessness. We're trying to get every sector of society to work together. We think that it's very possible to end homelessness. It won't happen overnight, but we also know that if someone who is important or famous, who has a lot more influence than I have, says that this is unacceptable, it will happen—such as if Bill Gates or President Bush said that we have 800,000 Americas living on the streets, 3.5 million over the course of the year, with 40 percent of the homeless population being families, and 25 percent being children under the age of eighteen, and it's unacceptable. Someday we're going to luck out, and there will be a president or business leader or philanthropist or a famous person who is going to say that homelessness is my number one priority. Join with me and let's end homelessness in America.

I am very hopeful. I wish that we could do this sooner than ten years from now. We know what needs to be done, we simply have not been able to mobilize the whole country the way we should.

◀ Face-to-Face Interaction ▶

I speak to high school and college students a lot, and I always ask people in the audience how many of them have ever volunteered in a shelter or a soup kitchen on Christmas, Thanksgiving, Easter, or another religious holiday. Something like 75 percent of today's young people have had a face-to-face encounter with a homeless person, which is quite remarkable, more than any other population group. So young people are having a lot of direct contact with homeless people in a controlled and friendly environment. And many Americans, on their way to work, play, or school, come across homeless people. So Americans know that homelessness is an important issue. There was a poll done by the Associated Press that found that 90 percent of Americans consider homelessness to be either a serious or very serious issue. The American people are volunteering, they're concerned about this issue, but I just don't think this concern has been communicated to our public officials for whatever reason. It could be that the general public is lobbying for lower gas prices but not lobbying to house homeless people, because Americans tend to wait until it happens to someone they know, or they tend to think, Why should I be concerned? I'm not going to get concerned until something impacts me or my family. So that's why it's easy to walk by a person living on the streets.

◄ Homeless People and Young People ►

We do a nonpartisan campaign every two years called You Don't Need a Home to Vote. We've found that even before we go into a shelter to register people, about one third of the nation's homeless are registered to vote, and when we have organized educational forums and get-out-the-vote drives in different communities, we've been able to achieve a 55 percent voter turnout. If there is anything beneficial about being homeless, it's that you have time on your hands, and many homeless folks go to the library, and they get on the computer, and they have time to read the *New York Times,* so they know who the president is, and they're up to date on current affairs. So I think that the two groups of people who will ultimately end homelessness in this country are the homeless people themselves, who will not necessarily be marching on the streets but will be getting involved with helping themselves and with one another, and young people, who will be making those connections at an early age when they do volunteer work.

Thirty years ago no parents would let their teen go down to the skid row area to work at a soup kitchen. Now it's become a family affair, and churches and synagogues frequently send teams of people down to shelters and soup kitchens, and parents bring their children along. The children volunteer and interact alongside their parents, and there are more young people volunteering than let's say in the 1960s, when you had people who were activists, but they weren't always doing volunteer social work. It used to be that social workers and volunteers were primarily women and that's still true today, but it used to be something like 90 percent women and 10 percent men. Now it's closer to 60 percent women and 40 percent men.

◀ **Say Hello** ▶

The next time a citizen of the world sees a homeless person on the street, it's important to say hello, to get to know their name, to buy them a cup of coffee, and to acknowledge their existence. You're likely to walk by the same person every day. If every world citizen were to get to know a homeless person, we would all be a lot better off. All people need to know that others care about them. We can't feel good about ourselves and our society if we have people living on our streets.

Joe Trippi ➤ **on Politics**

JOE TRIPPI, currently a senior adviser on the John Edwards campaign, was heralded on the cover of the New Republic as the man who "reinvented campaigning." He began his political career working on Edward M. Kennedy's presidential campaign in 1980, and also worked on the campaigns of Walter Mondale, Gary Hart, Richard Gephardt, and Howard Dean. In 2004, as National Campaign Manager for Howard Dean's presidential campaign, he pioneered the use of online technology to organize what became the largest grassroots movement in presidential politics, raising more money than any Democratic presidential campaign in history, all with donations averaging less than $100 each. Trippi's innovations have brought fundamental change to the electoral system and will inform how all future political campaigns are run. He is the author of The Revolution Will Not Be Televised: Democracy, the Internet, and the Overthrow of Everything. *We were interested in what he had to say about political campaigning in the future because he is one of the people who will truly shape how campaigning is done and ultimately whom we elect to run our government.*

The Internet, mobile devices, social networks, and viral media will all enable and create a radical shift in our politics over the next five to ten years. Television once took the people out of politics. Money, and raising lots of it, became more and more important because candidates who bought more television ads won. The Internet, social networks, and new media are putting back into our politics what television took out: the people. Television's power to isolate people in their homes is giving way to the power of people to use new media and new technologies to connect and communicate with one another. Politics will be turned upside down over the next five to ten years. Top-down big money and big media politics are going to lose ground and give way to a new bottom-up politics fostered by these empowering technologies. Millions of people will be able to connect with one another and form powerful volunteer armies in support of the candidate or issue of their choice, raising more funds than today's political parties are capable of using the tried-and-true big donor dinner.

◀ The End of a Two-Party System ▶

There is a strong chance that within the next ten years these advances will portend an end to one or both of the major political parties. Both parties' platform conventions are already obsolete—with the party adopting the platform of the candidate it nominates and not the other way around. Two of the remaining reasons a candidate needs a political party—the organization that party has across a region or the nation and the contributor base that a party has as well—will become obsolete over the next five to ten years. Candidates will soon be able to rally more volunteers and organizers using the Internet, mobile devices, and social media than either political party can rally through its various committees.

There is only one medium in the world that allows five million Americans to contribute $100 each in one day to a candidate. The Internet makes it possible. Millions of cell phone users can make it possible in an instant. Not television. Not a political party. One candidate will be able to rally that many Americans to contribute and join his or her campaign in one day because of the changes we will see in the next five to ten years. People, and big numbers of them, able to connect with one another will be more important than a candidate's ability to connect with big money.

•　　　•　　　•

◄ **Future Candidates** ►

Just as radio gave way to television, a new kind of candidate will emerge. During the 1960 Nixon-Kennedy Presidential debate, those who listened on the radio were sure that Vice President Nixon had won—those who watched the same debate on television were sure the younger and more vibrant looking John F. Kennedy had won the debate. On radio it mattered what a candidate sounded like, but for the last forty to fifty years, because of television, looks have mattered more. Over the next five to ten years that will change again, and in a surprising direction. Broadcast television has evolved our politics into one of phoniness—consultants and candidates have perfected the art of "faking it" for a thirty-second television ad or a ninety-second carefully scripted debate response. No more. The Internet, social networks, and viral media will create an environment over the next five to ten years in which only the most authentic candidates survive and win.

What drives our politics will have moved from what a candidate sounds like, to what a candidate looks like, to who the candidate really is. And the fakes need not apply. No one can fake it twenty-four hours a day, seven days a week. Candidates will have to be who they really are and be comfortable in their own skin to succeed, because any public moment could be captured by a citizen and immediately shared with millions of other citizens. Voters will have to like a candidate's "warts," because no candidates will be able to keep all their warts hidden all the time. This will become increasingly clear as video cell phones become ubiquitous. Today's pundits fear that the Internet, social networks, mobile video devices, and viral media will create a new class of super-cautious candidate—but they will be proven wrong.

◀ The Coming Challenges for Political Candidates ▶

The next five years are likely to be a very dangerous transitional period for candidates as candidates, citizens, and the news media adjust to the new reality created by ubiquitous citizen-generated media and viral media. Falling asleep in a Senate hearing, uttering a racial slur, saying something controversial at an event that is "closed to the press"—these things can no longer be done with impunity. No event will truly be closed to the press, because any citizen is capable of committing an act of journalism with his or her cell phone camera today, and this power will only increase.

The next five years will prove particularly dangerous to politicians who are blind to the changing communications landscape. Just as television brought us the slick TV candidates, whom the camera "loved," over the next ten years we'll see a shift in which the authentic candidate survives and wins. Slick, programmed, and scripted candidates will not prosper in this medium. A candidate who knows he has flaws and is capable of laughing at them will fare better than a candidate who thinks he can keep citizens from seeing them.

And while the country is ready to elect a minority president today, it is not likely to happen until the end of the ten-year period—2016. Colin Powell would have been a formidable candidate prior to the invasion of Iraq. That said, Barack Obama looks to be coming up short on the experience front and will not win the presidency in 2008. In 2012, the president will be running for re-election, and in 2016 that president's vice president will be running for office. The system is stacked against anyone who is not already in the pipeline, regardless of color. I think bottom-up politics will be in full force by 2016, so it may be possible that that force will thrust a minority into the presidency—that would be my bet for when it happens.

•   •   •

◀ Looking to Our Peers ▶

One of the biggest barriers to getting people to vote or participate in the process is their belief that nothing they do will change anything. This attitude is prevalent today, and is likely to be the same in the future. Often those that don't participate also believe they are the only ones who feel the way they do about what needs to change in our nation's politics. However, peer-to-peer communication will increasingly have more power than traditional institutions will have. Five friends e-mailing you about the movie they saw over the weekend—all of them telling you the movie sucked—will have much more influence over you than the millions of dollars the movie studio spends on advertising telling you the movie is the greatest movie you will ever see. You're not going to go to the movie.

So, too, is participation in politics—six or seven friends engaging you to participate is far more likely to move you to get involved than candidate advertising, Let's hope more voices are heard in the political process in the future.

Chad Trujillo, PhD ➤ **on Astronomy**

Astronomer **CHAD TRUJILLO** *studied the orbits of the numerous trans-Neptunian objects (TNOs), and in 2005 it was announced that he, along with Michael E. Brown and David L. Rabinowitz, had discovered 136199 Eris, the first TNO known to be larger than the planet Pluto. The TNO was later revealed to have a moon. Trujillo received a BS in physics from MIT and a PhD in astronomy from the University of Hawaii. Trujillo was later a postdoctoral scholar at the California Institute of Technology (Caltech) and is currently an astronomer at the Gemini Observatory in Hawaii, where he studies the Kuiper belt and the outer solar system. While we can only imagine what else may be out there, Trujillo and his colleagues are actually changing the way we think about the universe.*

Astronomy is primarily technologically limited—not just in the solar system area that I study, but also extragalactic study and all of astronomy. We are limited by our observations, and that ability is pretty strongly correlated with technological advances. There was basically a revolution in astronomy in the eighties, when people started using CCD technology instead of photographic plates, and now the forefront in many aspects of astronomy is in the infrared detectors and studying things in light that you can't see with your eyes. Different wavelengths that were harder in the past to study due to technological reasons are just kind of opening up now.

When a star forms there's a lot of dust around it, and previously we couldn't really see through that dust at all because we were just looking at optical wavelengths, which is what your eye is sensitive to. But looking at these other wavelengths in the near and mid-infrared, you can probe deeper into these regions and find out more about how stars form and that kind of thing. I know in extragalactic astronomy people are studying very high red-shift objects, which means objects that are very far away. There are some interesting things to do with those in infrared as well; the older objects are starting to fall into this infrared regimen. I don't mean to pound on the infrared, but that's the kind of thing that's a developing technology now. Certainly in solar system astronomy the most interesting things to study are those places we can visit. For instance, we just launched the New Horizons, and that's going to Pluto, which is right on the outer edge of the solar system. Technology is a huge factor in that.

◀ Public versus Private Exploration ▶

Certainly it would be great if we started more exploration in the private sector as opposed to the government sector. The government sector is great, because they have access to a lot of resources, but the private sector has a lot of flexibility that the government doesn't have. The problem is that it's really hard to go to space—just basic physics makes it hard to do—so it's not like we're all going to have these space cars in ten years that we can drive over to the corner store on the Moon.

I think the overriding thing that people want to know about is how things turned out the way they did. How did galaxies form, how did the universe form? How did galaxies form in the universe? How did stars form in the galaxy? And ultimately how did planets form around stars? And how did we get here? I think that's kind of the overriding exploration in astronomy, but it's a long trip between saying that and actually the day-to-day or year-to-year of what astronomers do. We might work a year and get a tiny piece of a really large puzzle, and we don't even have the box top to figure out what it's supposed to look like. So it's a long exploration.

◀ The Definition of a Planet ▶

In the next ten years, I think the definitions will be made. When we made our discovery, we didn't even have a definition of what a planet was. Astronomers were meeting and discussing this and trying to come up with an actual definition of what a planet might be, and the whole debate was sort of forced by our discovery that, hey, there's a tenth object in the solar system and it's larger than Pluto. We were calling it a tenth planet because it orbits the sun, and it's bigger than Pluto, and Pluto was considered a planet. But instead Pluto was demoted from a planet to a dwarf planet, and so was our object. It may turn out in the future that both of these objects and anything else bigger than Pluto might be considered full planets again, too. There are all kinds of definitions that people are discussing, and certainly in the next ten years that will probably be a big issue. I think even in a couple of years we will have a definition. We might have to revise it depending on what's found in the next decade.

◀ The Future Impact of the "Tenth Planet" Discovery ▶

Now we have another body that is bigger than Pluto, and there are a few other bodies out there that we've found that are maybe two thirds the size of Pluto or so. Studying this group of bodies will actually give us a window on how Pluto formed, which has been kind of a controversy for a long time. These bodies are right on the outer edge of the solar system. They've been frozen basically since the beginning of the solar system, four and a half billion years ago. We hope that by comparing these bodies, we can find out if there are some common things among them, and we're hoping it will give us a kind of doorway into how the solar system formed. This outer edge is really analogous to how paleontologists study fossils to find out about dinosaurs. Our study group is frozen on the outer edge of the solar system, with fairly little modification since the solar system formed.

I'm mostly an observer, and usually the theorists come up with the theories, and the observers test them or constrain them. One of the big questions is what happened early on in the solar system. We know that the planets formed, but we don't know where they formed. We know they probably moved around some, but *how much* is a good question. Did they swap places? That's a possibility. Or did these things on the outer edge, did they actually come from the inner solar system near earth? Were some of them maybe thrown out, away from the sun, and they're out there now, but they didn't start there? Maybe there are also objects that started out there and remained out there on the outer edge. Those types of things are what we are after, and it seems like studying the large bodies and comparing them makes sense. By comparing the big ones to the small ones, maybe we can unravel some of what happened in the solar system formation process. Ultimately, we want to connect this with other stars. So right now, anther big area in astronomy is how other stars formed, and how many of those stars might have planets, and what types of planets they might have. There is this big gray zone between our solar system and other solar systems. There's a lot that we just don't understand. There are a lot of differences that we see between the two, but we are hoping that by studying our solar system and other solar systems we'll be able to draw some parallels between the two.

◀ **Giant Telescopes** ▶

We have now around the world maybe ten telescopes that are really big—like eight- to ten-meter-diameter primary mirrors. The next step is thirty-meter-diameter telescopes, and when that kind of telescope comes online, I think we are really going to see a revolution in astronomy, because it's basically limited by our observational ability. A thirty-meter telescope is at least ten times better than a ten-meter, and probably much more. So when you make the factor-of-ten improvement in your ability to measure something, you really explore unexpected regions, unexpected things, unexpected ideas, unexpected places. I think in the next decade or so we're going to see some really interesting things.

A big obstacle to that is funding. It takes a lot of money to build one of these giant telescopes, and it takes a lot of politics. How do you build it? And who gets to build the pieces of it and where do you put it? All of that is kind of logistics, but it's logistics that take a long time to work out and a lot of money, and that's the big obstacle. But I think it's something that almost all of the astronomical community wants, so it seems likely that it is going to happen.

It's hard to even say just how much it is going to help, because we're going to be able to see in a matter of hours or less things that take days to see now. We're going to be exploring whole new regions—the faintest, farthest galaxies, and then in our solar systems, the really faint things that we just couldn't study before.

In the next few years, the Pan-STARRS program will be coming online. That's going to be this large all-sky survey, and it's going to be finding lots of extragalactic things of interest—supernova and gamma-ray bursts and that kind of thing. They are also going to be finding literally millions of new asteroids that we've never seen before and many tens of thousands of Kuiper Belt objects on the outer edge of the solar system. The project will certainly find some really neat stuff that we never expected.

◀ **Funding Fears** ▶

For me, one of my biggest hopes, probably since I started in astronomy about ten years ago is, hey, wouldn't it be fun to find something bigger than Pluto, and now we've actually done that. I don't think

I'm finished. I'm just trying to keep my eyes open for something else that is interesting.

My worry is that a lot of astronomy is supported by public money—the government appropriates money, and that's a large reason we get things done in astronomy. My fear would be that the money might start not being appropriated to astronomy because of other budget needs. Right now, the United States is really on the forefront of astronomy, but if funding is reduced that's not going to be the case.

For instance, Europe has a very good funding system, and they have a lot of good telescopes. We all attend the same meetings, but they are our competition, and if we start to fall behind, if we start funding less in astronomy, then they could certainly surpass us.

Steve Ward, PhD ➤ on Computers

STEVE WARD *is professor of computer science and engineering at MIT, where his recent teaching and research activities have concerned the areas of computer system architecture. His research projects have had frequent and widespread practical impact; the 1979 Nu machine became a model for microprocessor-based workstations, its seminal UNIX port and system software is the progenitor of numerous software products, and the NuBus has become an industry standard. His software projects have included the Curl language for delivering application services as web content, and he is currently exploring alternative "organic" programming models for adaptive systems whose behavior mimics that of organisms rather than conventional computers.*

Two issues that are important to consider are first, intellectual property in the information age, and second, the "computers are no damned good" problem. I'll deal with the latter issue first.

◄ Computers Are No Damned Good ➤

Computers are essential to modern life in civilized places. One can't do banking, buy gifts, stay informed, or communicate effectively without a serious dependence on the technology of computers and the networking that interconnects them. The problem is this: There's simply no effective way for normal people to have reliable access to the services of computers and networks. We're forced to buy

machines, configure them with software, debug configuration conflicts, viruses, and other crashes, back up our files, and take responsibility for a host of other tasks that we, as consumers, are ill-equipped
to handle.

It's common to assign blame for this situation to a number of
readily available targets: software industry quality standards, Microsoft, and consumer economics that favor function over quality in
the marketplace. Each of these may be a contributing factor, but I
argue that the real culprit is our obsolete model for the delivery of
information services, by which I mean banking, e-mail, and the other
computer-Internet functions we've come to depend on. Rather than
each setting up our own computation center and becoming its sysop,
we need to relegate local hardware to absolute commodity status
and allow maintenance responsibilities to migrate back over the wire
(e.g., to service providers), where backups, software installation, and
other such chores can be handled transparently to us. In effect, we
might demand the equivalent of a dial tone from the external network that supports the devices we deploy, say, at home, and get fast
service if we call and say, It's broken.

This is a harder problem than it may seem, for at least two reasons.
First, for technical reasons (e.g., support for high-quality interactive
medial) there must be software (and hence computers) running local
to the end user. This fact limits the simple expedient of running
application code entirely on remote servers.

Second, the need to decentralize control of the system architecture (and its economics) introduces major complications. It would
be reasonably easy to establish a centralized distribution network for
carefully controlled, high-quality software so long as we didn't mind
its being under the control of a single entity. This is much the model
TiVo uses for software in its captive market. For many good reasons,
this model is inappropriate in the broad information services domain,
where we demand the evolvability and responsiveness that only free
market control can provide. This introduces both technical and economic challenges.

◀ **Intellectual Property** ▶

Our largely unsuccessful attempts to treat information as we do physical goods are at odds with the communication revolution we find ourselves engaged in. Unlike potatoes and oil, information has no natural conservation property that generates economic scarcity; by natural economic forces, information becomes asymptotically free. Virtually every measure we have tried—such as copy protection— to maintain the unnatural economic value of information involves communication restrictions. These are both counterevolutionary and futile—counterevolutionary because they fly in the face of the explosion of communication we now enjoy, and futile because there are no natural boundaries (like the "possession" of physical goods) to promote enforcement.

This situation is fundamentally problematic. If one believes, as I do, that artists, writers, and others whose contributions are informational deserve to be rewarded, we need to find and establish alternative economic models to provide that reward.

Existing representatives of these interests (such as the Recording Industry Association of America and the Motion Picture Association of America) advocate strong legal measures to support the artificial scarcity of tunes and videos. These measures are simply not tenable in the long term; new technologies for dicing up information and recombining it into unrecognizable pieces for distribution not only make the copying of information undetectable, they render the act meaningless as a legal distinction.

◀ **Alternate Economic Models** ▶

I believe there are alternative economic models that are consistent with emerging technologies, that put us on the right evolutionary curve (one that encourages rather than discourages communication), and that appropriately reward contributors. One example that I've given several talks on addresses software (rather than, say, tunes or movies), but I suspect similar proposals can be made for other forms of information.

The basic idea is this: Each PC user pays a monthly fee and gets access to any software he wants. His computer keeps records (there are some neat ways of doing this), which ultimately causes his monthly fee to be divided up on a pro-rata basis among the providers of the software he uses. In this scheme, software can be distributed freely on the Internet, with no restrictions whatsoever. If I like a program and send a copy to you, you can run it without restriction. If you use it a lot, its author will be rewarded.

The first time I talked about this proposal—to a large audience in Germany—I was called a communist by a member of the audience. The protestor argued, politely, that the scheme requires some central authority to set the flat rate and therefore bound the total software market. This leads to a controlled economy, which even then, decades ago, was out of favor in Germany.

My off-the-cuff response to the protestor, which I'm still inclined to defend, is this: The flat rate is set by a consortium of software providers, not a government agency. There is a natural ideal value; if it's too low, the software vendors leave money on the table; if too high, they discourage new customers. So by trying to maximize their profits, they gravitate to the appropriate monthly fee.

In fact, I think this yields the ultimate free market: it's superefficient, since any garage shop can compete with Microsoft at very little cost and any consumer can choose any software at any time.

Although I've talked about this kind of thing for years, I've never written it up. Several others have mentioned it, however; if you like, check out Phil Greenspun's Web site at http://philip.greenspun.com/wtr/dead-trees/53015.htm and go to the second page or so (look for my name). Mike Dertouzos also wrote about it in one of his books.

So in ten years, the computer industry will likely still be experiencing the turmoil it's currently in, or perhaps worse. Although people are starting to address the two problems I mention above, a decade is a short enough time that the prospect of either being completely addressed is pretty unlikely.

◀ Communication Bill of Rights and Other Hopes ▶

I would love to see something like a communication bill of rights articulated and established within United States and, if I'm fantasizing, international law. The idea is to guarantee my rights to basic communication, digital and otherwise, as sort of an extension of the First Amendment. Like the First Amendment, such a precedent would prevent the proposal of onerous and ultimately ineffective laws that interfere with communication.

I'm hoping that a generation of information appliances will appear that are largely invisible to the end user: Like plumbing, they just do their job.

Consumers will have reliable access to standardized services (e-mail, document production, and so on) without any need to provide maintenance chores. A number of service providers will compete largely on price and quality-of-service grounds, much as telephone companies do now. They'll share pre-competitive standards for software, which allow arbitrary providers to implement new functions and inject them into the competitive distribution network.

◀ Free Information Flow ▶

I think that forward-looking professionals, particularly those in the business of creating information, are well advised to explore new business models consistent with free information flow. These include flat-rate access, subscription-based services, and other alternatives to "selling" content.

Consumers should relax and enjoy the revolution. They are the ultimate beneficiaries.

Amy Ziff ➤ on Travel

AMY ZIFF, *a travel and media insider, joined Travelocity in 2002 as editor at large. She serves as a media resource for travel tips and advice and travel trend information, and she writes a regular travel column,* Travel Tips from A to Z, *and the Window Seat blog, http://windowseat. travelocity. As a Travelocity spokesperson, Ziff has appeared on* Today, Good Morning America, The Early Show, *Fox News,* and many *others, and she has been quoted in the* Wall Street Journal, Vogue, Good Housekeeping, and Redbook. *From what they want out of an exotic trip to fears about terrorism and disease, Ziff understands travelers' thoughts, hopes, and worries. We were interested in Ziff's insights because she has an unparalleled ability to stay in direct contact with consumers through e-mail, regular traveler polls, and trending and data analysis.*

The most dramatic change in the last ten years is the impact of the online travel business. The technology has made the world seem a little bit smaller. Now that research is so easy to obtain, it literally has put the dream of flight into every traveler's hands. Online travel has also made it much more possible for shoppers to find low prices, and so people who never traveled before can. Thirty million households were online in 2004, and the prediction is that it will be more than 46.5 million in 2009.

But think of it another way—the latest PhoCus Wright statistics say that 37 percent of all travel was or will be booked online in 2007, but more than half of the travel marketplace doesn't *yet* book online. In the next decade, we'll see those numbers shift so that the norm will be that most people *do* book their travel online. And that's pretty significant.

The Web has the power to expand the marketplace as well. It's motivating people who might otherwise just be armchair travelers (those who love to read *Travel + Leisure* and their weekly newspaper travel section) to get up and go. The Web puts the price point at your fingertips. With the technology today you can say, I really want to go to Australia, but not until flight prices drop. You can sign up for a product that will e-mail you when the price drops. Imagine, in ten years' time, you'll probably be able to book that same flight in an instant. Instead of seeing that the flight has dropped and going to the link to buy, you'll have previously stated what price range and dates you wanted and given your travel parameters, and it will check your calendar for availability, book the trip, and send a notice.

The technology of the travel industry is definitely changing a lot of aspects within the industry as well. The travel industry overall is in great flux. There are wars for customers between the online supersite stores (Travelocity and the like) versus the supplier sites (such as a specific airline) who want to own travelers directly. There are offline agencies as well, which will remain, though many will lose share over time.

As travel becomes more commonplace and the concept of a global world is more widely accepted by the masses, we'll see new destinations emerge. Already people are traveling to far places with greater ease. Hawaii is the average American's dream vacation destination. But what about Mauritius or the Maldives? Suddenly the possibilities for destinations will be infinitely larger and farther. The next ten years will bring low-fare air carriers to Asia. We're already seeing those being developed so there won't only be domestic low-fare airlines. The trend begins with low-cost offerings outside of the United States, as routes to South America and Europe have started to emerge.

With the huge business opportunities in Asia, and specifically India, we'll see that region influencing travel destinations. These places seem very exotic now, but ten years from now travel there will be much more common. And more people are tacking on vacations to their business travel, and that will keep happening.

◀ Planes, Trains, and a National Identity Card ▶

The airline industry is fascinating—it's so massive and complicated. The American airlines are in a critical place right now. There used to be six majors, and now it's considered that there are only five. It's hard to say which airlines will remain in ten years. My prediction is that they won't look the way they do today. As for who'll be on the scene in ten years, I would expect that we'll see a mix of both new and old players. The Concorde, or something like it, has to come back. Maybe it's just my wish, but I think it's one of those things that there will be enough of an interest in, and maybe that will become how first-class, business, or more elite travelers will go. We're already seeing business-class-*only* airlines enter the marketplace.

But all airlines, high and low end, will have to answer the billion-dollar question, which is how to fly without becoming prisoner to the costs. Fuel is one of the greatest costs to airlines these days, and maybe the answer will be in finding a more affordable energy resource.

And yet, with all that focus on aviation, I also expect that we'll see better transit alternatives across the United States. Fuel costs are so high that we're going to see some exciting things from an environmental standpoint. We have to. This is a time when green entrepreneurs can enter the travel space in ways they haven't been able to before. I hope that Amtrak will be sorted out, and high-speed-train options will come back into vogue. I'd also look for major increases in water travel as a method of commuting. And look at how phenomenally successful the Prius is, and all the other hybrid vehicles entering the marketplace. Hertz and Avis are among the car rental carriers to announce that they're adding green cars to their fleets. New York City plans to make their entire cab fleet hybrids by 2012, and that will be just the beginning. I think we'll see all kinds of alternative cars and vehicles, and that mass transit and common car rental options will change.

I also think that for all this travel, we'll settle on a national identity card of sorts. The statistics are that about 20 to 30 percent of Americans have passports, although with the new Western Hemisphere Travel Initiative, more citizens than ever are getting theirs. Expect passports to be updated. Not only will there be an identity card, if you don't require a full passport but still need the identification, but it's likely the format will be changed altogether due to all the new technologies that we can use to determine who people are—and that they are who they say they are. Imagine going to the airport and checking in at the e-kiosk by fingerprint or a retinal scanner rather than by credit card. Biometric data will be used in our daily lives in myriad ways. While the technology is getting far more sophisticated, the government needs to catch up.

◀ **Potential for Disaster** ▶

One of my fears is that the airlines will become so crippled by their expenses—even low-fare carriers—that they won't solve the fuel issue fast enough. I also worry that flying will become increasingly burdensome due to outdated air traffic control systems. In a world where we don't sort out pricing and efficiency, for a business with razor-thin margins and many airlines operating at a loss, it's a pretty ugly scenario to imagine. Does travel do a complete 180 and become prohibitively expensive, and do we all conduct conference calls and take virtual vacations? I suppose it's possible, but not likely. We've got too much invested in answering these questions and solving the problems. I think there will be critical shifts in how airlines operate and a new kind of carrier will emerge—something more radical than the low-fare carriers we have now.

My greatest fear is that there will be another major terrorist incident. No one wants to talk about it, but of course the thought is there. It's really frightening to think about what that could do. And at the very same time, watching people's reactions post 9/11, the Madrid and even the various London bombings, has been really interesting. After 9/11, the recovery to travel was very slow. I'd say that it took until summer 2005 to gain ground on where we were prior to 9/11. In December 2004, I could see the visible signs of recovery. There was suddenly this noticeable difference in how people were traveling. We were looking at people doing things that they did pre–9/11, and that was really exciting. Now, for better or worse, we've surpassed those numbers. The other terrorist events around the world haven't had nearly the same impact. At least American travelers are proving that they're very resilient. There are other worries for the travel industry beyond terrorism, such as the spread of disease. We saw with SARS how fast and far disease can travel in this day and age. That could be bad for the travel industry as a whole. While there have been scares with meningitis and TB, there hasn't been any sort of outbreak or epidemic. The one positive thing that can come from these occurrences is that they allow the system (air travel, the World Health Organization, the Center for Disease Control, etc.) to reflect on how well or poorly we respond and come up with ways to be better. I hope we'll be able to work globally to respond appropriately should we ever need to.

◀ **Extreme Travel** ▶

There are people who are pushing the extremes, but I don't know that those things will be affordable to the average person. For example, something like the Ice Hotel—there's one in Sweden and one outside of Quebec City—is out of the ordinary and very interesting to a lot of travelers who like to boast about what they've done. Would you want to sleep in a room that's always between twenty-six and twenty-eight degrees? But will the masses flock to an underwater casino or take a home-equity loan in order to go on a space flight?

We're living in a society that's always clamoring to have the new big thing and outdo everyone. Super-resorts with different self-created biospheres could be a way to experience various climates in one place, for example. Or eco-resorts that run fully on green power and are self-sustaining in every way, from the food that they harvest organically on their own land to the animals to green building practices and operations.

I expect to see an even bigger surge in small plane usage. As the masses move to the skies, the elite will go take another tier of plane. So first-class travel won't be in a jet, it will be in a private plane. The equipment will become more affordable, and you'll get plane shares—time shares in a plane—as a method of commuting. You'll have your own pilot. Prices for that are starting to make sense, and people who want a first-class experience do not want the hassle of going through security with everyone else—the whole cattle car experience. And there will also be the birth of the anti-low-fare carrier, which will be all business-class elite all the time, and they'll shuttle primarily between major business hubs on long-haul routes.

◀ Comfort with Technology ▶

I also think the convergence of technology will heavily influence travel. Your phone, your TV, your Gameboy—everything will be in one light device, and you'll be able to shop with your handheld, peruse destinations, and call up Asia while you're sitting on the subway. You'll be able to sit in your car and watch a video about a country you're interested in seeing. People's ability to think and see the world and travel will be so infinite and amazing.

You're looking at a customer base that is very comfortable in a highly technological world. It's a class of people who are going to graduate from college having always had a cell phone. Kids today have never known what life is like without e-mail, they get the majority of their information online, and they're very comfortable with the virtual scene. This helps to make their world smaller, while our parents might have been anxious about taking the family on a global vacation. It will become far more affordable and common for families to just pick up and go.

◄ **Preparing for the Future** ►

This is a time of incredible flux. I think we'll look back at this period of history and see it as the next industrial revolution—a technological revolution.

Yet it's in our nature as humans to be change-averse. Most people tend to want things to stay as they are. You can change so much, but do you *really* want to? It's that 60-plus percent of the population that has not migrated to the Internet because they don't want to change the way they do things. But they will. Slowly.

I think the way you can help yourself as a consumer is to try to be open and not afraid of it, but say this might help me and make my life easier. When you shop on the Internet, you're that much closer to better fares, cheaper fares, and you can actually talk to a person 24/7. Listen to your kids, because they'll be your leaders in this. I talk to families all the time, and the way families book travel is that the kid does the research online and then mom books it.

As a professional, it's about innovating and staying ahead of those trends. Particularly in the online industry and the travel industry, the big question is how do we fight being a commodity brand? The Internet has made things very much about price, but they'll have worked that out in ten years, or they won't be here. It's an interesting integration of old and new, and from the media perspective I'm fascinated by what's happening. Preparing is mostly being open and willing to look at things in a new way—knowing that the way we do things yesterday may not be the way we do things in the future. Be open to it.

◀ ACKNOWLEDGMENTS ▶

There wouldn't have been a *What's Next* without Richard Lovett, who came up with the idea and supported the writing of this book. Thank you for inspiring us and guiding us.

Kevin Huvane has been a source of incredible support and humor throughout this entire process. For many reasons, we thank him.

Many thanks to Bryan Lourd, Rob Light, David O'Connor, and Rick Nicita, who all offered support, help and advice.

For their support in this project, we thank Steve Lafferty and Bruce Vinokour.

Michael Rubel made sure we didn't get in trouble. And stayed on course. Many thanks to him.

Joni Evans conquers the world but still gives so much love, so much support and the occasional needed kick in the pants. Thank you.

Jennifer Rudolf Walsh always listens, always answers, and always has the best advice. Thank you so very much. And how do you do that?

Cassie Jones, you may know a lot about the future now, but you are a rare throwback to editors of the past, who took the time to make a manuscript just right. Thank you.

To Judith Regan, who believed in this book from the beginning. Thanks for all of your support.

Victoria Doramus came into this project late, but without her, we truly would have been lost. If she is what's next, we'll be okay. She called; she edited; she tracked down. She was fantastic. Thank you. Thank you.

Johnathan Wilber, thank you for coming to our aid when we needed it most. Again. And again. And again.

Amie Yavor went above and beyond to help in this project. We truly appreciate your help and encouragement.

Each of these individuals managed Herculean feats. Thank you to Andi McNicol, Thao Nguyen, Becca Topol, Emil Mertzel, Chris Gough, Ned Specktor, Mary Beth Brown, Maggie Dumais, Lisa Shotland, Roy Peters, Peter Jacobs, Jennifer Stanley, Michael Camacho, Hilary Hudson, Natalie Lent, Colin Sweeney, the Goldbergs, the Ericksens, and the Wards. Without their help and support, this book would not have come to fruition.

Elliot Thomson, outstanding friend, godfather, writer, and supporter, thank you.

Katie Tarses, you are an angel and a friend.

Thank you to the Goulds for lending perspective and endlessly listening.

Elizabeth Newman researched, interviewed, wrote, edited, and organized. She made the impossible possible on a daily basis, and she did so with intelligence, grace, and elegance. She was inspiring.

Despina Georgiou, Martha Magnuson, and Rebecca Mcquigg all deserve extra thanks for their part in researching, calling, and fact-finding.

To everyone in the Intelligence Group: Amanda, Barbara, Bayla, Clare, Cynthia, Ellen, Jill, Krista, Kristin, Liz, Margot, Melissa, Rebecca, Tristan, Victoria, Wallie—you seem to be able to predict the future better than anyone. You are true experts. Thanks for tolerating absences in pursuit of this project.

To Julie, Mark, and Luke Rowen for showing that in the future, friends become family.

Thank you to Jo for healing and love.

Thanks to Linda and Mitch Hart for endless tolerance and love.

And thanks to all of our family for enduring weekends and nights and holidays at the computer.

Hugs and kisses to Marcus, Jack, and Lilia who make Jane want the future to be as good as it can possibly be and understand when she can't be there for pickup.

Finally to all of our contributors, who gave their time, energy, and great thoughts on the future. We thank you.